# CHILDREN LIVING IN SUSTAINABLE BUILT ENVIRONMENTS

Urban living has dramatically changed over the past generation, refashioning children's relationships with the towns and cities in which they live, and the modes of living within them. Focusing on the global shift in urban planning towards sustainable urbanism – from master planned 'sustainable communities', to the green retrofitting of existing urban environments – *Children Living in Sustainable Built Environments* offers a critical analysis of the challenges, tensions and opportunities for children and young people living in these environments.

Drawing upon original data, *Children Living in Sustainable Built Environments* demonstrates how the needs, interests and participation of children and young people often remain inferior to the design, planning and local politics of new urban communities. Considering children from their crucial role as residents engaging and contributing to the vitalities of their community, to their role as consumers using and understanding sustainable design features, the book critically discusses the prospects of future inclusion of children and young people as a social group in sustainable urbanism.

Truly interdisciplinary, *Children Living in Sustainable Built Environments* forms an original theoretical and empirical contribution to the understanding of the everyday lives of children and young people and will appeal to academics and students in the fields of education, childhood studies, sociology, anthropology, human geography and urban studies, as well as policy-makers, architects, urban planners and other professionals working on sustainable urban designs.

**Pia Christensen** is Professor of Anthropology and Childhood Studies, University of Leeds, UK.

**Sophie Hadfield-Hill** is Lecturer of Human Geography, University of Birmingham, UK.

**John Horton** is Associate Professor of Human Geography, University of Northampton, UK.

**Peter Kraftl** is Professor of Human Geography, University of Birmingham, UK.

# CHILDREN LIVING IN SUSTAINABLE BUILT ENVIRONMENTS

New Urbanisms, New Citizens

*Pia Christensen, Sophie Hadfield-Hill, John Horton and Peter Kraftl*

LONDON AND NEW YORK

First published 2018
by Routledge
2 Park Square, Milton Park, Abingdon, Oxon OX14 4RN

and by Routledge
711 Third Avenue, New York, NY 10017

*Routledge is an imprint of the Taylor & Francis Group, an informa business*

© 2018 Pia Christensen, Sophie Hadfield-Hill, John Horton and Peter Kraftl

The right of Pia Christensen, Sophie Hadfield-Hill, John Horton and Peter Kraftl
to be identified as authors of this work has been asserted by them in accordance
with sections 77 and 78 of the Copyright, Designs and Patents Act 1988.

All rights reserved. No part of this book may be reprinted or reproduced or utilised
in any form or by any electronic, mechanical, or other means, now known or hereafter
invented, including photocopying and recording, or in any information storage or
retrieval system, without permission in writing from the publishers.

*Trademark notice:* Product or corporate names may be trademarks or registered trademarks,
and are used only for identification and explanation without intent to infringe.

*British Library Cataloguing-in-Publication Data*
A catalogue record for this book is available from the British Library

*Library of Congress Cataloging-in-Publication Data*
Names: Christensen, Pia Monrad, author.
Title: Children living in sustainable built environments : new urbanisms,
    new citizens / Pia Christensen, [and three others].
Description: Abingdon, Oxon ; New York, NY : Routledge, 2018.
Identifiers: LCCN 2017029068 | ISBN 9781138809390 (hardback) |
    ISBN 9781138809406 (pbk.) | ISBN 9781315750019 (ebook)
Subjects: LCSH: City children. | Sustainable urban development. | Sociology, Urban.
Classification: LCC HT206 .C47 2018 | DDC 307.76083—dc23
LC record available at https://lccn.loc.gov/2017029068

ISBN: 978-1-138-80939-0 (hbk)
ISBN: 978-1-138-80940-6 (pbk)
ISBN: 978-1-315-75001-9 (ebk)

Typeset in Bembo
by Apex CoVantage, LLC

*This book is dedicated to all children and young people experiencing urban change, and in memory of Professor Libby Burton*

# CONTENTS

| | |
|---|---|
| *List of figures* | *ix* |
| *List of boxes* | *x* |
| *Acknowledgements* | *xi* |

| | | |
|---|---|---|
| 1 | Introduction: New urbanisms, new citizens | 1 |
| 2 | Towards the interdisciplinary study of children and sustainable urbanism | 14 |
| 3 | Sustainable urbanisms in policy and practice | 39 |
| 4 | Living with sustainable urban technologies | 59 |
| 5 | Sustainable mobilities | 81 |
| 6 | Constituting communities: Welcoming, belonging, excluding | 103 |
| 7 | Vital politics: Children and young people's participation in public space and local decision-making | 130 |
| 8 | Making space for vitality in sustainable urbanisms: Childhood and play | 148 |

**viii** Contents

9  Conclusion: Towards a theory of children and
   sustainable urban vitalities                                  177

*References*                                                     *193*
*Index*                                                          *213*

# FIGURES

| | | |
|---|---|---|
| 1.1 | Case study development: Hettonbury | 8 |
| 1.2 | Case study development: Romsworth | 8 |
| 1.3 | Case study development: Nannton | 9 |
| 1.4 | Case study development: Tillinglow | 9 |
| 1.5 | Romsworth community workshop, Future Tree activity | 12 |
| 3.1 | The 'Egan wheel': components of 'sustainable communities' | 44 |
| 3.2 | 'Letchworth: The First Garden City' poster | 48 |
| 4.1 | Examples of eco-technologies in Hettonbury: Code Level 6 buildings | 61 |
| 4.2 | Examples of eco-technologies in Hettonbury: sustainable urban drainage systems – retention pond | 62 |
| 4.3 | Evidence of playful activity in the snow in Hettonbury | 66 |
| 4.4 | 'Weird' features on the Code Level 6 homes in Hettonbury | 73 |
| 5.1 | Spaces to play in Hettonbury: The Square | 92 |
| 5.2 | Spaces to play in Hettonbury: the park | 92 |
| 5.3 | Spaces to play in Hettonbury: courtyard | 93 |
| 5.4 | Spaces to play in Hettonbury: mews | 93 |
| 5.5 | Differentiated street surfaces around the park in Hettonbury | 95 |
| 8.1 | Who can afford to play? Example from India | 155 |
| 8.2 | Running through the fountains in Hettonbury | 158 |
| 8.3 | Partitioning bodies from the messy (and potentially dangerous) materialities | 162 |

# BOXES

| | | |
|---|---|---|
| 3.1 | Principles of the Freiburg Charter | 41 |
| 3.2 | Key principles from Farr's (2008) *Sustainable Urbanism* | 43 |
| 3.3 | India's vision for Smart Cities | 45 |
| 3.4 | 'Ideal' Communities | 47 |
| 3.5 | Letchworth: the first Garden City | 47 |
| 3.6 | New Towns | 49 |
| 3.7 | Exemplar city of sustainable urbanism: Curitiba | 50 |
| 3.8 | Exemplar city: Malmö, Sweden | 51 |
| 5.1 | The Woonerf ('living street') movement | 84 |
| 5.2 | Homezones | 84 |
| 9.1 | Evidence-based prompts for future participatory work with children and young people in the planning, design and building of sustainable urban spaces | 180 |

# ACKNOWLEDGEMENTS

We would like to thank the people who took part in the research on which this book is based. Over 250 people – predominantly children and young people, but also their families, schools, community groups and professional stakeholders – participated in the New Urbanisms, New Citizens (NUNC) research project, through sustained engagement lasting several months, if not years. We would like to express our profound gratitude to all of these individuals, and hope that this book does their experiences and voices justice.

Special thanks to the UK's Economic and Social Research Council (ESRC), who funded the NUNC research project (reference number: RES-062-23-1549). We also wish to extend our thanks for additional financial support for two other projects on which this book draws: the SHINE-TRUE project, funded by the Higher Education Collaboration Fund (HECF)/East Midlands Development Agency (EMDA); and the New Urbanisms in India project (reference number ES/K00932X/2).

We would like to extend our warm thanks to students and academic colleagues who at various points worked with us on the NUNC project and helped to ensure its success. In particular we wish to thank: Alan Prout, Clare Jarvis, Jen Dickie, Sarah Smith, Jane Ellis, Junyi Wu and Susana Cortes Morales.

We would also like to thank the project Advisory Group, who contributed to the intellectual development and societal impact of the NUNC project: Peter Hedges, Libby Burton, Alan Burns and Simon James, Martin Phillips, Hugh Matthews, Phil Mizen and Janet Jackson.

Finally, each of us would like to thank our family, friends and colleagues who have supported us during the whole process of undertaking and writing-up our research. Pia would like to thank: her children Tobias and Josefine, mother Yelva and brother Ronald. She would like to thank Chris for his ongoing support and happiness during writing this book. Thank you to colleagues at the Universities of Warwick and Leeds, and especially Tom Evans. Sophie would

**xii** Acknowledgements

like to thank: her husband, Chris, and parents, Sue and Alistair, for their ongoing support and colleagues both near and far who have played a key role in her development as an early-career researcher. John would like to thank family and friends, and particularly Rebekah Ryder for numerous interesting discussions about UK planning policy. Peter would like to thank Juliet, Emily, Adam, his parents and brother, Gavin Brown, Jenny Pickerill, and colleagues in Geography at the Universities of Leicester and Birmingham.

Unless otherwise referenced, all photographs were taken by the authors and are reproduced with their permission. Figure 3.2 is reproduced with kind permission from Letchworth Garden City Heritage Foundation.

# 1

# INTRODUCTION

## New urbanisms, new citizens

Over the past few decades, urban living has dramatically transformed the lives of children and young people. Rapid urbanisation, formidable physical re-composition of cities, and huge proliferation of the world's population (heading towards 70% urbanisation by 2050) are refashioning the interactions among demographics, environmental, social, cultural, economic and politics in towns and cities across the world (UN-Habitat, 2016). In many urban contexts the lives, mobilities and everyday experiences of children and young people are substantially impacted upon by large-scale urban extensions, including new innovative forms of urban sustainable development that seek actively to engage urban dwellers with the repercussions of climate change. Simultaneously, an ongoing international 'new wave' of multidisciplinary childhood studies claims to radically and affirmatively transform thinking about the spaces and politics of childhood and youth. This book aims to bring research and policy-making around urban sustainable development and childhood into productive conversation. It will do so by drawing upon rich empirical data from a large-scale interdisciplinary study of four newly built sustainable urban environments in southeast England, and upon cutting-edge research from other geographical contexts. In this way the book marks a step-change in scholarship on the everyday lives of children and young people growing up in new sustainable urban environments, based on theoretically informed empirical exploration.

### Structure and contributions of this book

The argument we develop is twofold. First, we demonstrate through interpretative analysis how 'new wave' materialist, nonrepresentational and posthumanist theorisations afford fuller, carefully detailed, practicable, new understandings of children and young people's mobilities, materialities, socialities, play and civic

**2** Introduction

participation. In particular, our analysis will provoke, extend and recast significantly, some key normative scholarly, political and popular assumptions about children and young people's play, (lack of) mobility, and (lack of) community engagement and participation.

Our research was animated by recent lines of new theorisations within a multidisciplinary childhood studies, which we discuss in Chapter 2. We have found that this scholarship (which some term a 'new wave' (Ryan, 2012, 2014), and which terminology we use for ease of reference) offers inspirational, exciting prompts to engage, in new and sustained ways, with children and young people's complex mobilities, socialities, embodiments, emotions/affects, and more-than-human relationalities. Indeed, these ideas helped us to acknowledge, articulate and engage more fully with children and young people's everyday lives in ways which were both intellectually revelatory (affording interconnected languages of affect–embodiment–materialities–biopolitics) and practically useful (for example, allowing us to share research findings in diverse engagements with urban planners and policy-makers). Simultaneously, in this chapter we argue that the full appreciation of the *vitalities* of children and young people's everyday lives require some key tenets of 'new wave' thinking to be critically re-evaluated and grounded anew within a politicised sensibility attuned to community affects, diversity of identities, inclusions and exclusions.

We substantiate this throughout the book drawing on examples from our ethnographic encounters with children and young people. A particular aim of the book is to capture both theoretical and policy/planning implications of researching children and young people's lives and experiences in diverse urban spaces. In this, we echo Christensen and James (2017) who argue that such endeavour raises powerful, yet complex new epistemological questions. In Chapter 2, we articulate five framing questions of 'new wave' scholarship. We argue that children and young people's everyday lives and experiences demand more cautious, critical engagements with the 'new wave' theorisation. In effect, then, the substantive chapters (Chapters 3–8) develop, and build towards, a critical re-engagement with the 'new wave' theoretical framework to establish a firmer ground in the lived, experiential, *vital* empirical details and politics of children and young people's everyday experiences and entanglements with the material built and natural environments of urban spaces.

As a second point of departure, in Chapter 3, we introduce and contextualise the concept, principles and international planning/policy context of 'sustainable' urbanism. We outline how this globalised turn has constituted a significant array of new urban spaces and – we argue, consequently – new experiences of urban childhood and youth. The scale, significance and motive force of sustainable urbanism is remarkable. Over three decades, one can trace the growth of particular modes of 'sustainable' urbanism through numerous international policy discourses, construction projects and design and planning interventions, which are impacting the lives of millions of children and young people. In reality sustainable design and planning interventions – deriving from particular Euro-American antecedents and exemplars – have been adopted in diverse, global sites of urban development and expansion.

A great deal of existing research has studied the underlying policy discourses and planning visions of 'sustainable' urbanism, but much less consideration has been given to the *actually existing* urban spaces, communities and experiences constituted via policies and visions of 'sustainable' urbanism. So, in the latter half of Chapter 3, and through the remainder of this book, we identify some characteristic features of *'sustainable' urbanism in practice*. In particular, we highlight three key sets of features:

1   built-in *sustainable urban architectures and radical technologies*;
2   urban *mobility and networks of connectivity* (for example, smooth and effective reduction of carbon dioxide emission through the creation of walkability indicies, cycling and public transport networks); and
3   community *participation, liveability, inclusiveness and conviviality*, which have been planned-in to 'sustainable' urban developments over the last decades.

Over the course of this book we explore how actually existing material, spatial and social features of 'sustainable' urban developments are impacting significantly upon children and young people's everyday lives. Through a series of in case studies we explore new build housing in south-east England and beyond.

In Chapter 4 we draw attention to the often taken-for-granted, sometimes playful, sometimes frustrating interactions with built-in *sustainable urban architectures and radical technologies*. We show that as 'smart' and 'green' new technological innovations are integrated into homes and communities in diverse contexts – from sites in England to new urban developments in India – there is a need for greater understanding of how people interact with these new features, and impact on how young people and their families may begin to imagine sustainable living in the future. We focus on lived experiences of sustainable urban architectures, including sustainable urban drainage channels, and the eco-technologies woven into the fabric of homes and streetscapes. Drawing on a materialist perspective – paying attention to the emotional, embodied and intra-active everyday lives of sustainable urbanism – we show how young people were inextricably connected to their local built environments, connected through observing, being with, wondering about, being critical of, touching eco-architectural forms and working out everyday routines and practices, involving interaction with new household technologies.

In Chapter 5, we explore attempts to enhance sustainable *mobility and networks of connectivity* in urban contexts. In particular we show how the mobilities of young people are intense, despite social and material boundaries that have previously been interpreted as harbingers of a *decline* in children's independent mobility. In contrast to the focus of earlier scholarship, we demonstrate how children and young people engage in 'walking' as an important, yet mundane everyday activity. The chapter then goes on to discuss the experiences and interactions of children and young people with the design and material features of streets, roads and other street users.

**4** Introduction

The chapter shows how self-contained road networks and certain design features importantly afford young people's everyday mobility. We focus on 'shared surface' streets that have been designed to equalise the status of pedestrians, cyclists and motorists in their use of the street and have been promoted as a step towards the democratisation of city space. However, as we will show, in its present articulation, the shared surface street does not straightforwardly foster benign and egalitarian relationships between children-as-pedestrians and adult motorists. In the chapter we argue that traffic movement involves complex interactions among intersecting humans, social, discursive and diverse materialities, and we specify how linguistic, affective and material orderings are important to children (and others) in their navigation of shared surface streets.

In Chapter 6, we consider notions of 'viable', 'meaningful', 'cohesive' or 'functioning' community which have come to be central to sustainable urbanism. We note that urban development supporting social sustainability features is characterised by policy and planning interventions designed to attract and accommodate a diversity of residents through providing 'mixed' housing stocks and convivial public spaces. However, children and young people have a particularly ambivalent presence within the sustainable urban policy and planning discourses: being at once superficially visible (in, for example, architects' drawings, visions documents, planning briefs and housing developers' brochures), yet still profoundly marginalised via the design and regulation of public and 'community' spaces. The chapter evidences how children and young people have profound and important (but often overlooked) roles in both the initial and ongoing constitution of community in newly built urban spaces: through everyday gestures of generosity and welcome, but also through everyday acts of boundary-maintenance 'them and us' and social-spatial exclusion. We particularly note how quickly intergenerational and intersectional discourses and exclusions based on age, social class and housing type emerged in the four case study communities. As in other chapters, the discussion is underpinned by the celebration of children and young people's rich, detailed, lively, playful everyday knowledge (achieved through outdoor mobilities in particular) and narratives of community, but rues the limited extent to which planners and policy-makers actually engage with this knowledge. The discussion of social exclusions, in the latter half of the chapter express such deep concerns, which we later frame as critical questions for 'new wave' theories in childhood studies.

Chapter 7 explores young people's experiences of *participation* in practice, in communities designed to ostensibly foster liveability, inclusiveness and conviviality. Through analysing young people's movements, interactions and voices in diverse community spaces, from self-purposed community centres to public spaces, we show multiple barriers to young people's everyday participation in their communities. We highlight spaces and moments of structural exclusion – the exclusion of young people's bodies and voices – excluding them from dialogues, negotiations and discourses. However, developing our arguments in Chapter 6, and through our attention to vital urbanisms, we highlight spaces, moments and encounters between young people, adults and infrastructures that shape community vitality.

Chapter 8 offers a final step towards a full appreciation of the *vitalities* of children and young people's lives in sustainable urban communities. It focuses upon an activity that is deemed to be a central, assumed element of children and young people's lives, especially in the Minority Global North: play. However, rather than seek to romanticise play, or see play as some kind of 'natural' solution to the creation of more vital, urban places, we carefully construct an argument for examining what we term *the space between childhood and play*. Reflecting upon a number of examples from our research, and from elsewhere in the world, we argue that a focus on the space between childhood and play opens up a number of opportunities for interdisciplinary childhood studies in sustainable urban contexts (as per Chapter 2). Specifically, we consider how playing comes to be conjoined with a range of key concerns for sustainable urbanism: everyday social relations; public space; nonhuman agency; social difference; and, the politics of vitality.

The conclusion (Chapter 9) develops our closing contribution that marks a critical return to the five questions we introduced in Chapter 2. First, however we summarise key findings from preceding chapters in a way that is designed to offer both conceptual and practical (especially, policy-oriented) insights. We critique recurring marginalisation of children and young people's experiences and knowledges in sustainable urban planning and policy practices. Against this grain, we offer a series of practical, evidence-based prompts, which we hope will inspire future engagement with children and young people in affirmative participatory processes to develop the vitalities of diverse sustainable urban spaces. Second, we re-engage with the five framing theoretical questions. We argue that sustained research encounters with children and young people prompt critical reflection upon 'new wave' materialist, nonrepresentational and posthumanist theorisations in multi- and interdisciplinary childhood studies. In the conclusion, we essentially stage a conversation between the framing precepts of 'new wave' scholarship and the vitalities, details and politics witnessed in our research. We suggest that this kind of conversation is not only extremely productive and generative of important new, critical and politicised insights – it is also essential to retain the vitality of academic 'new wave' debate.

## Research Context

The key empirical material discussed in this book derives from a major, four-year, interdisciplinary research project on which the authors collaborated. The New Urbanisms, New Citizens (NUNC) project was funded by the UK's Economic and Social Research Council (2009–2013). In this research we explored children and young people's experiences of newly built 'sustainable' housing developments in south-east England. The selected case studies exemplified the internationalised emergence of 'sustainable' urbanisms as key, characteristic, increasingly commonplace spaces of childhood and youth. The project was an avowedly interdisciplinary

**6** Introduction

collaboration, bringing together anthropologists, geographers and sociologists with shared, although disciplinarily disparate, interests in childhood and youth. The overarching aim of the project was to investigate relationships between sustainable community regeneration, children's experiences and mobilities in new urban environments, and their participation and citizenship in planning and design. The project addressed a series of objectives which set out to:

- develop our theoretical understandings of children's lived experiences in new, sustainable urban environments;
- investigate children's mobility patterns through their everyday uses of public and private community spaces;
- explore children's experiences of belonging to their community and the implications for their participation and citizenship; and
- inform the planning and design of sustainable communities *for all*, with an explicit focus on young people's everyday experiences of life in new urban environments.

The policy impetus for the project was the then New Labour government's major programme of investment in housebuilding in the UK, framed by the Sustainable Communities Plan. 'Growth Areas' in the southeast of England (see Chapter 3) were earmarked for the planning and delivery of hundreds of thousands of new homes (over three decades). However, following a major round of investment in ostensibly 'sustainable' urban development, this agenda was overtaken by economic and political events: specifically, the global economic downturn, during which the building of new housing slowed dramatically down; and a change to a Conservative government in 2010, leading to transformations in the political backdrop surrounding the planning of new build settlements (a period of decline followed by renewed commitment to large-scale housebuilding in early 2017). Nonetheless, these Growth Areas were the focus for substantial initial urban development, and continue to be regarded as exemplars of large-scale delivery of sustainable urbanism. The project focused on one of the designated Growth Areas. The Milton Keynes–South Midlands (MKSM) Growth Area encompassed an area of 4,850 km$^2$ located between London and Birmingham, England. When the Growth Area was first designated, the plan was to build in the region of 250,000 new homes. However, in practice, approximately 10,000 homes were built annually between the roll-out of the Sustainable Communities plan in 2003 and the housing market downturn of 2009. Although the Growth Area is now officially de-designated, the region is still a focus for large-scale housing development. Significantly, planning proposals and permissions in the region continue, to a large extent, to retain design features and principles characteristic of the Sustainable Communities Plan.

Within MKSM, four communities were chosen representing diverse forms and principles of new, sustainable urban development. In the book all community and personal names are pseudonyms to protect the identities, mobilities, lives and spaces of the children, young people and their families taking part in our research. The first case study, Hettonbury, was chosen for its status as exemplar for sustainable urban development in England. The new suburb represents a 'sustainable urban extension' built along a number of key principles for sustainable urbanism (see Chapter 3). The outline planning consent was approved in 1997 for 1,020 new homes to be built on a site proximate to a large town in the South Midlands. Notably, Hettonbury was planned and built using the process of Inquiry by Design – a complex, lengthy form of negotiation involving local authority planners, architects, private developers, local community members and various local voluntary organisations. The outcome of this process was a design code, which resonates reasonably strongly with the design parameters of the Sustainable Communities Plan (ODPM, 2003b). Hettonbury (Figure 1.1) contains sustainable features such as: a Sustainable Urban Drainage System (SUDS) incorporating residential drainage, porous paving, swales and retention ponds; photovoltaic (PV) and solar hot water units installed on the majority of houses; houses built to higher standards of environmental design (e.g. better insulation), with some exemplar 'Code Level 6' homes (see Chapter 4); urban architectures meant to foster social sustainability elements such as 'liveability' and 'conviviality' (see Chapter 6) – the courtyards, urban squares and public spaces, are linked by 'shared surfaces' to afford pedestrians the right of way over cars (see Chapter 5). At the time of writing in 2017, the Hettonbury development was still not fully completed.

The construction of the second community, Romsworth (Figure 1.2), began at around the same time in 2003, but it was built on distinctly different principles to Hettonbury. Despite having a similar number of homes, Romsworth has been created as a new self-sufficient development, built on former agricultural land approximately eight kilometres from the nearest town. It is an example of a standalone sustainable community, although it has never been badged as an 'Eco-town'. It is not possible to understand Romsworth without knowledge of its early planning history. The land on which Romsworth is now situated was sold by the landowner on the explicit premise that a *community* would be built there. Subsequent transfers of ownership occurred probably because developers were (somewhat unusually in the UK context) tied into actually building a *'community'* and not 'just another' new housing development. Eventually, the notion of community has become manifest in many important ways: through the comparatively early construction of local community facilities, including shops, cafe, community centre, a primary school, a doctor's surgery and a dentist (compare Romsworth, for instance, with Hettonbury, which at the time of writing still only has one small shop, a school and a community centre (see Chapters 6 and 7); through the design of houses, built largely in the style and masonry typical of the housing in surrounding villages; through advertising hoardings compelling home buyers to 'come and build a community'; through early and ongoing practices of community-making among residents, including efforts to welcome new neighbours and a vast array of community events. Although construction work took place during the

**FIGURE 1.1** Case study development: Hettonbury.

**FIGURE 1.2** Case study development: Romsworth.

**FIGURE 1.3** Case study development: Nannton.

**FIGURE 1.4** Case study development: Tillinglow.

**10** Introduction

entire period of the NUNC research, by the time of writing, Romsworth stood completed as a community.

The third case study, Nannton (Figure 1.3), typifies the majority of new build housing development, which took place in MKSM in the wake of the Sustainable Communities Plan. The development occupies a large tract of land covering around 2 km² on the edge of an existing town. Since 2000, more than 2,000 new homes, and associated roads and infrastructure, have been built by private large-scale housing developers and contractors. The development contains a mix of housing types, tenures and sizes. However, typically for large developments and given the economies of scale involved, the development comprised many houses built to the same template. Unlike Hettonbury – but like many housing developments built in south-east England, post the Sustainable Communities Plan, Nannton does not feature any visible or exceptional forms of sustainable architecture. Unlike Romsworth – but, again, typically for many Sustainable Communities developments Nannton is not particularly marketed or configured as a '*community*'. Indeed, promotion of the development has overwhelmingly focused on location and convenience for local, regional and national transport links. The development includes a school, shopping precinct and outdoor play and green spaces. Additional community resources were original planned. However, at time of writing, development of Nannton had stalled, such that the provision of community resources and spaces remains relatively modest, given the density, size and diversity of the population.

Finally, the fourth case study, Tillinglow (Figure 1.4), exemplifies a mode of housing development that has been commonplace, post the Sustainable Communities Plan and in many other geographical contexts. Small pockets of housing have been constructed on derelict, 'brownfield' (previously occupied by industrial premises or other usage) or 'infill' (occupying often awkwardly shaped plots in between existing urban development) land. At Tillinglow, around 100 high-density dwellings were constructed on a brownfield site on the edge of an existing housing estate. The Tillinglow development was delivered by a provider of affordable and 'shared-ownership' housing, and – like many new build housing developments of this scale and model of delivery – has been beset with challenges, litigation and negative publicity relating to the reportedly poor quality of materials, rapid erection and scant finish. The development includes elements of sustainable architecture such as Sustainable Urban Drainage System (SUDS) channels, photovoltaic (PV) panels and solar hot water units. However, the development did not include construction of new services and community amenities, and the site has relatively poor connectivity to adjacent housing estates.

In addition to our explicit focus on data from these four case communities, throughout the book we have drawn on a range of international examples of children living and growing up in spaces of sustainable urbanism. A notable example is data from the New Urbanisms in India: Urban Living, Sustainability and Everyday Life project, funded by the ESRC (ES/K00932X/2), which investigated the everyday lives of young people and their families in a site of urban transformation in India, led by one of the authors (Hadfield-Hill and Zara, 2017).

## Research methodology

The NUNC project team adopted a mixed-method approach to researching the lives of children (aged 9–16) in the four communities (Christensen et al., 2011) This large, interdisciplinary project was underpinned by ethnography, specifically, by up to six months participant observation in each of the four communities. Observations took place in a range of settings: in streets, squares, woodland and fields, and in public buildings and venues such as in schools; in community centres, at organised clubs, local festivals and activities, such as Scouts; and in children's family homes. This part of the research was combined with up to four interviews with each of the 175 children who took part in the research across the four communities. The interviews covered the following broad topics: 'my week' – getting to know participants and their everyday lives; mobilities (journeys, transport and play) within and beyond the communities; sustainability; community participation and citizenship. All of the interviews were recorded using a digital audio recorder and transcribed. Young participants (50 in total, either individually or in small groups) took the researchers on 'guided walks' around their communities. They led the researchers to important places (as they defined them): the walks and the informal conversations en route were recorded through a variety of media, including a GPS-enabled camera and a digital audio recorder.

In tandem with the observations and interviews, we integrated the use of GPS technologies. Young people were given a GPS device for a one week period to track their mobilities, at the end of the week the device was returned, the data downloaded and a follow-up interview arranged. Google Earth images, visualising the tracking data formed a key component of the mobility interviews, engaging young people in the analysis of their own data and mobilities. Finally, in each of the communities we co-organised a local workshop together with young participants. These events were designed to be participatory, and, in each community, were attended by 30–50 people, including child and adult residents, local community representatives, and a range of professional stakeholders (for instance the police, youth workers, teachers, local authority planners and councillors). The workshops included a range of activities: from presentations by the young people about issues that concerned them, to creative tasks (guided walk, treasure hunt, and the Future Tree) designed to foster discussion about key themes from the research (Figure 1.5). The workshops offered an opportunity for data production, and a safe dialogical space in which participants could undertake further exploration of controversial issues, conflicts, experiences, hopes and happenings as residents in the community.

We followed, and in some cases developed, ethical guidance for research with children and the young people. The research underwent full institutional approval

**FIGURE 1.5** Romsworth community workshop, Future Tree activity.

at the University of Warwick, and all of the researchers had the necessary checks for working with children in the UK. All research was consensual: the team obtained written parental or guardian permission for each child, as well as written consent from children themselves. Given the lack of formal guidance in the UK context on the use of GPS research tools with young people, the team formulated a new robust ethical protocol for GPS research with children. In addition, the research followed ethical principles and guidelines surrounding anonymity, confidentiality, withdrawal and data management.

The datasets from the project were analysed via NVivo. In writing this book, data from the NUNC project have been analysed alongside material from a range of other projects and sources. Thus, while the NUNC research forms a substantial resource for the thematic chapters, the book draws upon findings from a range of academic studies in contexts outside the UK (although it must be re-stated that specific studies of children in 'sustainable' urban communities, beyond the NUNC project, remain rare).

## Concluding statement

In essence this book is a call for research, policy and practice which is better attuned to the often-overlooked ways in which children and young people

Introduction **13**

constitute *their own* inhabitations and understandings of 'sustainable' urban spaces, *their own* everyday geographies of mobilities and encounters, and *their own* modes of everyday participation and citizenship. We note that so far children and young people's lived, embodied experiences, understandings and insights have been overwhelmingly absent from extant scholarly and policy discourse and debate around sustainable urbanism. Given this absence, our final argument is, at least in part, a methodological one. We argue for the necessity of carrying out in-depth, detailed and systematic mixed-methods research with children and young people in order to gain important and critical new insights about the lived – including deeply sensed and embodied – everyday impacts of sustainable urbanism. The key material and writing of the book essentially represents the efforts of interdisciplinary collaborative research including well-developed, ethically-led participatory practices with children and young people living in diverse, emergent contexts of sustainable urbanism. Herewith, we hope that this book will form a platform for future equally productive multi- and/or interdisciplinary ventures in the field.

# 2

# TOWARDS THE INTERDISCIPLINARY STUDY OF CHILDREN AND SUSTAINABLE URBANISM

## Introduction

A key perspective that underpins this book is that the everyday experiences of children and young people provide important new understandings of sustainable urbanism. In our research and throughout this book we do this through commitment to what Tim Ingold (1995) has called a 'dwelling perspective'; that is, research (such as ethnographic fieldwork) based on learning through personal engagement with the world (in all its variety). However, in advancing this claim, this chapter will situate our work within a large and well-established field of social-scientific research on children and childhood. For shorthand, in this text, we refer to such scholarship as 'childhood studies'. In our definition, childhood studies include work situated within sociology, anthropology, human geography, psychology, history and education. However, our theoretical framework draws primarily on the authors' background in social sciences perspectives. Childhood studies represents the major theoretical point of departure for both the book and for the authors, all of whom have researched and written under the broad premises of childhood studies for many years. Those premises are multiple, and well documented; however, the first part of the present chapter provides an overview for those readers less familiar with childhood studies and, especially, what became termed the 'new social studies of childhood' (NSSC). It then introduces a large subset of that work that has focused on *urban* and, to a much lesser extent, *sustainable urban* childhoods. At the end of the first section we argue for a more thoroughly *interdisciplinary* childhood studies as one that can better apprehend the complex and recursive inter-relationships between diverse childhoods and differently patterned forms of sustainable urbanism. For, while childhood studies scholarship has been characterised by striking theoretical consistency, much of the research has continued to proceed within disciplinary silos.

The second part of this chapter outlines what an interdisciplinary childhood studies might look like, and how it might enable academics and practitioners alike to grapple with pressing contemporary issues of climate change and sustainability, which we discuss in more detail in Chapter 3. It provides a thorough and critical assessment of a nascent 'new wave' (Ryan, 2012) or 'infra-paradigm' (Oswell, 2013) of childhood studies scholarship, using the former term (albeit not unproblematically) as a shorthand to bring together a number of key conceptual frames. We outline how these frames cut across both different disciplinary positions, and older and (especially) newer scholarship, the latter inspired by poststructuralist, feminist new materialist and nonrepresentational thinking. These frames are: mobility; othering, intersectionality and intergenerationality; emotion/affect; embodiment; materialities, biopolitics and nonhuman natures. While we can, of necessity, only outline each of these frames with relative brevity, our intention is to demonstrate how, *taken together*, these broad conceptual themes lay the groundwork for a more truly interdisciplinary childhood studies. Just as importantly, in so doing, this book constitutes arguably the first systematic attempt to theorise *and* empirically exemplify what a 'new wave' of childhood studies might look like. While it does not constitute such a 'break' from all of the key principles of NSSC as some authors may wish, this book – starting with the arguments in this chapter – nevertheless aims to instigate a major influence on intellectual agendas in contemporary childhood studies. The chapter closes by summarising how these agendas will in turn – as evidenced by the material in the remainder of the book – enable novel conceptual developments in scholarship on sustainable urbanism.

## A starting point for childhood studies: the new social studies of childhood

As Ryan (2012, 2014) observes, the academic study of childhood has a relatively long history, and one that initially saw little separation between 'social' and 'biological' (or 'scientific') modes of inquiry. From the work of Rousseau, into the nineteenth and early twentieth centuries, childhood scholars combined and contributed to the rapidly emerging disciplines of child psychology and development, education, and the biological sciences, often informed by spiritual doctrines (Hendrick, 1997; Jenks, 2005). By the early twentieth century, social reformers – and especially philanthropists concerned with the conditions of the urban classes – sought to intervene into children's social *and* physiological development through programmes ranging from the early playground movement (Gagen, 2004) to new educational approaches (Kraftl, 2006). Indeed, the health and welfare of society – and, of necessity, of children – was central to attempts to reform and redesign urban spaces along principles that, like the Garden Cities discussed in Chapter 3, offered the foundations for more contemporary forms of sustainable urbanism. Thus, for well over a century, scholarship and professional practice directed at children and young people have been entwined with that on (sustainable) urbanisms.

**16** Towards interdisciplinary study

While the New Social Studies of Childhood represent the major theoretical point of departure for the current volume, it is worth briefly noting that there are many important antecedents to that scholarship. Significantly, these carried forward the twin concerns of the work described above: on the one hand, a resolute focus on *urban* life; and, on the other, a commitment to understanding (if not addressing) the positioning of children and young people as 'other', as 'deviant', or even as 'criminal'. From the 1920s onwards, for instance, the Chicago School of Sociology produced formidable work within urban sociology, including in developing the symbolic interactionist approach. The Chicago School carried out a number of ethnographic studies of young people that examined the social and ecological bases of the shaping of human social behaviour (including the origins of deviance), tying their work into processual models (emphasising social structure and physical environment) of urban form (e.g. Wirth, 1938; Whyte, 1943). Whyte's classic study, *Street Corner Society*, became exemplary for urban ethnography, in its intimate, insightful portrayal of poverty and youth through exploring the social worlds and everyday lives of Italian young males in an inner city community in Boston, USA (Whyte, 1943).

During the 1960s and 1970s, Anglo-American sociological and criminological scholarship into youth subcultures sought not only to identify symbolic homologies between class and subcultural styles, but to engage in detailed (often participant- observation) research *with* young people, which emphasised their agency in subverting mainstream cultures. A commendable example is Stanley Cohen's (1972) analysis of the creation of the Mods and Rockers by the media and the workings of 'moral panic' in a society. During the same decades, work by geographers engaged in close analysis of children's experiences of, and place-making within, the city. Such studies include William Bunge's (1973) 'geographical expeditions' in Detroit and, particularly, Colin Ward's (1978) classic studies of children's everyday life and playing in city streets and urban wastelands. Ward's plea for the importance of informal learning, place and social justice brought him, on the one hand, to celebrate the 'resourcefulness and the intensity, variety and ingenuity' of children's experiences that contributed to the becoming-lively of urban environments. On the other hand his book was a testimony of how children's freedom in the city was being eroded by urban (re)development projects – that he saw as serving the financial benefits of housing developers and the interests of motorised traffic (connectivity and speed) (Ward, 1978). At this time many studies, particularly within environmental psychology focused on understanding children's relationships to the physical environment through a focus on the development of spatial cognition – fundamental spatial concepts and cognitive mapping of physical environments (Hart and Moore, 1973; Hart et al., 1973). Most scholars within this tradition would emphasise how children's learning about place was a function of intersecting identities and relationships such as age, gender and class (e.g. Blaut et al., 1970; Hart, 1979; Matthews, 1987).

The above review represents a small selection of the many studies that sought (theoretically, empirically and politically) to understand children and young

Towards interdisciplinary study **17**

people's experiences of urban life. For decades, diverse scholars were concerned to investigate the marginalisation and negative portrayal of young people – especially in cities. These concerns found support by the formalisation of the United Nations Conventions on the Rights of the Child (UNCRC) in 1989, and its subsequent ratification by the majority of the world's national governments (Skelton, 2007). However, although informed by these imperatives, the development of NSSC during the 1990s offered a far more coherent framework for the social-scientific study of childhood. While the theoretical advances of NSSC were many, we want in this section of the chapter to identify just two (for a far more detailed introduction, see James and Prout, 2015).

First, NSSC scholars offered critiques of developmental models of childhood that had been formulated by psychologists and others. Anthropologists and sociologists began to show that as they age, children seldom follow neat, universal and teleological models (such as those established by Piaget) and that the testing of children as objects rather than subjects of inquiry was both ethically and methodologically problematic. Thus, the first premise of childhood studies was that scholars needed to engage children more directly: to view them as subjects, as agents in their own right, and to listen to their voices and agency (James and Prout, 2015; Jenks, 2005; James et al., 1998). In other words children demanded *conceptual autonomy*, in epistemological and methodological terms, removed from other units of analysis (such as the family, generation, gender) and viewed as valid research subjects in their own right (Thorne, 1987; Corsaro, 1997; Christensen and James, 2000). Another was that there were moves to place children on an even footing with adults in research, such that in ethical, political and methodological (if not legal) terms, children were viewed in 'symmetry' with adults (Christensen and Prout, 2002). A third implication was to view children as 'beings' in their own right (James et al., 1998). This distinction was at the time a necessary step in the fuller recognition of the child as 'complete'. In concurrence, these writings insisted on the recognition of children as co-contemporaries (emphasising the value of life in the present) rather than in terms of futurity (emphasising value of life as future adult – as 'becoming'). This formed an important move away from any adultist bias found within the developmental perspectives (of primarily child psychology, medicine and education) that designated 'incomplete', unstable by nature and in the making – that is undergoing the 'law of growth' as inherent qualities of the child (Jenks, 2005). It is important to recognise that such scholarly 'overstatement' helped to establish the conception of children (as well as adults) as simultaneously *human beings* (quasi-citizenly subjects with status, rights, needs and responsibilities, with the capacity for stability, meaning-making, and agency in the world) and as *human becomings* (Lee, 2001; Uprichard, 2008; Worth, 2009).

A final and consequent implication was that children should be enabled to participate – to varying degrees – in both decision-making that affects their lives, and in the process of undertaking academic research (e.g. Hart, 2013; Christensen and James, 2000; Tisdall et al., 2006; Percy-Smith and Burns, 2013). Certainly, this first premise – one of moving beyond psychological frameworks

**18** Towards interdisciplinary study

to engage children directly in the process of research, including in participatory methodologies – undergirds the authors' original research, reported in this volume (see Chapter 1). However, the various implications of this first premise – especially in terms of voice, agency and participation – have also been the foci for critiques that have led to the 'new wave' of childhood studies scholarship, discussed later in this chapter.

A second, and related, original point of departure for childhood studies was the recognition of childhood as socially constructed. There is disagreement about the extent to which social factors condition childhood experience. However – again, in part responding to the rather biologically deterministic models of childhood development – the key consideration here is that childhood is not *simply* a natural phenomenon. Rather, childhoods vary over time and space; they are conditioned by societal expectations, cultural norms and discourses and emotional affects; and childhoods are literally and figuratively produced by (often adult) social practices and organisations. In a classic example, Jenks (2005) contrasts two principal ways in which children in European societies have been viewed: the Apollonian (naturally 'angelic') and the Dionysian (naturally 'demonic') child. Christensen (1994) and Valentine (1996b) demonstrate how such views of childhood colour our treatment of children – from their representation in media reportage to the rules that are imposed upon them by parents and other 'responsible' adults to their at the time often 'muted' voice within academic studies.

Simultaneously, it has been observed that the social construction of childhood often implies the institutionalisation of childhood at least in European and North American contexts (Qvortrup et al., 1994; Philo and Parr, 2000; Barker et al., 2010). Recent scholarship has shown, for instance, how emotions play a crucial and complex role in policy-making for and professional practices with children – from the influence upon policy-making of a society's general emotional preconditioning towards children, to the emotions of individual policy-makers that drive particular policy formulations, and from 'problematic' emotions in children that require intervention, to the shared emotions that emerge in the interaction between children and the practitioners who work with them, within institutional spaces (Blazek and Kraftl, 2015).

## Childhood studies in (sustainable) urban contexts

The preceding section demonstrated that there has been an enduring academic interest in children in urban environments. However, as the key premises of NSSC became increasingly influential within the social sciences, issues such as voice, agency and the social-constructedness of childhoods came to the fore in scholarship on specifically *urban* childhoods (for fuller reviews, see Hörschelmann and van Blerk, 2013; Skelton and Gough, 2013). At the same time, earlier interest in (especially) children's environmental cognition waned as critiques of psychological studies of childhood gained strength. This paradigmatic turn is perhaps most notable in the work of Hugh Matthews, whose work shifted within the space of a

Towards interdisciplinary study **19**

decade from detailed examination of children's mapping abilities (Matthews, 1992) to studies of children's experiences of and resistance to adult rules in urban spaces such as streets and shopping malls (Matthews et al., 2000). Indeed, Matthews's work during the late 1990s and early 2000s, as well as that by a number of other scholars (e.g. Valentine, 1996a; Skelton, 2000; Christensen and O'Brien, 2003), was instrumental in setting the agenda for scholarship on children in urban contexts. On the one hand, childhood studies scholars – and those working under the banner of sub-disciplinary children's geographies – emphasised how children's uses of urban space were constructed, designed, managed and monitored by adults, via what Holloway and Valentine (2000) termed 'spatial' (rather than 'social') constructions of childhood. Valentine's (1996a) classic study showed how, specifically in urban *public* spaces, children were viewed as both vulnerable (to 'stranger danger') and as a threat to the proper workings of civic society. Thereafter, many studies have examined how parents and other significant adults attempt to control children's everyday uses of urban spaces (e.g. Aitken, 2001; Pain, 2006) and researched children's place-making, for example how children carve out spaces 'of their own', places where they feel they belong, places for play, and places to express their social identities and relationships (Christensen and Mikkelsen, 2013). A cursory glance at back issues of journals like *Children's Geographies* and *Childhood* uncover a slew of studies – far too numerous to mention here – that similarly examine children's experiences of, and place-making within, diverse urban public spaces.

More recently, this scholarship has expanded to focus on a variety of political, environmental, educational and economic contestations that in many different geographical locations powerfully influence children's urban lives – from the lives of street children in Brazil (Ursin, 2011), to the social networks for survival in Addis Ababa (Eriksen and Mulugeta, 2016), to imageries and lived experiences of children living in 'alternative' urban settlements, such as Christiania in Denmark (Wasshede, 2017). This recent work has sought to take up a range of theoretical advances, which, perhaps inevitably, extend beyond and even challenge the main premises of NSSC, indicating the diversity and vibrancy of current scholarship in childhood studies (see also Prout, 2005). We return to these theoretical advances in the second part of this chapter in our discussion of 'new wave' approaches to childhood studies.

Here, we wish to highlight two interlinked empirical lacunae among the diverse range of scholarship on urban childhoods, which this book addresses in important ways. First, there is by comparison relatively little work that focuses on the *planning and design* of urban environments, especially outside of the contexts of the Minority Global North. Second, there is a dearth of research about children in/ and *sustainable* urban environments (see Chapter 3). In terms of urban planning and design, perhaps the most important body of work – from both academic and policy perspectives – has emerged from the 'Child-Friendly Cities' (CFC) programme. From a planning viewpoint, the United Nations' CFC website (www.childfriendly cities.org) brings together a wide range of resources, examples, toolkits and advice on developing cities with children in mind. The CFC approach is enunciated in nine 'building blocks', which bring together key elements of UNCRC and NSSC,

**20** Towards interdisciplinary study

including children's rights to basic services and amenities, and the inclusion of children's perspectives in decision-making that affects their lives. The CFC is also underpinned by robust academic work on urban childhoods in both the Minority Global North and Majority Global South. For instance, seminal work by Chawla (2007) explored the experiences of children growing up in diverse neighbourhoods in cities, with particular emphasis upon children's participation and their care for natural worlds.

In earlier work, *Growing Up in an Urbanising World* (Chawla, 2002) examined how, across eight countries, children from poorer communities could be better involved in the planning and design of their communities. This work demonstrates that – in a striking echo with the urban-based work taking place in the industrialising cities of the late nineteenth century – the rapid expansion of cities worldwide means that there are both *more children* living in cities than ever before, and that children are some of the most *vulnerable* to social and environmental threats. However, as more recent work has attested, children are also key agents for community resilience in cities (Karsten, 2005) nonetheless, still undervalued and often unrecognised as a resource in social and economic (re)production (Katz, 2004). What was (and still is) most striking about the *Growing Up in an Urbanising World* project was that it afforded one of the only major *comparative* studies of children's urban lives. However, it is evident that notions of 'sustainability' are not treated in any systematic conceptual or empirical way. The study is loosely framed within the (now dated) Brundtland Report *Our Common Future* (World Commission on Environment and Development, 1987) and its fallouts, rather than specifically addressing 'sustainability' as a subject of analysis. In the book the term 'environment' is referred to in discussions; these tend to focus on education for sustainability (EfS), environmental hazards, opportunities, threats, experiences and environmental 'features' of cities. This omission is not unique but perhaps symptomatic for the lacuna we observed in urban-based childhood studies scholarship as a whole: there is an apparent lack of up-to-date, critical, and conceptually informed studies about children in *sustainable* urban environments.

We will extend this observation by clarifying that there exist many studies about children and the environment, and, especially, about EfS and children's engagements with 'nature' (e.g. Chawla and Cushing, 2007; Malone, 2007; Satchwell, 2013; Huckle and Wals, 2015). Yet we would make two constructive-yet-critical observations, which are fundamental to the argument and analysis of this book. First, as we discuss in more detail in this chapter and Chapter 3, there are very few empirical studies that look beyond EfS and related forms of *learning*, to understand the *multifarious* ways in which children interact with the built and natural environment, ideas, policies and practices of sustainability. Building on arguments we have made elsewhere, and given the central importance of sustainable urbanism to contemporary urban planning (evidenced in Chapter 3), we contend that it is critical that future scholarship on children and sustainability include a focus on sustainable urbanisms and the multiple ways in which children interact with them, the way they see, touch, play with or perhaps ignore its built, technological and natural features (Kraftl et al., 2013; Horton et al., 2015). Second, contemporary theorisations and conceptions of 'nature' have shifted fundamentally over the past fifteen years (Hinchliffe, 2008; Taylor, 2013). Nevertheless, many childhood studies scholars deploy notions of nature that are ostensibly opposed to culture, which are often romanticised, and which see nature as a (de)finite resource, or entirely a social construction. Yet, theories of 'nature' have undergone radical transformation whereby the anthropocentrism of previous accounts has been displaced. We discuss the implications of this transformation for childhood studies in/of sustainable urbanism in the section on materialities, biopolitics and nonhuman natures, here below.

## Towards the interdisciplinary study of children and childhood

As we have demonstrated so far, studies of children and childhood have from the very beginning been a multidisciplinary endeavour. Indeed, despite different disciplinary lineages in, for instance, sociology and human geography (and still even more rigorously within parts of psychology, education and health), childhood studies scholars remain relatively uniformly committed to the founding principles of NSSC, as outlined above. However, notwithstanding a range of multidisciplinary conference sessions, publications and funded research projects, it is our contention that childhood studies have yet to become truly interdisciplinary. Decades of writing within the field have allowed us to reflect upon scholarship across diverse disciplines and found surprisingly little disciplinary cross-referencing and some (again, to be provocative) perhaps questionable assertions of 'novelty'. Yet we have observed parallel developments in the various disciplines that make up contemporary childhood studies, where there is, quite simply, far greater scope for interdisciplinary conversations to be had, and, we would hope, a sense(s) of synergy and *theoretical* purpose. Here we cite but two examples. First, there have been recent calls within sociology and the sociology of education in particular to 'spatialise' childhood and youth; however, notably within anthropology and, especially, human geography, there is a long history of many, varied, often nuanced and detailed accounts of spatiality. Second, we note the parallel but ostensibly separate attempts to introduce new materialist, nonrepresentational and posthumanist accounts of childhood within sociology, anthropology, geography, (environmental and early childhood) education, policy and youth studies. Most protagonists – with notable exceptions – have only rarely engaged with one another (but see a recent example of the establishment of an interdisciplinary research network the Common Worlds collective: www.commonworlds.net). In our view, these observations are symptomatic of wider challenges not only within childhood studies but also in its affinity to other fields of studies. For example, in this context we note, along with Skelton and Gough (2013), the deeply problematic lack of engagement between childhood studies and urban studies scholars.

In response to the challenges outlined above, we would urge a more *generous* mindset that holds the potential to be even more theoretically *generative* than have

**22** Towards interdisciplinary study

been the intra-disciplinary conversations already under way. Although cognisant of the need to preserve theoretical diversity, we argue that given congruent but essentially parallel developments in several disciplines, there is a space for a shared set(s) of theoretical sensibilities that could, in part, be grounded in the very 'new wave' theoretical developments that we outline in the next part of this chapter – around embodiment, emotion, spatiality, vitality and materiality. It is our intention therefore that this book will offer a series of steps towards interdisciplinary childhood studies that are, as a result, *both* theoretically ambitious *and* better-equipped to deal with the complexities of children's recursive inter-relationships with (sustainable) urbanisms. This book does not provide a final position in these debates, not least because as we discuss below, this book alone cannot take the potentialities heralded by the 'new wave' to their logical conclusions. However, through our own internal interdisciplinary conversations (from anthropology, geography and sociology – and importantly as committed childhood studies scholars), and through what we hope in this and other chapters is a generous attitude to working with scholarship from a range of disciplines, it is our intention that this book offer a springboard for future work in childhood studies. We also hope that the book will offer urban studies scholars a robust and exciting analysis centred on the concept of *vitality* for critically assessing the roles of children and young people in contemporary urban transformations towards a sustainable world. It will do so not only by developing but *exemplifying* these theoretical positions via in-depth empirical analyses from the NUNC research project (outlined in Chapter 1) and elsewhere around the world. In some chapters, we therefore spend considerable time focusing upon our own and others' empirical material, allowing children and young people's experiences – in association with a range of human and nonhuman 'others' – to come to the fore in our analyses of sustainable urbanisms.

## (Re)Constituting a 'new wave' of childhood studies?

During the mid-2000s, as childhood studies expanded, a range of scholars sought to supplement and, in some cases, problematise the founding principles of NSSC (notably, Prout, 2005). This more recent field of scholarship, still nascent, but equally cutting across several disciplines and international contexts – has been tentatively branded a 'new wave' of childhood studies (Ryan, 2012), or as constituting an 'infra-paradigm' (Oswell, 2013). Although cognisant of the pitfalls of naming scholarship – not least in describing work that has, in various disciplines, in some cases been under way since before 2000 – we use the term as shorthand in this book to describe a kind of gathering momentum around a loose grouping of theoretical approaches that include feminist new materialisms, nonrepresentational theory and actor–network theory (ANT).

In this 'new wave' scholars characteristically have begun to critically unpick premises such as children's voice and agency (as seen as individual or pre-given), and the emphasis on social constructions of childhood. Prout (2005), for instance, argues that childhood in late modernity must be approached as both complex and heterogeneous. In his book, Prout attempts to break down the nature/culture binary, drawing upon evolutionary and biological sciences to show how childhood is to be found in notions that do not separate the social and cultural from biology – the more-than-social (Kraftl, 2013, 2015) including to move beyond the 'social' as articulated in discourse, representation and neatly bounded categories and forms of identity ('adult', 'child', 'male', 'female'). As Prout (2005) argues, childhood experiences are comprised as much of posthuman, nonhuman materialities – toys, animals, drugs, food, desks, mobile telephones – as they are of social interaction. As actor–network theorists write (e.g. Latour, 2005), even if we accept that 'society' exists, we must recognise that social relations are always-already reliant upon and stitched together by nonhuman technologies, artefacts and 'natures'. For research that seeks to blur the nature/culture boundaries drawing on such posthuman and new materialism perspectives, see for example Rautio's (2013) research about the *stones* children carry in their pockets to the *food* that passes through bodies and becomes human (e.g. Bennett, 2010). This research seem to downplay the role of the social (as understood in most childhood studies writing) but only to recognise that scholarship *also* needs to attend to the bodily, material, emotional, affective interactions that humans have with one another and with nonhuman contemporaries. As a result, 'new wave' childhood theorists have sought to question the notion of 'the child' as a sovereign, individuated subject. Their argument is not simply that childhood is relational – experienced in intergenerational relationships between individuated 'children' and 'adults'. Rather, new wave theorists seem to – drawing on a range of nonrepresentational, critical feminist, posthuman theories – posit that human bodies (and subjects) are constantly being composed and decomposed through energy, materials, technologies, prostheses, and emotions that flow into, through and out of them (Horton and Kraftl, 2006b; Prout, 2005; Lester and Russell, 2014). It is after all often difficult to tell where one (human) body begins and another (human or nonhuman) body ends, which is perhaps most intensely embodied and experienced in childhood (Christensen, 1999, 2000).

The rest of this chapter sets out in more detail some key conceptual frames of the 'new wave' childhood studies – moving knowingly across work – that have either already been associated with 'new wave' theorising in childhood studies, or which we contend should be. However, in setting out this work, it is important to note certain caveats. First, that many of the authors cited below may not necessarily think of themselves as being part of a 'new wave' of childhood studies – indeed, some of the work included pre-dates the (still nascent) usage of this term. Second, that although we use the term to assemble a range of theoretical and interdisciplinary perspectives, we do not endorse the uncritical identification (or celebration) of a 'new paradigm', since the reasons for identifying such paradigms can be as much about the politics of academic endeavour as they are about identifying actual theoretical innovation (for a stinging critique of such manoeuvres, see Gratton, 2014). Rather, since the term is already in circulation, we use it tentatively, critically, and, we hope, generatively, to bring together some divergent but nonetheless cognate theoretical work in childhood studies. Finally, we also note that some critics have already

**24** Towards interdisciplinary study

unpicked the apparent novelty of work in the 'new wave' – arguing in particular that the biosocial dualisms that new wave theorising purports to overcome have been posited artificially, and that in the very early scholarship mentioned earlier in this chapter (by Rousseau and others), such dualisms were never present (Ryan, 2012). We agree to an extent with this assessment, but also note that the argument to think beyond biosocial dualisms has arisen within the specificities of contemporary academic and societal contexts. That is, the tenets of the NSSC – and its emphasis upon the *social* side of the biosocial equation – are now so pervasive that the impulse to go beyond the biosocial has constituted an important first step in dealing with the rather lopsided approach to childhood propounded by most childhood studies scholars. At the same time, a range of philosophical approaches – not present in the time of Rousseau – have developed in conversation with the particular social and political imperatives of the present moment. These range from the designation of a new geological epoch – the Anthropocene – in which the impacts of humans upon the earth appear far more profound than was hitherto assumed, to the advent of new scientific knowledges and biotechnologies that are deployed to construct, survey and control life in ways thought unimaginable just a few decades ago (see, for example, Rose, 2009).

With these caveats and considerations in mind, the rest of this chapter outlines the key theoretical frames that we consider helpful starting points – both for interdisciplinary 'new wave' theorising in childhood studies and, specifically, for our analysis of childhoods in sustainable urban contexts. These frames are:

*   mobilities;
*   othering, intersectionality and intergenerationality;
*   emotion/affect;
*   embodiment;
*   materialities, nonhuman natures and biopolitics.

Given the space available in this chapter, we do little more here than introduce some of the key features of each conceptual frame, specifying the (sometimes subtle) difference that 'new wave' approaches might instantiate compared with the major premises of NSSC. In the conclusion to this chapter, we propose the idea of 'vitalities' as an overarching frame for the new wave and, indeed, for our analysis in the rest of the book. We exemplify and develop all of these ideas in greater detail throughout the analytical chapters that follow.

## Mobilities

The first conceptual frame is that of mobility, which pervades all aspects of (urban) life (Cresswell, 2006). As we argue in Chapter 3, in many contexts, policy and planning approaches to sustainable urban streetscape design have been strongly underpinned (if not justified) by deep concerns about *children and young people's* apparent profoundly limited and declining mobility. Over several decades academic, policy

Towards interdisciplinary study **25**

and media debates in Europe and North America have regularly voiced anxieties regarding children and young peoples' limited access to and use of outdoor environments (Hillman et al., 1990; O'Brien et al., 2000; Louv, 2005). Frequently, children and young people's limited outdoor mobilities are positioned as an epochal shift from a recently gone idealised past. In the UK for example, there is certainly evidence to support this impression. The UK Department of the Environment's (1973) study of 50,000 observations of children's outdoor mobility found that the street was a popular location for children's play: of the children in the study, 75 per cent played on the roads, pavements and other paved areas in close proximity of their homes; children were frequently observed walking, running, using wheeled vehicles, play equipment and ball games (ibid.). However, by 2005 it was suggested that only 15 per cent of children played outside on streets in the UK (Department for Transport, 2006; Lacey, 2007). Thus it is widely argued that, as societal perception of heightened risk and uncertainty rose through the 1990s (Beck 1992; Giddens 1991), children became the population group perhaps most affected by perceptions of risk in public spaces (Pooley et al., 2005).

Much research has explored how parental fears and anxieties have increasingly centred on, and delimited, children's outdoor play and mobility (see, for example, Hillman et al., 1990; Valentine and McKendrick, 1997; Valentine, 1997; Jackson and Scott, 1999; O'Brien et al., 2000; Bringolf-Isler et al., 2010; van Loon and Frank, 2011). Likewise, there is much evidence to suggest that new modes of auto-mobile everyday family life have meant that children are now predominantly driven by car to and from their activities (Zeiher, 2001; Barker, 2003, 2009). As a consequence, it is widely suggested that children spend significantly less time outdoors, with limited freedom to negotiate urban environments for themselves (Christensen and O'Brien, 2003), and that contemporary city streets constitute unfriendly environments because of street crime, traffic congestion and the lack of open recreational spaces (Ferré et al., 2006; Christensen and O'Brien, 2003; McKendrick, 2000). Hamilton-Baillie (2008), for example, argues that many urban streets have become confusing and unwelcoming because of heavily engineered signs, rules and regulatory markings. Elsewhere, Karsten's (2005) study of generational change argues that spaces previously inhabited by children playing on their own have increasingly become populated by children accompanied by adults. These trends, in combination, are argued to be 'fostering a new type of neighbourhood in which public space is increasingly child-free' (Platt, 2012: 196).

While these lines of argument have been hugely significant in prompting and framing policy and academic discussions in relation to children and young people's mobilities, it is our contention that children and young people's *own* experiences of community mobility have only recently been acknowledged within this discursive context. Admittedly, there have been many studies (several cited above) that have examined children's *urban* mobilities, in the broadest sense, often framed by notions of 'independent' mobility (Mikkelsen and Christensen, 2009; Skelton and Gough, 2013). However, children and young people's experiences of mobilities in

**26** Towards interdisciplinary study

*new, sustainable* urban developments – within the kinds of increasingly global policy and design imperatives discussed in Chapter 3 and Chapter 4 – have gone relatively unacknowledged. In the following section we explore children and young people's experiences of mobilities in our case study communities, and particularly their encounters with aspects of 'shared surface' street design that are, for reasons outlined previously, a key pivot for sustainable urban design.

Importantly, in our search for understanding the *vitality* of sustainable mobility we move on from socio-historical perspectives that tend to focus on children's lack of independent mobility (see Chapter 5). Our move towards an 'open-minded' theoretical stance entails changing notions of movement, childhood, agency, scale and heterogeneity towards perspectives less dominated by dichotomous oppositions. We stand by the notion of children's everyday mobility as local, immediate, bodily, emotional, social, and material, but also already interwoven in policy, planning, political and economic networks across diverse scales (see also Ansell, 2009). In order to take this position we build on Cortés-Morales and Christensen's (2015) intervention that (at the time of writing) represents the most comprehensively argued impetus for childhood and mobilities studies to recognise the interdependent multiple forms of mobilities, actors and actants at diverse geographical scales. In this perspective children's mobilities are accomplished through the distributed, combined or collective agency of heterogeneous entities that include technologies, humans and nonhuman entities of different kinds, such as parents, siblings, friends, pets, transport means, transport policies, public infrastructure, urban street design and planning. In this context we recognise children's mobilities as constituting a continuum of interconnected scales of movement that are (partly) given by the past, and shaped by the present, but, critically, *also* imagined in the prospective future of twenty-first-century urbanisms where cities are moving from the car-centric to the human-scale (see Chapter 5).

## *Othering, intersectionality and intergenerationality*

A key, underlying principle of childhood studies scholarship has been that childhood is constructed *in relation* to adulthood. That is, adults do much of the political, imaginative, practical and representational work of constructing childhoods in order to clearly distinguish children from themselves. In the parlance of 1990s identity studies, these are acts of Othering: powerful discursive regimes in which marginalised groups who do not conform to (what is usually) an adult, male, white, heterosexual, middle-class 'centre' are ostracised through often inaccurate and sweeping representations of their identities. Such representations further reduce any political agency those Others (in this case children) may have won, while increasing their reliance upon the central Self (adults). We have already discussed the effects of such endeavours in especially urban public spaces, wherein young people are deemed to exist in some kind of liminal zone that sees them as not-quite-adults, who pose a threat to the stability of civic life (Sibley, 1995).

Indeed, as we noted earlier in this chapter, there exist a plethora of studies examining how children's experiences in and mobilities around urban spaces are structured by unequal intergenerational power relations. In the later chapters in this book, we consider whether and how children are (or continue to be) 'Othered' in the more contemporary and rather more particular circumstances of sustainable urban communities.

Importantly, however, the conceptual bases of scholarship on the Othering of children in urban spaces run rather deeper than some empirical studies might suggest. Here, it is useful to briefly expand on two key terms that have become increasingly important to childhood studies scholars: intergenerational relations and intersectionality. Lena Alanen's (2005) work on *intergenerationality* is probably some of the most influential. Seeing parallels with theories of gender relations, she argues that relationality is an important feature of 'doing generation' (ibid.: 71). She argues that, in parallel with gender orders and gendered divisions of labour, these ways of doing generation create 'generational orders' (ibid.: 66). Such orders operate across spatial scales: from the micro-scale interactions between parents and children or teachers and pupils, to widely held beliefs (and laws) that structure and perpetuate the social order *over* generations (Alanen and Mayall, 2001).

It has been repeatedly argued that intergenerational relations – and the generational order – have received considerably less attention within childhood studies literatures, and within wider studies of age, than children themselves (e.g. Hopkins and Pain, 2007; Vanderbeck, 2007; Punch, 2015). There are several reasons for this but the predominant one has been a pressing (political) urge to emphasise children's agency – ostensibly finding such agency *everywhere*, as a 'universal, unitary phenomenon' (Oswell, 2013: 280), without necessarily excavating its relationality or critically considering what agency actually is (Hammersley, 2016). Nevertheless, our approach to adult–child relations in this book is inspired by a relatively small vein of research that *has* sought to critically examine the nuances of intergenerational relations. Some of the most important examples stem from the Majority Global South, where scholars have examined the sheer *diversity* of ways in which adults and children relate. Often, these ways of relating extend beyond the roles ascribed to 'adult' and 'child' in the Minority Global North, as children either take on tasks such as familial caring roles or paid work that might be assumed to be adult-like, or as children and adults share different responsibilities within and beyond the home (Evans, 2012). As Punch (2015) has repeatedly and persuasively argued, these are not forms of intergenerational but *interdependent* relations that stretch or even dismantle the predominantly European and North American conceptions of the child, and of agency, that have been propounded in childhood studies (Klocker, 2007). Nevertheless, it is important to avoid a romanticisation of such relationships as necessarily reflective of a more progressive or equitable social order. For instance, depending on a child's birth position, they may be ascribed particular roles that foreclose certain possibilities – in some Majority World contexts, the youngest sibling may be expected to remain at home to care for their parents (Punch, 2015).

**28** Towards interdisciplinary study

As Hopkins and Pain (2007) argue, the concept of intergenerationality can be complicated further by a focus on *intersectionality*. The concept of intersectionality began to gain credence after World War Two, as black feminists expressed increasing dissatisfaction that early wave feminisms saw all women as uniformly oppressed by men. Rather than emphasise a 'global sisterhood', black women scholars articulated how women's lives (and their marginalisation) varied enormously depending on their social, historical and geographical positioning (Crenshaw, 1991; Brah and Phoenix, 2013). The essential philosophical and political argument beneath this observation is that different forms of social difference – ethnicity, gender, age, sexuality – *intersect* as forms of power that produce individual subjectivities, which in turn 'place' individuals at different points within social hierarchies. No-one is 'just' a man or a woman.

As with theories of voice, agency and, indeed, generation, the concept of intersectionality has migrated from feminist academe to childhood studies and, indeed, to youth studies (e.g. Dunn and Farnsworth, 2012). The result has been a series of studies – undertaken especially with older young people – that seek to complicate and specify the experiences of young people who are never 'just' young (Willis, 1977). A particularly noteworthy line of inquiry has been around intersections of ethnicity, youth and gender, specifically in recent efforts to understand the shifting experiences of young Muslim men and women in a British context marked by intensifying Islamophobia (Dwyer et al., 2008; Hopkins, 2009; Hemming and Madge, 2012; Kashyap and Lewis, 2013).

As much as intergenerationality and intersectionality offer important frames for understanding childhood and youth, these terms also have potential limitations. As Horton and Kraftl (2008) argue, both terms have been deployed – perhaps somewhat against the intention of those who initially developed them – as relatively bare place-holders for stable identity categories that can simply be 'ticked off' or combined in ever-more-complicated permutations. The result is – as Brown (2012) puts it rather acerbically – a kind of 'oppression Olympics', wherein scholars appear to compete to study ever-more-specific and (it is assumed) ever-more-marginalised social groups. The moral and political imperatives to work with these groups may be completely sound. However, mirroring debates about childhood studies (King, 2007), the question is whether the political and empirical impulse to search for and research these groups has overtaken or even replaced a considered reflection upon the conceptual value of 'intergenerationality' and 'intersectionality'. In picking up this point, Staunæs (2003) argues, in a study of youth identities in a school setting, that we should not *start* with a sense of *a priori* identity categories that *then* intersect with other identities, but with the lives of (young) people themselves, in order to examine how performances, discourses and feelings of subjectivity may or may not *produce* intersectionalities. This critical assessment resonates well with Punch and McIntosh's (2014) argument about intergenerationality. There are, in other words, multiple intersectionalities and intergenerationalities, which are contingent upon social action rather than ascribed in advance. Therefore, our task as childhood studies scholars is not only to map or advocate for different forms of intersectionality and intergenerationality in practice, but to ask what those practices *do* to develop or challenge the ways in which we conceptualise those terms.

A final question – not yet broached in any significant way by childhood studies scholars – centres around what 'new wave' studies of intergenerational relations and intersectionality might look like. On the one hand, the 'new wave' might simply usher in more complexity: to the categories of generation and intersecting identity groups, we can add nonhuman forms. Empirically – at least for those who would follow the insights of ANT – this would mean placing nonhuman materialities alongside or into the relationships that compose 'adults' and 'children'. However, the insights of the new wave run deeper than this. New wave theorising has the potential to revolutionise what we mean when we think of 'identity' or 'subjectivity'. No longer interested in focusing on individuated human subjects, there is equally no need to be tethered to traditional identity categories, since to be so exhibits too great-a-measure of anthropocentrism. On the other hand, then, as we argue in the conclusion to this chapter, we need to ask whether the resolutely *social* languages of intergenerationality and intersectionality need to be expanded, overhauled, or – and this probably sounds like heresy – replaced with other ways of theorising the relationality and complexity of (human) life. In this book, and in particular in Chapters 7–9, we move some way along the path of imagining how these languages might sound – at least, in the context of children's engagements with sustainable urbanisms.

## *Emotion/affect*

A turn to emotion in the social sciences was also in large part influenced by feminist scholars, critical of the masculinist, 'rational' and dualistic thinking of academic endeavour (Rose, 1993; Williams, 2001). Indeed, the inclusion of emotions in (and of) research has become a central feature of research with demographic groups marked out as somehow marginalised – women, ethnic minorities, LGBT groups, as well as children. Childhood studies scholars have mobilised a bewildering array of theories of emotion, and we can again only scratch the surface here. Before outlining some of these approaches, it is worth making two observations. First, as will become clear, a focus on emotion (and later affect) is by no means the property of a 'new wave' – indeed, many studies pre-date the new wave by some significant margin. Second, there are considerable disagreements both between and within disciplines about how 'emotion' and 'affect' should be defined and differentiated. For the purposes of this section, we view – alongside perhaps the majority of social scientists – 'emotion' as a nameable embodied property (like happiness or sadness), that can be felt and, crucially, *named* by an individual. In contrast, we define affect as something shared between one or more actors (human or nonhuman), which is more akin to a kind of 'atmosphere' (like hope, security or homeliness) (Anderson, 2009).

Childhood studies scholars have examined emotions in diverse ways (for different reviews, see Kenway and Youdell, 2011; Kraftl, 2013). Here, we distil four

**30** Towards interdisciplinary study

important considerations. First, emotions and emotionality are arguably central to the social construction of childhood. That much should be evident from the preceding sections of this chapter – whether in terms of 'fears' about children's safety in public spaces, or the kinds of hopes (Kraftl, 2008) and aspirations (Brown, 2011) that are frequently proscribed on behalf of young people. In other words, the social construction of childhood is a highly emotive praxis. Second, and related, emotions have become entangled with policy-making and professional practices for children, in manifold ways (Horton and Kraftl, 2009a; Blazek and Kraftl, 2015). For centuries, adult experts have used children (and generational futures) as justifications for particular interventions – from the early American playground movement (Gagen, 2004) to policies for social inclusion (Mizen, 2003). As Blazek and Kraftl (2015) note, critical scholarship in this vein has assessed when and where adults intervene (or choose not to intervene) into or on behalf of children's emotions, and/ or on the basis of *their own* emotions about children (Reay, 2000). Third, there exists a wealth of studies focusing on children and young people's own expressed emotions – often in response to the very fears and hopes that adults have on their behalf (Blazek and Windram-Geddes, 2013; Rosen, 2015). For instance, related to the mobilities literatures discussed above, several studies examine children's own senses of risk in their everyday lives, finding a range of fears that are both resonant and dissonant with those of adults (Nayak, 2003; Christensen and Mikkelsen, 2008). Elsewhere, several authors have examined children's emotions about participatory processes that are intended to make them feel included – but which do not (e.g. Kiili, 2016). Fourth, many studies focus on the role of emotion in the production of young people's identities and subjectivities. Some studies examine children's emotional responses to citizenship education and other programmes designed to regulate their subjectivities (and, indeed, their emotions) (Wood, 2013; Kallio and Häkli, 2013). Other work has examined feelings of humour, fear or anger in young people's 'narratives' of identity (e.g. Valentine, 2000) and (sub)cultural belonging (Geldens et al., 2011).

A far smaller body of work has focused on affect (for a review, see Blazek and Kraftl, 2015). Again, we can discern between two distinct strands. On the one hand, some (rather limited) scholarship has explored how adults attempt to create particular kinds of atmospheres in order to engender certain kinds of outcomes. For instance, Kraftl's (2006) study of a Steiner School demonstrates how the design and decor of a kindergarten combined with the everyday practices of teachers to generate visual, tactile and olfactory feelings of 'home'. Such feelings were, specifically, achieved through practices like bread-baking that aimed to fill the room with smells redolent of (particular kinds of) home. On the other hand, there have been more established lines of inquiry into children's role in and experiences of affect. Here, given the rather more distributed definition of affect we are using, it is immediately problematic to claim that these are studies about children's voice or agency. Instead – while voice or agency might emerge – the emphasis is upon how children are but one set of agents – human and nonhuman – in the production of affective atmospheres. In an early study, Harker (2005) observes how affects

Towards interdisciplinary study  **31**

of playfulness were woven between bodies – his own and those of children – during his time at an early childhood setting. Indeed, there has been considerable attention to institutional and especially education settings in work on affect, not least as it enables analysis of how affects are produced, negotiated and resisted and, thus, of how affects are laden with and constituted through power relations (e.g. Watkins, 2011).

There has, however, been far less attention to how affects are produced and experienced by children in *urban* settings. Hence, in this book, we mobilise many of the above theorisations of emotion and affect to add nuance to existing understandings of children's experiences of urban life. We use theories of emotion and affect to extend accounts of where, when and how 'sustainability' is configured within children's urban lives. Moreover, we seek to develop theories of emotion and affect through our attention to sustainable urbanisms, and vice-versa, asking what are the emotionalities and affectivities at play as sustainable urban policies, designs and technologies meet children's everyday lives.

## Embodiment

Children's bodies have been an important empirical and theoretical focus for many years – indeed, some of the earliest works by NSSC proponents covered this ground, with a particular focus on the contexts of children's health (Lee, 1999; Christensen, 2004b; James and Prout, 2015). Building upon these foundational texts, children's bodies have, since then, been theorised in diverse ways by social scientists (for overviews, see Woodyer, 2008; Evans et al., 2009; Cook and Hemming, 2011). Here, we focus on three such approaches, noting that we deal with biopolitics of childhood in the section on materialities. First, and again developing the founding premises of NSSC, children's bodies have been understood as socially constructed. A key early assumption, underpinned by feminist politics, was that a focus upon bodies in both research and practice with young people was a progressive one, mirroring concerns with 'voice' and 'agency' (Evans et al., 2005; Ecclestone and Hayes, 2009). Second, education scholars have explored the emotional and affective components of embodied interactions between children and teachers in the classroom (Probyn, 2005; Zembylas, 2009). These studies – focusing on how bodies *feel* – resonate with work on emotion, affect and intergenerational relations, which were all discussed above (see also Davies and Christensen, 2015, on children's personal lives and intimate relationships). Third, bodies may be made flesh (Evans et al., 2009) in particular in and through institutional spaces such as schools and orphanages (Disney, 2015; Kraftl, 2016). This approach corresponds most closely with 'new wave' theories, where a focus on the *socially* constructed body of the child is replaced (or supplemented) with recognition of the fleshiness of bodies, constituted as they are by both 'human' and 'nonhuman' materialities, such as toys, clothes, pharmaceuticals and food (Prout, 2005). In exploring the elision of the bio, the social and the political, attention has been paid recently to how new neuroscientific knowledges have been deployed in schools in order to

**32** Towards interdisciplinary study

reformulate the very embodied physicalities of children's learning (Pykett, 2012; Gagen, 2015), and to how anti-obesity programmes politicise and seek to intervene into the everyday eating and exercising habits of particularly shaped bodies (e.g. Pike and Kelly, 2014).

In practice, many studies of children's bodies have also attended to emotions and affects (and vice versa), since those facets of human experience are ineluctably entwined. Our approach in this book is no different. However, as becomes evident in our discussion of the final frame – materialities, biopolitics and nonhuman natures – we also seek to extend beyond recent work on embodiment. Specifically, we are interested not only in the embodied practices of individual children, or groups of children (and adults). Nor do we merely seek to move beyond biosocial dualisms by attending to the nonhuman materialities through which children experience the city. Rather, we want to (begin to) find ways to conceptualise and empirically investigate what we term *the embodiment of sustainable urbanisms*. This entails not only starting with *children*, but with the multiple energies, flows, processes and materialities – the multiple 'metabolisms' – of the sustainable city itself (Heynen et al., 2006; Kennedy et al., 2011). Doing so does not of necessity entail a return to an imperialist, masculinist, iconographic view of the city-as-body (Grosz, 1999). Instead, it entails an attentiveness to how the planning and materialisation of the city is constituted by, and envelops, the bodies of children as individuals, and as they are massified as 'city life'. Drawing on our discussion of vitality and life-itself (below), Chapters 3, 4 and 7 are particularly important with regard to our development of this argument.

### Materialities, biopolitics and nonhuman natures

In considering the four previous theoretical frames for this book, we have argued – largely implicitly – that the 'new wave' of childhood studies presages a radical overhaul of the ways in which we understand and position 'the child' in childhood studies (Hackett et al., 2015; Eßer et al., 2016). In tandem with the above frames – and particularly those on embodiment, emotion and affect – we seek in this last section to outline, in turn, how some of the latest theorising on materialities, biopolitics and nonhuman natures inform our thinking in this book. While there are considerable differences within and between these strands of work, it is worth considering them together because they lead us to perhaps the key philosophical question that undergirds this book: what are the forms of life – the *vitalities* – through which children's entanglements with sustainable urbanism are imagined, designed, experienced, felt and materialised? In other words, rather than (re)articulate an interest in 'children's everyday lives' *in* sustainable urban communities, we ask what are the multiple ways in which children's lives are (and are not) recursively *produced* in, through and with the everyday lives of sustainable urbanism.

First, recent scholarship on *materialities* has perhaps been some of the most vibrant and important in ushering in a challenge to the doxa of the NSSC. Certainly, beginning with Prout's (2005) seminal work, the influence of ANT has

Towards interdisciplinary study **33**

been to attempt to reconfigure or, ideally, to overcome biosocial dualisms in childhood studies. As Prout argues, it is a 'requirement that childhood studies move beyond the opposition of nature and culture [to] a hybrid form [wherein] children's capacities are extended and supplemented by all kinds of material artefacts and technologies, which are also hybrids of nature and culture' (Prout, 2005: 3–4). In this revised model, children are – like other social actors – deprived of (some or even all of) their cultural and agential capacities, and some of those capacities are in turn translated into or through objects (Turmel, 2008; Rainio and Hilppö, 2017). As Horton (2012) argues, this move entails a relatively radical re-think of the status of objects in children's lives: from a sense of their representational or symbolic *meaning* (as in many studies of children's popular cultures) to their everyday *mattering* – what those objects do, with/in the lives of children, that takes on the status of something noteworthy or emotionally significant, albeit not necessarily tied to a nameable identity or (sub)cultural grouping.

ANT approaches have more recently been supplemented with approaches from posthumanist, feminist and new materialist philosophies (e.g. Haraway, 2008; Bennett, 2010; Braidotti, 2011). Nonetheless, a range of studies have grappled with Prout's challenge to theorise and empirically investigate the materialities of children's lives (or, lives lived with, through and in materialities). Some of that work has – not without attracting critique – proceeded through an intense focus upon the micro-scale, often ephemeral interactions between children and things (Woodyer, 2008; Mitchell and Elwood, 2012). For instance, Rautio (2013, 2014) engaged a small group of children in a series of encounters with a box full of objects, leading to detailed observations about how and why children carry stones in their pockets, or how they become encased by rollable sleeping mats in such ways that it becomes difficult to discern whether the 'agent' propelling them both is the child or the mat (rather, they operate *together*). Elsewhere, in an urban context, Kullman (2014) examines an 'ordinary' piece of street furniture to examine the detailed ways in which children interact with the materialities of the street. He argues for diverse 'child-pavement entanglements' (ibid.: 2864) that include patting dogs and checking the road is safe before crossing. For him, these entanglements are entrained in a wider ethic of care for the city (expressed by children), which structures children's mobilities (also Kullman, 2015; Cortés-Morales and Christensen, 2015).

A second response to Prout's work has been a (re)turn to children's bodies – or, rather, the embodiments of childhood (Wilhelmsen and Nilsen, 2015; Hackett et al., 2015) – with an increasing interest in *biopolitics* (Kraftl, 2015). In many ways, and echoing our critical observations about the 'new wave' at the beginning of this section, recent approaches to theorising the child's body-as-materiality are not new. Early work by Nick Lee (2001) examined how children's bodies were positioned within and produced by medico-legal practices and technologies. Later, in his study of children's sleep and the soft toys that they and their parents use as transitional objects to facilitate sleep (Lee, 2008), he makes perhaps the clearest case for how a 'new wave' of childhood studies moves beyond the status of the child as a discrete subject for analysis. He observes that this is 'a view of the "person" as

**34** Towards interdisciplinary study

an emergent property of certain open-ended interactions between a hybrid assortment of elements' (ibid.: 61). In turn, this is 'a generalized constructionism . . . that discusses *childhood* as an emergent property of interactions between persons, discourses, technologies, objects, bodies, etc.' (ibid.: 59, emphasis added). Later still, Lee argues for how such forms of constructionism are productive of political – and specifically *biopolitical* – modes of ordering childhood (Lee and Motzkau, 2011). Focusing on a range of technologies – including the 'mosquito' box, a device that emits a high-pitched whine that only young people can hear, and which is intended to repel them from particular public spaces – they argue that the elision of the biological with the political has, of late, afforded some of the most powerful and potentially insidious ways of 'constructing' contemporary childhoods, and of Othering children (ibid.). Concomitantly, there has been increasing interest elsewhere in the biopoliticisation of childhood, focusing upon arenas of education and health and especially the deployment of the 'psy-disciplines' (Wells, 2011: 19) through a 'psychiatrisation of childhood' (Philo, 2011: 33–34). Policies aimed at biopolitical interventions into the lives of children in their early years – and their parents – have come under particular scrutiny (e.g. Gagen, 2015; Millei and Joronen, 2016).

Interest in the materialities and embodiments of childhood has been accompanied and in some cases combined with a focus upon the *nonhuman natures* that constitute children's lives. Indeed, such scholarship has arguably constituted some of the most theoretically challenging, empirically rich and politically progressive work in what we are framing as a 'new wave' of childhood studies. Focusing on early years education settings, scholars such as Affrica Taylor (2013) and Veronica Pacini-Ketchabaw (2013) posit that children's bodies (and child-subjects) are constantly being composed and decomposed through energy, materials, technologies, prostheses, and emotions that flow into, through and out of them. For instance, Taylor (2013) has shown how children are literally entangled with the animals – domestic or wild – with whom they co-exist in Australia. In a Canadian context, Pacini-Ketchabaw and Clark (2014) follow the 'hydro-logics' of water as it moves through the micro-scale of the human body to the macro-scale of the continental watershed. This work is particularly important because it extends most explicitly beyond micro-scale, ephemeral experiences to articulate far wider senses of 'what matters' (Ansell, 2009; Kraftl, 2013). In their work, Taylor and Pacini-Ketchabaw are particularly inspired by postcolonial theorising that enables them to re-think relations of settler colonialism and indigeneity, towards educational praxes that may lead towards decolonisation and/or or alternative ways of imagining human relationships with and as 'nature'. As Pacini-Ketchabaw and Clark (2016: 100–101) lyrically evoke:

> Just as we observe that waters shape our physical landscape, we can easily imagine that waters can carve out crevices in our pedagogies, make room for other ideas, other ways of being and becoming with water. This carving is not finished yet. We continue to learn how to live with a wounded and flooded water table.

We develop theorisations of materiality and the nonhuman in Chapters 3 and 7, in combination with the four previous theoretical frames.

## Conclusion: towards a critical appraisal of the vitalities of childhoods in/of sustainable urban lives

The purpose of the conclusion to this chapter is to set out a series of propositions that we unfold in greater depth in the chapters that follow. Our propositions are centred upon the notion of *vitality*, which, we argue, characterises well our *interdisciplinary* approach to understanding children *and* sustainable urbanisms, across geographical contexts and scales. Our understanding of the term vitality is, on the one hand, based on a broader or combinative view of the five frames we discussed above. In other words, for us, these frames amount to a powerfully integrative, albeit non-totalising and non-holistic, approach to understanding the movements, (social) differences, embodiments, feelings, materialities and nonhuman natures that go some way to constituting children's lives. Indeed, these are just some of the speeds and slownesses, energies and flows, and constellations of matter and meaning that make up life-itself.

On the other hand, we are informed by the explicitly vibrant- and vital-materialist thinking of postfeminist, posthuman philosophers such as Jane Bennett (2010), Rosi Braidotti (2011) and Elizabeth Grosz (2011). Bennett's work is particularly important, because it casts in a still wider light the debates about agency that have dogged childhood studies in recent decades. Hers is a task to find a way to express the flux of life-itself 'beyond the default grammar of human agency' (Bennett, 2010: 119). Her work has (at least) three key features, which are instructive for our purposes. First, hers *is* an optimistic view of vitality that, although not rooted solely in the rather more spiritual vitalisms of the nineteenth century, nevertheless enables a certain *enchantment* with the world to pervade her work (also Bennett, 2001; Geoghegan and Woodyer, 2014). Thus, we engage in a kind of Foucauldian affirmative critique, in which our critical faculties as academics are not blunted, but, rather than finding fault, we seek to identify critical or creative points of articulation for future possibility. As Foucault (1997: 322) has it:

> I can't help but dream about a kind of criticism that would try not to judge but to bring an oeuvre, a book, a sentence, an idea to life; it would light fires, watch the grass grow, listen to the wind, and catch the sea foam in the breeze and scatter it. It would multiply not judgments but signs of existence; it would summon them, drag them from their sleep. Perhaps it would invent them sometimes – all the better.

Second, Bennett's work offers perhaps the clearest explication of exactly *how* more-than-anthropocentric grammars of agency might look. Her book *Vibrant Matter* (Bennett, 2010) offers a range of examples of how human and nonhuman

**36** Towards interdisciplinary study

lives are ineluctably entangled. In one example, she helps us to understand the lively matter of food as it enters, moves through, becomes part of, and leaves the human body (also Mol, 2008). In another, she witnesses the vibrancy and motility of metals at the molecular level, as they demonstrate a surprising capacity to vibrate *in order to* preserve their internal relationalities *as* metal. In the chapters that follow, we are inspired by Bennett's more-than-human languages, we seek to uncover how children are articulated with the policies, technologies, flows and energies that constitute sustainable urbanisms. As Bennett herself recognises, this is no easy task – in fact, it is an eminently exhausting one, since it requires a decentring of the human from our modes of thinking and writing. It is also not one that we can always accomplish, although our methodology has privileged ethnographic participant observation other data material is based upon methods (like interviews) that privileges the voices of human agents. Yet our analysis offers at least a set of steps towards a more-than-social understanding of sustainable urban lives that envelop children, and are composed through them.

Third, Bennett's is, despite her emphasis on enchantment, not a call for a nostalgic or romanticised notion of vitality. Nor is it a treatise on a kind of uniform life force through which all things are created equally, even if in an analytical sense they are, initially, placed on a horizontal plane (akin to ANT). Rather, in her search for an ecologically just philosophy for our times, Bennett is clear:

> If I live not as a human subject who confronts natural and cultural objects but as one of many conative actants swarming and competing with each other . . . eco health will [sometimes] require individuals and collectives to back off . . . and sometimes it will call for grander, more dramatic and violent expenditures of human energy.
>
> *(Bennett, 2010: 122)*

Thus, there are, quite clearly, some times and spaces where, despite the horizontality and hybridity of ANT, postmaterialism and, indeed, 'new wave' childhood studies, we must (still) attend to *human* agency. It is also the case that, even if our purview of (child-)subjectivities is radically overhauled or at least expanded, the ability to act may (still) be cut across by older and entrenched power relations according to class, gender, ethnicity, and far more besides (Grosz, 2011). This is why we are committed to both *retaining* and *expanding* the traditional remit of NSSC – whether in terms of attending to children's voice, agency and participation, or to the kinds of questions about intergenerational relations and intersectionality that, as we argued above, should remain central to studies of childhood and youth.

In this book, we seek to develop these and other ways of theorising *vitalities* in the particular contexts of sustainable urbanism. Efforts to build sustainable cities (most obviously in the smart cities movement) represent perhaps some of the grandest examples of what some term 'geo-engineering' (Dalby, 2014). These are not just 'light green' but large-scale, technological responses to the present environmental moment (another example would be large-scale green energy generation). Just as scholars disagree on the appropriateness of such responses to the challenge of the Anthropocene (Yusoff, 2013), there is huge diversity in terms of the 'science' involved in sustainable urbanisms around the world. Our central question is, however – building on the theoretical arguments outlined in this chapter – whether and how theorisations of *vitalities* can help us to better understand the multiple lives of sustainable urbanism, and, particularly, the entanglements of children with/in those lives. In this light, and in closing this chapter, we wish to raise five questions. Those questions are prompted by a consideration of how theories of vitality might further develop each of the five frames presented in the previous section, as part of an expanded and more nuanced 'new wave' of childhood studies. We do not necessarily answer all of these questions in full, since their implications stretch well beyond the confines of one book. However, they offer some starting points for our analyses:

1   In what ways can we conceive of children's *mobilities* as core to the vitalities of sustainable urbanism? Here, we refer to the multiple mobilities that they constitute, that constitute them, and that cut across their lives, at various scales. These may be movements of people, things, technologies, animals, data, and more, operating in shifting constellations in the production of urban lives.
2   How might we re-theorise processes of *othering* and, especially *intersectionality* and *intergenerationality*, in order to respond to the challenge of vital thinking? In other words, taking the work of Bennett and others seriously, we need to recognise that theories of vitality offer a radical conception *beyond* the human subject (and thus the individual child) that constitutes a serious challenge to terms like intergenerationality and intersectionality. However, rather than arrogantly dispense with these terms, we ask what it might mean to theorise and to exemplify intersectionality and intergenerationality *vitally*. How do those terms operate in the constitution of vitalities and, in the context of sustainable urbanisms, who will 'back off' and who will 'expend energy' (following Bennett's challenge, cited above)? In what ways can we think of nonhuman actants as *part* of intersectional and intergenerational processes?
3   Set against the engineering, data-based, planning and architectural knowledges required to construct sustainable urban places, what is the role of *emotion* and *affect*? If sustainable urbanisms are also intended to be *liveable* forms of urbanism, to what extent must they *feel like 'actually alive' and vital places*? Can we engage in forms of affirmative critique that identify where – for children, who make up a significant population group in most cities, and who are arguably the group who spend most time in public spaces – there are examples of sustainable urbanism that *just feel right*? And how can we convey to diverse audiences of policy-makers, planners, NGOs and community groups why this might *matter*?
4   How are the *bodies* of children (con)figured in sustainable urbanisms? To what extent are children and young people present in planning documents, design

**38** Towards interdisciplinary study

codes, community consultations and the material features of sustainable urban places? How can and do sustainable urbanisms literally sustain the *vitality* of children's bodies, in intimate relationships with other bodies – through food, water, shelter, energy, clothing, and opportunities for learning, playing and working? And to what extent do these extend beyond the overwhelming focus on EfS in scholarship on children and the environment?

5    How can we take (more) seriously the theoretical, ethical and political challenge to attend to our ineluctable entanglements with *nonhuman materialities* and *natures*, in the specific contexts of sustainable urbanisms? What can a focus upon children do to help us understand, value and plan for *progressive* forms of sustainable urban vitalities – and how would we know what these look and feel like? And, finally, given persuasive critiques of the very notion of sustainability – and its deep co-implication with and sustenance of neoliberal political-economic orders – to what extent might theorisations of what we might term *vital urbanisms* supplement, extend or even replace those of 'sustainable urbanisms'?

# 3

# SUSTAINABLE URBANISMS IN POLICY AND PRACTICE

## Introduction

The turn towards sustainable urbanism is constituting new forms of urban spaces on an international scale. As we will show, these urban spaces afford new experiences of childhood and youth, raising profound new questions for academics, practitioners, policy-makers and professionals working within sustainable urban development contexts. In this chapter we discuss the conceptual, political and practical underpinnings of international policy and planning visions on sustainable urbanism, illustrated by key examples of sustainable urban policy-making in the UK. Most significantly, in the latter part of the chapter we turn our attention to the lived experiences and perspectives of young people as residents of *already existing* sustainable urban spaces and communities.

We thus introduce some characteristic features of what we call *sustainable urbanism in practice*, which are our focus in the following chapters. In particular, we highlight three key, recurring sets of features, which have been widely built-in to sustainable urban developments over the last decade. These include *sustainable urban architectures*, urban *mobility and connectivity*, and community *participation, liveability and conviviality*. Over the course of the book we explore how these actually existing material, spatial and social features of sustainable urban developments enter into children and young people's lives, drawing on our own research carried out in the UK and from further examples of research undertaken worldwide. We should clarify, from the outset, that this book's focus upon communities, policies, architectures and technologies which have been named 'sustainable' does not *endorse* these features as necessarily sustainable in any functional or intellectual sense; in choosing our case studies we are guided by language and policy which identifies these places as 'sustainable' and we recognise that the extent to which large-scale urban development can ever be sustainable is, at least, deeply contested. Rather,

**40** Policy and practice

our aim is to foreground perspectives hitherto subdued in debates about sustainable urbanism, via a series of interdisciplinary dialogues. For example, this interdisciplinarity is manifest in our bringing together of the anthropological project (amplifying the hitherto muted voice of social groups in recognition of a *multiplicity* of local experiences, perceptions and actions in the understanding and meaning of sustainable urban environments), with geographers' in-depth exploration of spatialities (in recognition of the impossibility of understanding society without understanding the physical (and social) spaces that are produced by people and that, in turn, produce them). Throughout the book we show how the inclusion of the perspectives of children and young people enrich understandings of 'what matters' in the development of new sustainable urban environments and demonstrate how children's multi-sensory bodily and practical engagements underline the co-constitutional qualities of the natural, built and social environments.

## Principles and visions of sustainable urbanism

'Sustainable urbanism' is an umbrella term for diverse, international policy, planning and design practices that seek to deliver, and foster a step-change towards increasingly environmentally, socially and economically sustainable urban environments (see Jenks et al., 1996; Satterthwaite, 1999; Williams et al., 2001; Williams, 2007; Farr, 2008; Wheeler and Beatley, 2014). Typically, these practices are explicitly rooted in the United Nations' (1987: 1) principle of sustainable urban development: that is, urban change, growth and capacity-building which 'meet[s] the needs of the present without compromising the ability of future generations to meet their own needs'. Three widely influential agendas for sustainable urbanism serve to illustrate the kinds of concerns and objectives which are central to policy, planning and design interventions in this internationalised context of sustainable urbanism.

First, in the European Union, the Freiburg Charter – developed through collaboration between international urban planning/architecture experts and elected representatives of the south German city of Freiburg – is widely mobilised as a template for viably enhancing the sustainability of existing urban settlements (see Mössner, 2015a, 2015b; Mössner and Miller, 2015). The Charter outlines twelve key, guiding objectives for urban policy-makers and planners (see Box 3.1), which especially emphasise the importance of compactness, neighbourhood-development, connectivity, transportation, decentralisation, participation and biodiversity. This vision of a 'compact city where everything is close to hand' is intended to function as

> a guideline, whose principles can provide pointers towards a forward-looking urban development and urban planning policy for other cities, districts and networks. These deliberations are intended to inspire others to think about the issues and to explore them within many different local environments. The Charter's principles are not strict rules, but rather basic ideas that are designed to provide food for thought and inspiration to act.
>
> *(Academy of Urbanism, 2012: 5)*

Policy and practice **41**

---

## BOX 3.1 PRINCIPLES OF THE FREIBURG CHARTER

### I. Developing a city of diversity, safety and tolerance

Balanced age and social structures with functioning neighbourhoods; Construction of varied dwellings and work facilities for all parts of the population; Promotion of innovative forms of accommodation; Creation of manageable units and open spaces; Provision of public and private infrastructure, specifically for all generations; Care, leisure and educational services, particularly for the very young and the elderly; Integration of all sectors of the population taking into consideration their ethnic origin.

### II. Developing a city of neighbourhoods

Decentralisation of opportunities for: living and working; social and care infrastructure; education and culture; leisure and recreation; access to green space; sustainable resource management.

### III. Developing a city of short distances

Making all essential services accessible on foot; Prioritising public transport, footpaths and cycle routes over private motor cars; Supporting and facilitating shifts to renewable, emission-free forms of motor transport.

### IV. Focusing urban development along public transportation routes

Carefully and consistently increasing urban density along public transport routes; Locating services around the stops of tram lines or other public transport nodes.

### V. Valuing spaces of education, science and culture

Fostering investment and innovation in universities, research institutes, schools and cultural venues; Supporting collaborations between organisations and disciplines for the development of new technical, economic and social models for urban living.

### VI. Maintaining and modernising commerce, economy and employment

Maintaining and modernising existing developments; Attracting pioneering, innovative businesses; Counteracting desire for greenfield development by offering a concept of in-town development.

## VII. Preserving nature and environment

Conserving habitats for animal and plant life, the natural quality of soil, water, air and climate, and historically grown cultural landscapes; Developing natural environments as positive spaces for living and leisure; Conducting expert investigation into potential impact on nature, environment and climate as part of all planning processes; Making existing buildings more energy-efficient, introducing a more efficient, interconnected energy supplies and switching to renewable energy sources.

## VIII. Demanding design quality

Ensuring that planning decisions cultivate the unique character of a city and develop it further while complying with the highest design quality standards; Ensuring that local communities have ownership and control of public spaces, in order to manage claims on use and prevent misguided developments; Closely supervising planning processes for prominent buildings; Fostering collaborative, transparent processes for all important construction and plans.

## IX. Long-term visioning

Ensuring that 'the face of a city [is] not subjugated to short-lived fashions and political u-turns'; 'Preserving the old and daring to embrace the new!'; Ensuring careful resource management to afford 'continuity, quality, sensitivity, identity and innovation for a particular place' in urban development.

## X. Fostering a culture of communication and participation

Developing 'a collective vision' of the city through ongoing, participatory open discourse; Integrating extensive ongoing communication between citizens and stakeholders into planning processes; Ensuring that methods of participation are appropriate and take into account the unique characteristics of each local context.

## XI. Ensuring reliability and fairness

Making the city a trusted 'reliable partner' for citizens and private investors, giving each of them equal rights and duties.

## XII. Nurturing cooperation and partnership

Providing spaces for collaboration between private and public stakeholders, and making best use of ideas contributed by them; Providing innovative models of financing, subsidy and incentivisation for public and private partners;

> Engaging research institutes, universities and industry in innovative urban development processes.
>
> Source: Adapted from Academy of Urbanism (2012)

Second, in North America, Farr's (2008) *Sustainable Urbanism: Urban Design with Nature* has been widely deployed as a planning and visioning tool, particularly for neighbourhood-scale interventions which seek to constitute more sustainable urban forms. Farr recommends the use of five groups of planning objectives (see Box 3.2) and associated performance measures. He notes that the emergence of sustainable urbanism essentially marks an attempt to apply, upscale and popularise practices which emerged via earlier (often localised and explicitly counter-cultural) urban reform movements and environmental activisms, particularly those focused on 'green buildings' (Kilbert, 2004; Pickerill, 2016), 'smart growth' (Geller, 2003) and 'new urbanism' (Katz, 1993). This brand of sustainable urbanism challenges urban planners and policy-makers to harness 'the power of thoughtful urbanism to induce people to voluntarily live a more human-powered and less resource-intensive lifestyle . . . to enhance the inherent sustainability of a walkable, diverse urbanism integrated with high-performance buildings and infrastructure' (Farr, 2008: 10). As in the Freiburg Charter, key precepts of Farr's *Sustainable Urbanism* (Box 3.2) include participatory, neighbourhood-scaled planning interventions relating to compactness, biodiversity, connectivity, conviviality, architecture, liveability and community life.

---

## BOX 3.2   KEY PRINCIPLES FROM FARR'S (2008) *SUSTAINABLE URBANISM*

- Constituting urban compactness – optimising building and housing densities to enable neighbourhood walkability, proximities, access to services, and viable, efficient transport and traffic systems.
- Planning-in sustainable corridors – creating and preserving networks of 'corridors' for habitats, biodiversity, transport, infrastructure within neighbourhoods.
- Nurturing biophilia – creating and preserving opportunities for human access to nature, strengthening and making-tangible human interdependence with natural systems and cycles (e.g. through interventions to make systems of food production, energy supply, and water/waste management visible and comprehensible).
- Building high performance buildings and infrastructure – reducing impacts of planning/architectural practices on neighbourhood environmental impact, and planning-in best practice in terms of energy-efficient and eco-friendly technologies in built environments.

**44** Policy and practice

- Masterplanning sustainable neighbourhoods – creating communities 'in formats that are compact, complete and connected, and ultimately more sustainable and satisfying' (Farr, 2008: 127) through participatory design interventions to constitute knowable neighbourhood edges and centres, enhanced walkability and connectivity, mixed land uses and provision of community spaces.

In a similar vein, more recently, the principles of new urbanism encouraging walkability, connectivity, mixed-use and diversity, mixed housing, quality architecture and urban design, traditional neighbourhood structure, increased density, green transportation, sustainability, and quality of life have been integrated into new urban developments across North America and increasingly replicated in Majority World contexts (e.g. Hadfield-Hill and Zara, 2017; see also Box 3.3 on Indian Smart Cities).

Third, in the UK, the 'Egan wheel' (Figure 3.1) has been widely used as a planning and pedagogical tool to reflect upon the preconditions for 'sustainable communities' (see Bell and Lane, 2009; Manzi et al., 2010; Rogerson et al., 2011; Chanan and Miller, 2013). In 2003, Sir John Egan chaired a national review of skills and evidence relating to sustainability within the built environment and planning professions. The 'Egan wheel' (ODPM, 2004: 18) has been widely reproduced

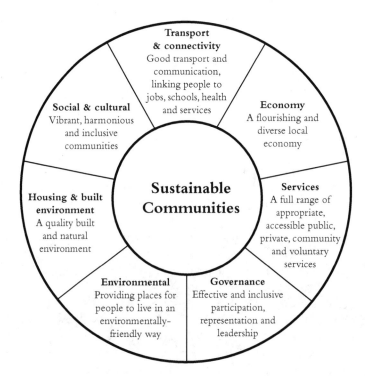

**FIGURE 3.1** The 'Egan wheel': components of 'sustainable communities' (ODPM, 2004: 19).

from the synthesis of their findings. The wheel identifies seven key constituents of sustainable communities, which are that built environments

> meet the diverse needs of existing and future residents, their children and other users, contribute to a high quality of life and provide opportunity and choice. They achieve this in ways that make effective use of natural resources, enhance the environment, promote social cohesion and inclusion and strengthen economic prosperity.
>
> *(ODPM, 2004: 18)*

In the UK, the Egan wheel has arguably been valuable in expanding public and professional understandings of sustainability: beyond discourses of eco-friendliness, towards more holistic understandings of the interdependency of environmental, political, infrastructural, housing and economic issues. Certainly, as we show in the following section, its objectives relating to urban planning/design, participation, biodiversity, community inclusivity, conviviality, liveability came to be prioritised within national policy imperatives relating to Sustainable Communities in England.

Concepts of sustainable urbanism have come to be internationally significant in urban planning and policy. For example, sustainable urbanism is a core goal of global multilateral urban development strategies such as the European Union Leipzig Charter on Sustainable European Cities (EU, 2007) and United Nations' Human Settlements Programme (UN-Habitat, 2009) and Urbanisation and Development Programme (also known as 'Habitat III'; UN-Habitat, 2016). As such, ideals of sustainable urbanism have been brought to a range of urban development contexts internationally (Rapoport 2015a, 2015b). For example, discourses of sustainable urbanism have specifically underpinned national policy agendas worldwide, including the Indian Smart Cities programme (Government of India, 2016), China Sustainable Cities Programme (UN-Habitat, 2009), and across Europe (Lafferty, 2001), including the Sustainable Communities plan in England (ODPM, 2003a, 2004). A proliferation of exemplars of large-scale 'sustainable' urban developments (HCA, 2009; Mapes and Wolch, 2010), and plans to construct sustainable urban spaces on a vast scale in China, Singapore (Government of Singapore, 2012) and India (Lavasa, 2012) evidences the continuing significance of sustainable urbanism for understanding urban lives and communities in diverse international settings.

---

## BOX 3.3 INDIA'S VISION FOR SMART CITIES

In 2015, the Prime Minister of India Narendra Modi launched the Smart City agenda, one which advocates 'urbanisation not as a problem, but as an opportunity'. The Government of India (2016: n.p.) define Smart City as cities which 'focus on their most pressing needs and on the greatest opportunities to improve lives. They tap a range of approaches – digital and information technologies, urban planning best practices, public–private partnerships,

**46** Policy and practice

and policy change – to make a difference. They always put people first.' This campaign has emerged from a need to address some of the key threats which face India's urban areas, such as growth and migration to towns and cities, access to energy, water and deepening social inequalities. With cities bidding for an allocation of central funds, at the time of writing, 90 of the cities have been selected (see Government of India, 2017 for the list) and projects are being implemented. The strategy for 'smart' implementation is fourfold:

- Retrofitting existing urban infrastructures to make urban spaces 'more efficient and liveable'. This would be applied to an area of 500 acres and identified in consultation with citizens.
- Redevelopment, of an existing area of the city with the co-creation of a new layout with enhanced infrastructure using mixed land use and increased density. This would be applied to an area of more than 50 acres, identified by Urban Local Bodies and in consultation with the local populace.
- Greenfield development, will see the application of 'smart solutions' to a 'previously vacant area using innovative planning, plan financing and plan implementation tools'. This would be applied to an area of more than 250 acres.
- Pan-city development, advocates for 'smart solutions' to be applied across the city, to existing infrastructures (Government of India, 2017).

Examples of 'smart' approaches to urban development include: CCTV surveillance; smart bus stops; smart paving; online system of water connections; smart e-rickshaw charging station. There is an overt focus on technological fixes to urban problems – as cities across India implement their 'smart' projects, the impact on citizens and, importantly, children and young people needs due consideration. In this context, this book reports on findings from the New Urbanisms in India project (www.new-urbanism-india.com) to provide additional international comparisons in terms of young people's experiences of new sustainable urbanisms (Hadfield-Hill and Zara, 2017).

Against this backdrop the discourses, visions and policies of sustainable urbanism have been the focus of a large body of international research and scholarship (for literature reviews see Wheeler, 1996; Koglin, 2009; Flint and Raco, 2012; Zheng et al., 2014). In the UK, for example, a great deal of work has sought to historicise the notion of sustainable urbanism, tracing an almost canonical genealogy of regional and national urban planning vision, as illustrated in the examples throughout this chapter. Scholars highlight the incorporation of the healing properties of light and air in the utopian nineteenth-century urban developments conceived by wealthy philanthropic industrialists in a moral commitment to improve the personal and family health and poverty of their workforces vis-à-vis the desperate urban decay dominating this era (see Box 3.4).

Policy and practice **47**

These observations were also driving the early twentieth-century 'Garden Cities' movement with its plans for the development of a thriving and green suburb through combining the qualities of town and countryside (see Box 3.5). The regeneration of public space as a base for democratic civic engagement, the formalisation of the profession of urban planning, the rhetorics of urban regeneration, emphasis on regional economic growth, and transformative architectural modernism came together in the postwar 'New Towns' Act (Box 3.6).

---

## BOX 3.4 'IDEAL' COMMUNITIES

In the UK, a series of utopian, nineteenth-century 'ideal' or 'model' urban developments are often cited as antecedents of more recent turns to sustainable urbanism (Alexander, 2009). Communities such as New Lanark, Port Sunlight and Bourneville were designed by wealthy industrialists to provide accommodation and public spaces for their workforces. These projects were typically motivated by a combination of religious faith, moral philanthropism and/or sound business sense. Industrialists such as utopian socialist mill-owner Robert Owen, liberal soap magnate William Lever and the Quaker Cadbury family of chocolate-makers were concerned that the inner-urban living conditions of their workers had become over-crowded, polluted and unhealthy (and perhaps, therefore, deleterious to their capacity to labour). Like the many modern(ist) planners and architects who followed them, they viewed new, carefully planned communities as an opportunity to address the social and moral problems that, in their view, afflicted the urban working classes. A large body of research has explored how the resulting communities were designed to offer improved housing conditions, access to education, and to allow the healing properties of light and air to flood into urban spaces through design interventions and new outdoor spaces (Gold, 1997; Fishman, 1999; Worpole, 2000).

---

## BOX 3.5 LETCHWORTH: THE FIRST GARDEN CITY

Ebenezer Howard (1850–1928) is widely figured as one of the most influential thinkers in the history of British urban planning. Nearly a century after his death, his notion of the 'Garden City' remains a resonant and evocative motif in planning theory and policy (TCPA, 2011, 2014), and is widely described as a precursor to ideals of sustainable urbanism (Alexander, 2009). Howard was persuaded by the socialist principle that everyone – regardless of their social class – should have some kind of access to land. However, he was not persuaded by the centralised socialism of many contemporary utopian socialists. Thus, he sought to emphasise the importance of a system of planning that would enable the development of new towns, but limit their size as part of a decentralised pattern of urban settlement (Hall and Ward, 1998). Howard's solution – the 'Garden City' – was one which, today, many would brand as 'sustainable'. He recognised the benefits of urban life – as a cradle for culture, politics, employment and sociability – as well as its many contemporary ills. Similarly, he viewed the 'country' as a place of beauty, fresh air, and bright sunlight, but one lacking employment opportunities and still caught in a generally oppressive class system. Thus, the Garden City – the 'town-country', as he termed it – would combine the best of both worlds (Howard, 1898: 10). Howard determined that each new Garden City development should have a fixed upper population limit (of 32,000), and be based upon a relatively small site (of 1,000 acres, meaning a radius of just 1.2 kilometres). Thus, anticipating the logics of contemporary sustainable urban planning, cities would be comprised of what would later be termed 'neighbourhood units': dense, walkable communities, with employment and services located proximate to homes (although for a critical review of these principles, see Lawhon, 2009). Howard's influence was felt in the construction of the first new towns in the world: Letchworth and Welwyn Garden Cities, both north of London. Howard's ideas have been direct or indirect inspirations for new urban developments around the world, in countries as diverse as the United States, Brazil, Australia and Bhutan.

**FIGURE 3.2** 'Letchworth: The First Garden City' poster. We thank Letchworth Garden City Heritage Foundation for permission to reproduce this image.

## BOX 3.6 NEW TOWNS

In the aftermath of the Second World War, the planning of new large-scale urban spaces was positioned as a key strategy to address issues of housing shortage, bomb damage, inner-urban poverty and regional differences in economic development in the UK (Raco, 2007). The 1946 New Towns Act allowed for the planning and development of new urban spaces: these New Towns were designed to be self-contained and located at some distance from London and other large metropolitan areas to ensure their (relative) economic independence (Hall and Ward, 1998). Each development was designed to contain diverse housing types and community facilities while accommodating diverse socio-economic groups. Planners were encouraged to design-in discrete self-contained neighbourhoods, and road layouts enabled an unprecedented degree of 'planning for the car' (Hardy, 1991). Thus, New Towns were meant to be socially and, to an extent, environmentally sustainable. Moreover, they were also intended to be financially sustainable. They were realised through innovative funding models – principally, Development Corporations (Thomas, 1996), which necessitated cooperation between the State and the private sector, and which were to become increasingly prevalent in future efforts to build new, sustainable urban places in the UK from the 1990s onwards. The period 1947–1968 saw the planning and construction of 28 New and Expanding Towns. Reflections upon this large-scale planning intervention are strongly polarised between nostalgia for a hopeful era of modernist planning solutions and dismay at the high levels of deprivation in many New Towns, fifty years on. It was not until the election of the New Labour Government in 1997 that the UK saw attempts to build new urban places on this scale.

However, in the work of 1980s Urban Development Corporations (Gold and Ward, 1994) developing the logics and strategies of place promotion, branding and economic competitiveness became key. This was followed by Tony Blair's political proclamation of 'liveability' as a key objective for urban policy and planning. Once again the urban agenda was to address the socially and environmentally constructed urban ills. Blair outlined the political project as one of targeting anti-social behaviours to improve community social cohesion and improving aspects of the environment through the preservation of open green spaces. This agenda became further articulated and detailed in the neoliberal politics underpinning the 2003 Sustainable Communities Plan (Raco 2005, 2007) that explicitly formulated an agenda for large-scale urban housing and development schemes grounded in principles and objectives of a sustainable urban agenda. As we discuss below, this plan formed the immediate policy context for the New Urbanisms, New Citizens project discussed throughout this book.

As we have demonstrated, there is a strong sense of cross-fertilisation of ideas and initiatives in the creation and regeneration of sustainable urban landscapes

**50** Policy and practice

internationally. In the work of Rapoport (2015a) it is striking how the global sustainability agendas that put the natural environment centre stage seems to have accelerated such 'internationalisation'. Not only is there a wealth of small- and large-scale projects on sustainable urbanism across the world, but the internationalisation process has also become centralised, as the masterplans guiding developments worldwide are the work of a small elite group of international and global architecture, engineering, design and planning companies based in Europe and North America. As Rapoport (2015a) shows, such masterplans set out ambitious and innovative solutions for land use, designs and technologies. However, the international turn to sustainable urbanism that often signifies the debates of the last decade frequently seems to overwhelmingly focus upon multi-award-winning 'exemplar' developments (Lara, 2010; cf. Robinson, 2002). Indeed, it is rare to see anything about sustainable urbanism without encountering the practically omnipresent examples such as Curitiba in Brazil (Box 3.7), Copenhagen in Denmark and Malmö in Sweden (Box 3.8). The focus on exemplar developments has undoubtedly been important in fostering public and academic attention and understanding of sustainable urbanism.

---

### BOX 3.7  EXEMPLAR CITY OF SUSTAINABLE URBANISM: CURITIBA

The city of Curitiba, in the south of Brazil, is widely hailed as an exemplar of sustainable urbanism in a high-density, rapidly growing Majority World context. Under the charismatic 22-year Mayorship of former urban planner Jaime Lerner (who is himself often described as an exemplar of visionary civic leadership towards sustainable urban development) the city has implemented a series of strategic plans since the 1970s which have won numerous international awards for excellence in sustainable urbanism (United Nations, 2013). Specifically, the city is lauded for:

- large-scale masterplanning of land use, road networks and public transport to produce a relatively low-cost integrated network of dedicated express bus lanes, encouraging popular use of public transport and apparent reductions in car use, despite high levels of automobility within the region;
- pioneering municipal recycling schemes to collect metals, plastics, paper and glass through the 'Garbage that is not garbage' initiative;
- municipal projects to protect water quality, harvest rainwater and develop public open spaces around urban drainage and flood-control systems;
- successful incentive schemes to engage 'hard-to-reach' communities in environmentally sustainable behaviours – for example through trading schemes where favela dwellers and fishermen could exchange waste for public bus tickets, food, football tickets or cash; and
- introduction of flocks of 'municipal sheep' to public parks and open spaces to mow grass and provide income from sales of wool which funds participatory community projects.

## BOX 3.8 EXEMPLAR CITY: MALMÖ, SWEDEN

Malmö, in southern Sweden, is widely cited as an exemplar of city-scaled sustainable urbanism in a Global North context. The city is known for strategic civic investment in environmentally sustainable technologies and programmes, after the decline of heavy shipyard-based industries. Successive city administrations have worked to brand the city as a distinctive 'testing ground for new environmental technology', with a commitment that Malmö will be 'climate neutral' by 2020 and entirely reliant upon renewable energy sources by 2030. Specific innovations showcased in the city include:

- experimental development of smart grid technologies for domestic power, heating and cooling, and public engagement with energy consumption and production projects;
- exploratory investment in large-scale windpower generation and smaller community windpower projects;
- city-wide implementation of household organic waste recycling to biogas;
- civic procurement strategies to increase public, municipal and corporate engagement with organic, fairly traded and ethically certified foods, beverages and consumer goods – for example through strategies to serve organic, ethical and 'climate-smart' foods in all city schools, pre-schools and health/municipal services;
- initiatives to reduce car parking spaces and foster public engagement with carpool schemes (e.g. through flexible, smartphone-mediated booking and payment systems for car hire);
- city-wide provision of high-quality dedicated cycle lanes and services for cyclists; and
- extensive, pioneering investment in green roofing and sustainable urban drainage systems, and extensions of these schemes to 'future-proof' the city against projected sea-level rises due to anthropocentric climate change.

## Actually existing urbanisms: sustainable communities in the UK

We suggest that the longstanding, international body of research exploring discourses, visions and exemplars of sustainable urbanism has too often overlooked the actually existing built environments and communities that are constituted via turns toward sustainable urbanism. So one key aim of this book is to call for – and to evidence the benefits of – greater attention to the specific kinds of urban spaces and experiences constituted by particular sustainable urban policy contexts. In particular, there is much scope for scholars to move beyond the widely cited and idealised 'exemplar' cities to explore in more depth different forms of provincial and suburban developments that appear to represent less distinctive and to some extent 'mundane' forms of sustainable urbanism (although one of the communities we examine *has* been vaunted as an exemplar, albeit not on an international scale).

## 52 Policy and practice

A key aim of this book is therefore to engage with empirical evidence from diverse sustainable urban spaces constituted within a range of locations and contexts. We want to highlight the importance of understanding sustainable urbanism as a broad variety of forms and as more than a mere result of policy visions and planning objectives such as those outlined in the previous section. Thus we go beyond the kinds of exemplars illustrated in the preceding case studies, to embrace a wider understanding of the influence and interactions between the material (location, built and natural environment) and the social that is the diversity of people and population groups and their actual lives, practices and experiences, wishes and needs.

As a stepping-stone for understanding the local, perhaps mundane, everyday geographies of actually existing sustainable urbanisms, it is vital to examine the specific national, local and regional policy contexts that frame the predominant research evidence presented in this book. As outlined in the Introduction, the New Urbanisms, New Citizens research project explored the experiences of children and young people growing up in new build sustainable housing developments in the context of the UK Sustainable Communities Plan (ODPM, 2003a). In effect, the Sustainable Communities Plan (and subsequent Sustainable Communities Act of 2007) instigated a major programme of large-scale planning for sustainable housebuilding and urban extension, focused in four 'Growth Areas' in south-east England (each earmarked for approximately 300,000 new homes by 2031). As per the Egan wheel (see Figure 3.1) the plan was centrally committed to a wide-ranging concept of 'sustainable' urban development, combining social, economic and environmental facets of sustainability in the planning, design and construction of new urban spaces (ODPM, 2003a, 2004). The Sustainable Communities Plan (ODPM, 2003a) combined a number of substantial, interlinked objectives:

> to accommodate the new homes we need by 2021 . . .; to encourage people to remain and move back into urban areas . . .; to tackle the poor quality of life and lack of opportunity in certain urban areas as a matter of social justice . . .; to strengthen the factors in all urban areas which will enhance their economic success . . .; to make sustainable urban living practical, affordable and attractive.
>
> *(ODPM, 2000: 37)*

In practice, urban development in Growth Areas tended to take four specific, recurring forms: exemplar 'sustainable urban extensions', showcasing sustainable design features in newbuild suburban developments; new stand alone sustainable villages; large-scale and somewhat interchangeable urban extensions developed by volume house builders, not explicitly marketed as sustainable; and small developments of new housing on urban brownfield or infill sites. Moreover, we note that all kinds of Sustainable Communities were overwhelmingly characterised by four key, recurring kinds of planning and design interventions. Each of the following interventions explicitly and directly drew inspiration from principles, visions and exemplars of sustainable urbanism as outlined in the preceding section.

Policy and practice **53**

First, as in many contexts of sustainable urbanism, in the UK, sustainable communities were characterised by a building-in of a suite of sustainable architectural and technological features within large-scale urban developments. The 'mainstreaming' or 'upscaling' of sustainable urban architecture was figured as central to fostering a 'step change' towards more environmentally sustainable household and community behaviours (RIBA, 2003; TCPA, 2006, 2007). The inclusion of innovative technologies was strongly incentivised, as policy-makers, planners and architects were encouraged to 'explore what low carbon, sustainable places might be like now and in the future', and understand 'strategic urban design, masterplanning and the management of buildings, spaces and places . . . [as] essential parts of any sustainable development' (CABE, 2007: 2–3; also DCLG, 2007). In practice, the most visible manifestation of this policy/planning context was the incorporation of 'high performance', 'energy-efficient' features into new domestic architecture (Edwards and Turrent, 2000; Lerum, 2007; Schmidt, 2009). Thus it became increasingly common for large-scale housing developments to include features such as sustainable construction materials, energy-efficient boilers, photovoltaic cells, solar water heaters, superinsulation, sedum roofing, wind turbines, passive solar retention, compost bins or biofuel systems (see Hadfield-Hill, 2013; Horton et al., 2015). Such features were valorised as prompts to foster education for sustainability, behaviour change and public understanding of environmental issues (Boardman, 2007; Shaw et al., 2007; Schreiner and Sjoberg, 2005; Zero Carbon Hub, 2013). The policy/planning context was also characterised by attempts to design 'high performance' infrastructures and landscapes that would be attractive and safe but that would also enable the effective functional management of non-human agents – water, plants, animals, pollutants, etcetera – in integrated systems such as sustainable urban drainage systems.

Many new housing developments (ranging in size from 100–10,000 homes) including these kinds of sustainable urban architecture and landscape features were established in the wake of the Sustainable Communities Plan (see Catto, 2008; TCPA, 2009; Barratt Homes, 2013; RUDI, 2013). Their development was paralleled by the emergence of regulatory mechanisms and rating systems (such as BREEAM and LEED), which came to constitute a language and logic of 'high performance' sustainable urbanism (Birkeland, 2012; Kubba, 2012). In the UK, an emphasis upon technological and architectural aspects of sustainable urbanism – exemplified in many Sustainable Communities developments, and the valorisation of ratings systems like BREEAM – has been widely debated, not least for an uncritical adherence to norms of large-scale housing supply and an elision of sustainability with neoliberal modes of governance that, for many commentators, renders 'sustainability' a meaningless cipher for contested processes of regeneration, private financing and responsibilisation (Raco, 2005; Cochrane et al., 2014). However, while Sustainable Communities have been extensively critiqued in discursive, political and regulatory terms (O'Riordan, 2004; Evans and Honeyford, 2011; Kraftl, 2014) we note (again) that remarkably little research has explored the ways in which built and technological features of sustainable urbanism are actually

**54** Policy and practice

integrated into or forming new household practices in particular sustainable communities. In Chapter 4, we specifically highlight the ways in which children, young people and families in our case study communities – and in actually existing sustainable urbanisms elsewhere – experienced, narrated and (mis)understood diverse 'high performance' sustainable architectural and landscape features.

Second, as in many visions of sustainable urbanism, most developments were structured by a range of planning interventions relating to urban mobility and connectivity. Most of these newbuild developments were, to some degree, masterplanned with the express intention of fostering urban 'compactness' (ease of everyday walkability and mobility within the community) and 'connectivity' (ease of travel to/from nearby areas, services and places of employment) (see Jenks et al., 1996; de Roo and Miller, 2000; Department for Transport, 2004c; Lucas et al., 2010). These masterplans also sought to enact existing UK policy commitments to plan local and regional 'integrated' transport networks, with the aim of 'extend[ing] choice in transport and secure mobility in a way that supports sustainable development' through:

- integration within and between different types of transport – so that each contributes its full potential and people can move easily between them;
- integration with the environment – so that our transport choices support a better environment;
- integration with land use planning – at national, regional and local level, so that transport and planning work together to support more sustainable travel choices and reduce the need to travel;
- integration with our policies for education, health and wealth creation – so that transport helps to make a fairer, more inclusive society.

*(DETR, 1998: 15)*

In this context, urban planning initiatives delivered via Sustainable Communities formed an important part of national policy imperatives to develop more sustainable travel futures. In particular, it was hoped that the planning of sustainable communities would facilitate behaviour change such that walking, cycling and public transport could become:

more convenient, attractive and realistic choice for many more short journeys, especially those to work and school. Because being active is especially important for children, we want to train them to walk and cycle in safety and confidence. This will:

- help to reduce car use and help to tackle social inclusion, making towns and cities safer and more pleasant places to live;
- help to reduce congestion and improve air quality; and
- increase levels of physical activity and improve public health. Moderate physical activity such as walking and cycling helps reduce obesity, heart disease, stroke, cancer and diabetes.

*(Department for Transport, 2004a: 6.3)*

Notably, the design of new urban streetscapes became key to realising these objectives. Many new developments included streetscape design features which intended to encourage the notion of streets as 'shared surfaces' for all, wherein pedestrians, cyclists and vehicles can co-exist happily and safely (Department for Transport, 2004b, 2007; CABE, 2008). Thus, for example, plans for many new developments proposed numerous walkable pathways, 'convivial' public spaces, traffic-calming measures and supposedly 'shared surface' thoroughfares. In so doing, considerable attention was given to the 'legibility', 'walkability', safety, curve radii, sight-lines and 'Connectivity, Conspicuity, Convenience, Comfort, and Conviviality' of routes within new communities (Department for Transport, 2004c: 7; Hamilton-Baillie, 2008). Exemplar projects such as 'Homezones' (see Box 5.1 in Chapter 5), or earlier antecedents such as the 'woonerf' (see Box 5.2 in Chapter 5), were widely mobilised in emphasising the importance of 'reclaiming the street' from cars and responding to the needs of diversely mobile local communities, including children, young people and families.

In the above contexts, a great deal of academic, policy and media debate in Europe, North America and Australasia has (sometimes rather uncritically) diagnosed an apparent decline in children and young people's access to outdoor space (Hillman et al., 1990; O'Brien et al., 2000; Karsten, 2005; Louv, 2005). A wealth of research has highlighted how parental fears and anxieties have normatively centred on children's outdoor play and mobility (see, for example, Hillman et al., 1990; Valentine and McKendrick, 1997; Valentine, 1997; Jackson and Scott, 1999; O'Brien et al., 2000; Bringolf-Isler et al., 2010; van Loon and Frank, 2011). Indeed, children's safety and their attendant mobilities have often been central to planning interventions in sustainable communities that seek to foster different, more hopeful, civic relationships between the diverse mobilities of motorists, cyclists and pedestrians, and have typically been hailed as unequivocally positive. However, we are struck by the way in which children and young people have rarely been consulted about their experiences of living with such planned interventions. In Chapter 5, we explore how children, young people and families engage, in diverse ways, with specific elements of local 'shared surfaces' with examples drawn from our research in the case study communities. In so doing, we seek to engage far more critically with the principles and assumptions that underpin contemporary forms of street design that, in turn, are such central features of sustainable urban planning around the world.

Third, planning interventions expressly designed to foster civic participation, conviviality and inclusion were a distinctive, characteristic features of many new-build developments in the UK during the Sustainable Communities era (Marsden, 2008). Central to this policy context was an aspiration to develop 'vibrant, harmonious and inclusive communities' (ODPM, 2004: 19), characterised by 'a diverse, vibrant and creative local culture, encouraging pride in the community and cohesion within it', and abundant in 'effective engagement and participation by local people, groups and businesses' and local 'sense of place' (ODPM, 2003a: 5). In practice, in the UK, policy-makers, planners and developers sought to realise these aspirations through some very specific local actions. As suggested in the preceding

**56** Policy and practice

paragraph, one widespread strategy in the Sustainable Communities context was the planning of all manner of supposedly 'convivial' streetscapes and public spaces: designing streets, pathways, squares, parks, plazas and courtyards such that they enabled (or channelled) residents' everyday, 'neighbourly' encounters with one another. Another key strategy, widely encouraged in aspirational planning documents in this context, was the provision of opportunities for local communities to participate in the planning, design and stewardship of particular elements of newbuild developments. Thus, planners and developers were expected to organise consultative decision-making processes and to foster dialogic engagement with various local residents' groups and decision-making fora. Moreover, planners and developers were encouraged to build-in an infrastructure of community spaces, meeting places and recreational facilities where a local nexus of community involvement and volunteering might develop.

Fourth, in many Sustainable Communities projects, developers were explicitly placed under a planning obligation to build 'mixed' or 'balanced' communities (DETR, 2000a, 2000b; Social Exclusion Unit, 2000; ODPM, 2003b). This notion of 'mixed community' entailed the construction of 'a well-integrated mix of decent homes of different types and tenures to support a range of household sizes, ages, and incomes' (ODPM, 2003a: 5). In practice, then, most Sustainable Communities comprised a purposeful (it was hoped cohesive) mix of different housing types, tenures and sizes, with social and affordable housing 'pepper-potted' (theoretically undetectably) among other housing types that should foster both social inclusion and the kinds of conviviality or 'liveability' discussed above. Notably, again, the implications of these interventions for children and young people have rarely been considered. So, for example, in Chapter 7, we consider the extent to which children and young people engaged with formally constituted spaces of community and participation in newbuild communities in south-east England, while Chapter 6 specifically explores the ways in which children and young people understand and articulate residential 'mixing' within their communities.

## The need for research with children, young people and sustainable urbanisms

Having identified some key features of sustainable urban developments, our key concern in this book is to consider how the material, spatial and social features of newbuild, sustainable urban developments are sensed, experienced, lived and narrated by resident children and young people. We have already briefly indicated some of the ways in which the chapters in this book engage critically and constructively with actually existing sustainable urbanisms, through the experiences, voices and actions of children and young people.

Critically, from an academic perspective, while much has been written about the policy and planning discourses of the Sustainable Communities Plan and its antecedents (Raco, 2005, 2007, 2012; Alexander, 2009; Cochrane, 2010), relatively little research has explored empirically the urban communities constructed via this

Policy and practice **57**

particular large-scale policy intervention. Throughout this book we specifically explore, and call for further, research and practice with children and young people in contexts of sustainable urbanism. For a series of reasons, we argue that there is still a pressing need for research on *children and young people* in relation to such contexts. At a global scale, over the past few decades, urban living has dramatically changed in character, leading to significant changes in the lives of children growing up today. Rapid urbanisation, the formidable physical re-composition of cities and the huge proliferation of urban populations associated with changing economic, political and social forces are refashioning children's relationships to the towns and cities in which they live, and the modes of living as a young person within them. Urban living has become particularly pertinent to contemporary childhood: UNI-CEF's *State of the World's Children* report (UNICEF, 2012) estimates that more than 40 per cent of the global child population now lives in cities. Yet children's experiences of cities are hugely diverse, in part because cities have changed dramatically in terms of their size, layout, infrastructure and planning. The past thirty years have seen many forms of urban restructuring and renewal: from gentrification to suburbanisation, from 'new', sustainable cities to green retrofitting, from the demolition of residential high-rises to the reinvention of city centres, and far more besides. Globally, scholars have highlighted the enormous speed with which cities in some parts of the world are growing – both through State-sanctioned projects like the newly built 'sustainable' and 'Smart' cities in India and privately financed developments. The world's cities are places of extraordinary dynamism and opportunity but also inequality, risk and failure – not only in the best-known 'global cities', but in what Robinson (2005) has termed 'ordinary cities', too.

It is our contention that the policy and planning shifts which are labelled 'sustainable urbanism' have constituted some unprecedented forms of community, infrastructural, domestic and regulatory spaces, which are (and are becoming increasingly) central to the everyday lives and experiences of children and young people around the world. This book will consider children and young people's experiences of these new forms of sustainable urbanism. Although our focus is upon case studies from the particular contexts of England's Sustainable Communities Plan, we suggest that the following chapters should be salient to any examples of sustainable urbanism, and we draw on a range of case studies taken from outside the UK to illustrate our arguments. On one level, this book addresses the often-overlooked experiences and voices of children and young people in sustainable urban contexts, and considers how sustainable planning interventions affect their lives. However, we also call for research and practice which is attuned to the often-overlooked ways in which children and young people constitute *their own* everyday inhabitations, mobilities, socialities and participatory practices with/in contexts of sustainable urbanism: how children and young people *constitute actually existing sustainable urbanisms*. The underlying argument of the book is that the design and layout of sustainable urban spaces do not necessarily *determine* the lives of children and young people; rather, children are important agents in the production of urban places (while, simultaneously, they experience marginalisation and

**58** Policy and practice

disenfranchisement through the architectural and social designs that frame those places). Through the book, we present a critical analysis of the challenges, tensions and opportunities for children and young people living in contemporary sustainable urban environments: from their crucial role as 'community-builders' in new urban places, to their role as consumers using and understanding sustainable design features of their homes and communities, to their diverse and critical roles in relation to formal strategies of community participation and cohesion. We thus critically examine the prospects for including children and young people as a key social group in sustainable urban design, planning projects and strategies, via the recognition of children and young people as citizens in their own right. In Chapter 2, we argued that the constitution of an interdisciplinary conceptual framework is required in order to understand, more fully, the complexities of children and young people's everyday lives in new sustainable urban spaces. That involves important, sometimes unsettling challenges of *both* conventional understandings of childhood and youth *and* the principles and presumptions of 'sustainable' urbanism itself.

# 4

# LIVING WITH SUSTAINABLE URBAN TECHNOLOGIES

In the previous chapter, we discussed some key principles and policies underpinning international attempts to build cleaner, greener and more environmentally sustainable urban living. As we argued, in response to such sustainable policy and planning visions, new *eco-technologies* – often labelled as 'green' or 'smart' – are increasingly designed-in to homes, streets and neighbourhoods across diverse contexts. Typically, smart infrastructures refer to technologies that are interconnected, efficient and responsive to human needs. For example, in India the rhetoric of the Smart City has become a cornerstone of the government's urban policy to support local economic growth and enhance quality of life through the implementation of smart energy systems, green transportation and smart buildings (Government of India, 2016). Advances in sustainable urban technologies have been driven by global technology innovators, such as for example IBM, who offer 'smart' solutions (including Big data and cognitive computing capabilities) to urban problems including: security and surveillance; heating, ventilation and cooling; water management and parking systems (IBM, 2015). Yet 'eco-technologies' extend well beyond 'smart' solutions, encompassing disparate, often separate technologies – from PV panels to porous pavement designs, and from sustainable drainage systems to combined heat and power plants (CHP).

Given the proliferation of such new sustainable urban technologies within public and domestic spaces, there is a need for greater understanding of how residents interact with the new eco-technologies and architectural forms of sustainable urbanism in their everyday lives. The scant research that does exist focuses largely on residents' experiences of living in small-scale, grass-roots eco-housing projects or even individual buildings (e.g. Pickerill and Maxey, 2009), rather than larger-scale 'mainstream' developments that are the focus of this book. Existing research has identified a variety of perspectives regarding the importance of *perceived comfort* in eco-homes, and gendered divisions of labour in the

**60** Sustainable urban technologies

maintenance of the home (Pickerill, 2015, 2016). Other scholarship, although relatively tentative and, notably, not involving children and young people, has focused on the importance of research on the *materialities* of sustainable consumption. For example, Hobson (2016) examined sustainable citizenship and environmental education, through a focus on the Sydney-based sustainable living programme called 'GreenHome', 'a community education programme that aims to inform and assist individuals in making small but environmentally significant lifestyle changes' (Hobson, 2016: 321). As we argue in this chapter and elsewhere, however (Horton et al., 2015), there is a need to extend research on sustainable urban technologies *beyond* the mantras of environmental education – quite simply because residents' lives and concerns exceed those of environmental awareness and knowledge. We are therefore inspired by Shove et al.'s (2012) work on the importance of engaging with social practices and interactions with ordinary household technologies in the home and, more recently, by Marres (2015: xi) in thinking on *material participation*, encouraging us to consider 'how everyday things, technologies and settings [are] invested with the capacity to engage'. Lane and Gorman-Murray (2016: 2) also prompt us to look at household items and the interactions between them – to move beyond the culture–nature binary to witness a co-agentic relationship 'to consider how aspects of the human and nonhuman world act in conjunction with one another'.

However, with the integration of eco-efficient technologies into *mainstream* housing developments, there is a need for research to work with broader and more fluid notions of the family to include the contribution of children and young people (Christensen, 2004b; Snow et al., 2015). Given the interdisciplinary conceptual frames that we introduced in Chapter 2, particularly important here is the notion of family practices that centres on the 'doing' of family rooted in the everyday (Morgan, 2011). Family practices are those cultural activities (such as, cleaning, cooking, watching TV, playing games, bed time, waste disposal, etc.) at the heart of family members' everyday experiences. Family practices carry a sense of routine and regularity and are meaningful to both children and adults. Given their centrality and constitutive character it is important families to be able to sustain these practices. It is evident that many such activities and practices involve technologies and tools of various kinds. Here, we focus on children and family practices involving diverse eco-technologies and how they become (or not) interwoven into the everyday life of families, as they try (or not) to establish sustainable routines (Christensen, 2004a).

In this chapter, we define 'eco-technologies' as the full gamut of architectural, urban design, environmental management and digital technologies that are built into sustainable urban spaces. Mindful of the dominant attention to the perspectives of policy-makers, planners, campaigners, practitioners and to some extent adult residents in previous research on eco-housing and green architecture (see Chapter 3; Kraftl, 2012; Faulconbridge, 2013) our discussion explores from the outset the perspectives of children and young people. We draw on data from the New Urbanisms, New Citizens project, supplemented with examples from other

Sustainable urban technologies  61

geographical contexts. One of the four case studies, Hettonbury, has been identified as a state-of-the-art exemplar of sustainable urban design, and incorporated a range of cutting-edge sustainable urban technologies. This provided an important opportunity to explore children and young people's encounters with and responses to the new eco-architectural and technological features and, therefore, most of the discussion centres upon Hettonbury. Here, we critically discuss examples from multiple sites of eco-architectural encounters within the community: the school, where eco-technologies have been integrated into the building design; outdoor, landscaped spaces, where on an everyday basis, children and young people interact with features such as 'Code Level 6' buildings and sustainable urban drainage systems (SUDS; see Figures 4.1 and 4.2); and, in family homes, where eco-technologies come to form part of (or not) the fabric of everyday domestic life. While, at least in Hettonbury, the implementations of architectural features and technologies are lauded as successful examples of eco-technological innovation, we will argue that an attentiveness to how these spaces are lived, interacted with and understood – indeed, how they can also go unnoticed or be misinterpreted – provides new insight into how sustainability measures are taken up and understood by their users, which is after all a crucial aspect of the success of new eco-technologies. Our aim – in line with our interdisciplinary conceptual approach to childhood studies *and* sustainable urbanism – is to advocate for a focus on living with sustainable

**FIGURE 4.1** Examples of eco-technologies in Hettonbury: Code Level 6 buildings.

**FIGURE 4.2** Examples of eco-technologies in Hettonbury: sustainable urban drainage systems – retention pond.

eco-technologies through highlighting the embodied, aesthetical, affective and sometimes taken-for-granted ways in which young people experience and interact with eco-technologies and designs.

The chapter begins with a review of literatures on education for sustainability (EfS) and a call for closer attention to everyday experiences of architectural and technological geographies of sustainability that encompass, but *extend beyond*, EfS. The chapter then progresses to explore: first, sustainable technologies as part of everyday routines and practices; second, how the appearance and subtleness of eco-technologies and architectural forms elicited a suite of anxieties about their 'weirdness'; third, how children and young people's experiences of the functional and technological complexity of sustainable urban technologies resulted in them and their families disengaging with and sometimes renouncing (particular features of) sustainable urbanisms.

## Moving beyond education for sustainability

It is not particularly controversial to argue that the vast majority of extant research on children, young people and sustainability has focused on education – on the kinds of knowledge and attitudes that might enable children (framed as 'future global citizens') to become responsibilised for the planet's future environmental conditions. Although environmental education goes by various names, we use the term 'education for sustainability' (EfS) as shorthand in this chapter. Extant EfS research has, generally, proceeded on two fronts. First, the majority of discourse and academic research on children, young people and sustainability is framed by a fairly *formal* education for sustainability (EfS) agenda (Schreiner and Sjoberg, 2005; Malone, 2007; Satchwell, 2013). Indeed in many Minority Global North contexts, EfS has been placed high on national curriculum agendas, as a means towards meeting global sustainability goals (Chawla and Cushing, 2007; Malone, 2007; Malone and Tranter, 2003; Zelezny, 1999). The focus is on how sustainability is taught, learnt and valued within formal education (Walshe, 2013), as well as upon how children may become key agents of change in intergenerational transmissions of environmental knowledge (Kola-Olusanya, 2005; Damerell et al., 2013; Grønhøj and Thøgersen, 2012). However, as we have argued elsewhere (Horton et al., 2015), a focus on *education* – although important – effaces the manifold ways in which children encounter sustainability in their everyday lives in the form of, for example, the eco-technologies prevalent in sustainable urban environments. Thus, in this chapter we ask how sustainability is practised and experienced by children in their everyday life with friends, with family or on their own.

Second, environmental education is often set within the premise that young people's interaction with 'the outdoors' will encourage them to be environmental stewards (Malone and Hasluck, 2002; Louv, 2005; Ridgers et al., 2012). More critical scholarship – which has proceeded through the new materialist lenses of the 'new wave' of childhood studies (Chapter 2) – has emphasised how children's outdoor experiences are constituted through entanglements with other humans, nonhuman 'companion species' and materialities (e.g. Rautio, 2013; Pacini-Ketchabaw and Clark, 2016). Notably, this scholarship has sought to extend beyond debates about children's (apparent) lack of connectedness with nature and EfS, to question how children's environmental experiences articulate questions of colonial power and gender (e.g. Taylor, 2013; Taylor and Blaise 2014; Taylor et al., 2013). Notably, however, little of this work has taken place in the (arguably far broader) contexts *outside* educational spaces – and, in particular, in sustainable urban settings. In this light, Bennett's (2010) work on 'thing-power' is particularly influential; her work guides our thinking about the multiple materialities that constitute young people's everyday experiences of sustainable urbanism. By considering the drainage systems, the wind turbine, the co-habitants of the swale system, the solar panels, gadgets, bricks, mortar, colours and codes we seek to get closer to how children experience and navigate these eco-architectural forms.

In this chapter, then, we challenge and significantly extend this literature to uncover a far greater diversity of ways in which young people's lives are entangled with 'sustainability', broadly understood. We focus upon how eco-architectures are experienced, practised and felt by their users – the children and families whose lives jostle up against and interact with these eco-materialities. A deeper look at eco-architectural encounters yields important insights into the embodied,

**64** Sustainable urban technologies

emotional, and everyday engagements that, recursively, shape attitudes and experiences to sustainability. In this chapter, and in developing new wave approaches to childhood, we position young people as part of a co-existing socio-material assemblage, in which they co-exist *with* eco-technologies in sustainable urban places (Horton et al., 2015; Hadfield-Hill, 2013). We build on Shove et al.'s (2012) work on social practices with ordinary technologies in the home, and upon recent scholarship in the geographies of architecture, which has analysed the everyday practices of inhabitation that are critical to the ongoing constitution of built forms (Jacobs and Merriman, 2011; Kraftl, 2015). We are interested in young people's *everyday architectural geographies of sustainability*: the bodies that touch energy-saving devices at school; that play in SUD systems outside their homes; and those that wonder about the function of the solar panels on the roof of their house.

## Sustainable urban technologies: play, routine domestic practices and taken-for-granted interactions

In this section we argue that despite the seeming uniqueness of sustainable urban technologies, they quickly became enveloped within everyday routines and personal rhythms involving friends and family – leading to an underlying taken-for-grantedness. Hettonbury, given its recognition as an exemplar of sustainable urban design, provided an ideal opportunity to explore young people's lived experiences of eco-technologies and sustainable architectures. In this development both domestic housing and public buildings such as the school and community centre were designed to meet the UK's Code for Sustainable Homes to varying degrees ranging from the minimum requirements to the highest level of accreditation, Code Level 6. In this context, children and young people played with, walked past, touched, sat on and looked at various sustainable urban technologies from glazed frontages to sedum roofs, sustainable urban drainage systems and solar hot water tubing. For many children, the route to school would include journeys past Code Level 6 eco-homes and around or through the SUD (Sustainable Urban Drainage) systems. As we have shown elsewhere (Horton et al., 2015) children's accounts of living in a place with sustainable urban technologies were strongly polarised – with one in four participants expressing positive attitudes of 'coolness' akin to science fiction design. This is in contrast to the majority of children who expressed strong views about the 'weirdness' of sustainable features dispersed through their community.

Movement and play were key ways in which young people engaged with the sustainable features. Children's bodily and sensuous interactions were essentially embodied *playful* forms of interaction. As we argue in Chapter 8, *play* is in our view key to a research agenda seeking to understand children, youth and sustainability. Yet there is little evidence of extant research that focuses on how children (or adults) *play with* or intuitively engage with – rather than learn about – sustainable technologies. Indeed the only brief reference to a playful engagement with such

Sustainable urban technologies  **65**

technologies is noted by Marres, who refers to play in her analysis of the eco-friendly kettle. For her, such gadgets have 'acquired special salience . . . for raising awareness and involving people in issues of climate change . . . [whereby] they are presented as a playful means to get people to consider the environmental consequences of their everyday activities in terms of energy use' (Marres, 2015: x). What then of young people's playful engagement with the eco-materialities of their communities? In Chapter 8 we will discuss how play is constitutive of the more-than-human liveliness of sustainable urban communities.

Here we highlight children's everyday interactions with the SUD system – often designed as drains, channels, ditches and swales (Susdrain, 2012) – to show how children's everyday routines and playfulness are entwined with the materialities of sustainable urban technologies. The SUD system was a key feature of the urban design of Hettonbury meaning that the children and young people would spot these features from their bedroom windows, walk past them on their route to school and describe them as good places to be with friends; as Zane and Rachel explain:

> my brother likes to go in them . . . we play in them as well . . . we play catch, who can get the furthest up and stuff.
>
> *(Rachel, female, 9)*

> I always walk around the river thingies to get some exercise each day.
>
> *(Zane, male, 10)*

Academic literature on swales and SUD systems often report on the biodiversity potential of such environments (Briers, 2013); however, wildlife was only one part of the assemblage. Through children's play – as it (re)combined with these ecosystems – the SUDS became a space of vitality. This liveliness was constituted through the coming-together of weeds, muddy paths, sticks, the children, the butterflies, ladybirds, bikes, and more (compare Taylor et al., 2013). Children would crouch down next to the ponds, search for tadpoles, watch dragonflies hover, follow the water-boatmen scurrying across the surface, pick up ladybirds, run soil through their fingers and build mounds on the banks of the swales. Many young participants spoke of the games they would play in and around the landscaped channels – whether it be running up and down, sitting on the barriers to chat, playing tag, riding their bikes, 'jumping them' and using planks of wood to create bridges. The SUDS were focal points for children's everyday playing, explorations and excitement.

Away from the SUDS, a wind turbine, constructed on the edge of a large playing field in Hettonbury, also provided a focal point for children's play.

> Both on the pavements and on the main field, fun had been had, playing in the snow [Figure 4.3]. Two large snowballs sat proud on the pavement snowball fights and other fun times had been had in the field.
>
> *(Field notes, Hettonbury)*

**66** Sustainable urban technologies

> This morning I took a walk through the field, admiring the new wind turbine. It glistened in the sunshine, but it was not turning, I wondered if it was faulty or just not yet operational. From the footprints in the snow it was obvious that a number of people had been up close to the turbine. One person had circled it, as if playing a game.
>
> *(Field notes, Hettonbury)*

These field notes were recorded in Hettonbury, the morning after some snowfall; they mark – albeit in a bare way – the multiple ambiguities that may or may not tie together 'children', 'play' and 'nature' in particular ways. Note, for instance, the researcher's careful use of terminology ('person', not 'child'): we probably *assume* that it is children that have made these snowballs or left playful footprints in the snow around the turbine – but we do not *know* this for sure. Note also the absence of any humans in these vignettes, other than the researcher – the evidential bases for play are represented by the material conditions of the snow – how it has been marked, how it coheres in snowballs, how it preserves its former interactions with humans given its particular crystalline properties at a given temperature (not ice, nor slush, nor meltwater). The researcher was moved to use the passive voice

**FIGURE 4.3** Evidence of playful activity in the snow in Hettonbury.

Sustainable urban technologies **67**

('fun times had been had') in order to witness these interactive (or intra-active) fun times (Barad, 2007; see especially Bennett, 2010). Note that it is hard to call the snow in its imprinted, balled-up state 'natural', but neither is the snow 'human'. Instead, 'we follow water [*as snow*] as it converges with the water-child [*and/or water-adult*] encounters we include. We attend to what might come back, change direction, bend, reflect, diffract and form through those convergences' (Pacini-Ketchabaw and Clark, 2016: 99; italicised terms in parentheses our additions). In the above vignettes, what has diffracted and formed through these convergences is a trace of *playing*. Finally, note that this extract begs us to question our notions of 'sustainable urbanism'. All the while play has diffracted in the snow, it has *taken place about* the wind turbine. In a literal sense this playful action has taken place around the turbine's base. In a technological sense, the turbine articulates another form of interaction between humans and 'nature' – our capacity to harness the power of the wind to produce energy to power sustainable urban places. Apparently, that capacity and the agency of the wind/turbine is incidental to playful encounters with the snow; the turbine seems to stand as a dispassionate fulcrum for a playful circumnavigation in the snow. Yet the researcher's field notes hint that something else is taking place around the turbine. They – like many members of the community – were not sure if it was even working. As we discuss at length later in this chapter, there were a range of questions, concerns and, ultimately, frustrations around the turbine that threatened to lead to children's disillusionment with sustainable urban technologies. Critically, at this juncture, we want to point out that some (but far from all) of their encounters with and learning about these technologies came through their *play*, in the community. We will pick up on this argument in more detail in Chapter 8.

Notwithstanding the importance of outdoor play, young people's everyday routines and interactions with sustainable urban technologies should not be seen in isolation from the family, indeed, many of the moments identified above took place together with siblings and other family members. However, this was particularly evident when stepping inside the home and researching the everyday routines and interactions with sustainable features and materialities. For instance, Goodchild et al. (2014) use Social Practice theory to understand how 'ordinary people' use and inhabit eco-homes. Using in-house videos and interviews, the researchers analyse the relationship between the body and space, giving a unique insight into movement and sensations of temperature variations within the home. The look, design and tangibility of eco-technologies are also considered to be prompts for behaviour change. Jelsma (2003) discusses such technologies as 'moralising machines', whereby objects, things, artefacts prompt humans towards certain behaviours. Hobson (2016: 325) suggests that the recycling bin, for example, 'necessitates sorting requirements and changes to routine around which reflections of correct behaviour are negotiated . . . they solicit practices that forge specific socio-material relations, which are fundamentally questions of ethics.' Through the materiality and their very presence in family spaces of consumption, the bins, the light bulbs, the eco-efficient kettle, require co-engagement.

**68** Sustainable urban technologies

Indeed, the most commonly discussed family practices in Hettonbury included *turning off the lights* and *recycling*, where children and young people reflected on the various intra-active familial practices (Barad, 2007), prompted by the technologies of the house. In the account below, Sasha (aged 10), Imogen (aged 14) and Izzy (aged 14) explain recycling in terms of the rubbish-sorting practices and processes including the allocation of various responsibilities among family members:

> . . . the plastics in one box, the glass in another . . . all the bits in the garden like the flowers go in the brown box and then the black box is just like stuff in bags, like crisp packets and that . . .
>
> *(Sasha, female, aged 10)*

> My mum puts all the bins out but I'm expected to sort my rubbish like into plastic . . .
>
> *(Imogen, female, aged 14)*

> Sometimes I have to do it in the morning, so I put the bins out before I go to, go on the bus . . . recycling, I'm on Wednesdays, Louis' on Thursdays and Lucy's on Fridays.
>
> *(Izzy, female, aged 14)*

Grønhøj (2006) argues that, among wider attention to family practices (Morgan, 2011), we need specifically to understand the dynamics of environmental practices within the household. Indeed, it is here we will draw attention to how EfS *does* become relevant, albeit as just one *part* of wider forms of engagement with environmental issues and technologies (see also Uzzell, 1994; Kola-Olusanya, 2005). In the course of our research, we asked families, *who* in their household would encourage sustainable practices within the home. Parents highlighted readily that they saw themselves as the driving force behind the everyday recycling and sustainability routines, often citing the financial benefits of sustaining these as the rationale. However, this was not seen by children as a unidirectional responsibility, from parent to child. Children made numerous references to their personal efforts to encourage their siblings and parents to 'turn off the lights' or 'unplug' electronic devices. They also described how they would initiate conversations within their family and friendship groups in order to better understand the meaning of the sustainable features of their homes and communities:

> I talk to my mum about it sometimes like one time I asked her about solar panels. I said 'why do you really need solar panels?' and we talked about it for ages.
>
> *(Maya, female, aged 9)*

> Technology . . . I talk with my dad like how they get solar panels up there and energy, double glazing . . . all the technology . . . [and] thinking about what the future's going to be like for children when they're older.
>
> *(Ellis, female, aged 10)*

As we highlighted in Chapter 1, there are few systematic studies of children's experiences of living with/in newly built, 'sustainable' urban communities. Therefore, broader, international comparators are difficult to find. Nonetheless, and paralleling our observations about the predominance of EfS research on children and the environment, there *are* numerous international examples of projects based in schools that have integrated eco-technologies into their design (see for example Howe Dell School, UK; The Green School, Indonesia; Herwig Blankertz Vocational School, Germany). The Argonne Child Development Centre in San Francisco, for example, was the city's first solar-powered school. It was designed to ventilate naturally in the summer and utilise passive solar gain in the winter (Williams, 2007). However, everyday usage of the building negated the functioning of these technologies as they were intended. For instance, in situations where teachers used electricity instead of the natural daylight in the classroom, Williams (ibid.) found that 'naptime' was controlled by the turning on and off of electric lights, rather than raising and lowering the blinds to allow the natural sun and daylight to govern the children's sleeping patterns. This raises important questions about the form and functionality of eco-architectural buildings and end-user practices, which can often be in conflict. There is a taken-for-grantedness in this example; indeed Williams (ibid.: 201) argues that 'achieving sustainable results . . . require[s] enormous time commitments working with city officials, district representatives, janitors, teachers, parents, children and neighbours . . . all these important people will either help or hurt the progress of sustainable building'. This example raises important questions about the level of deliberate thought and practice that eco-technologies require of their users. On the one hand, it would appear that simply designing-in such technologies in a way that does not intrude into people's lives can lead to a sense in which users assume their houses will save energy or other resources on their behalf – however they choose to use them. On the other hand, if technologies require too great a level of user involvement, they may not be so readily adopted. Such tensions were evident in Hettonbury. Despite the outwardly visual nature of the eco-architectural features, we found a *'taken-for-granted'* attitude towards sustainable urbanism among young residents, both within the home and the wider community, to which we now turn.

## The 'problem' of taken-for-grantedness in children's and families' engagements with sustainable urban technologies

Children's 'taken-for-grantedness' was observed on guided walks around Hettonbury. Often children did not point out or comment on the sustainable urban technologies surrounding them. Even when they had only lived in the community for a short period of time they seemed to have become accustomed to the sometimes 'unusual' appearances of eco-technologies. During the guided walks only one of the participants specifically directed us to the 'glass house' (one of the Code Level 6 homes), identifying it as an important feature of her community. On a particular occasion the 10- and 11-year-old children took part in a

**70** Sustainable urban technologies

'community walk' – an exercise during the local primary school's 'Sustainability Week', where teachers and community representatives took the children for a walk around the local area to identify 'sustainability' in their local area. However, it soon became apparent that both teachers and children were unaware of the many sustainable features of their community. During the walk, the group passed the Sustainable Urban Drainage Systems (SUDS), solar panels and Code Level 6 eco-homes; yet none of these overtly sustainable features was remarked upon by the children or their teacher, as illustrated in the following extract from the research field notes:

> The teacher turned to me (the field researcher) and asked if I had anything to add – I had, because we were standing by a SUD and its function had not been mentioned. I decided to point out the SUD's and explain their function to the children and their teacher. After this, at subsequent stops the teacher explained features of the natural environment and I spoke about the structural features (e.g. SUDS, gabions, house types, wind turbine, bat house, eco homes).
>
> *(Field notes, Hettonbury)*

Differences, however, emerged in the data between those who lived in the new phase of the development and those children living on the adjacent, older housing development; the participants living in the latter part of the community would highlight the differences between the two parts of the community in terms of the lack of eco-features where they lived compared with the technologies which were integrated into the new phase of development.

Returning to family practices in the home, we were intrigued that eco-technologies were not regularly highlighted by the children and young people taking part in the research (particularly by those living in Code Level 6 eco-homes). As part of the project, energy devices were lent to six families to monitor their household consumption – in an attempt to create an observable link between the sustainable technologies and the human. The energy monitors allowed families to collect, monitor and, importantly, see the efficiency of their homes and practices. As we have shown, there is an assumption, a taken-for-grantedness, that the sustainable urban architectures will do the work on behalf of the human. In the quote below, Lisa and Sasha explain their experimentation with the monitoring device, turning on electronics in the house and seeing the cost and usage escalate:

> Every time mum switched the kettle she ran in and went [pulls a face] . . . I liked turning the lights on and going and look at it.
>
> *(Lisa, female, aged 9)*

> 'when all family comes round, they ask what it is my mum shows them and that and then we turn something on and then it will do it, it will go

up . . . how much are we using now? How come it is 9p now? . . . How come it is 17p now? . . . Now it is 12p. Now it is 10. [Sister was upstairs during the interview using an electric device.]

*(Sasha, female, aged 10)*

From the follow-up interviews it was clear that this device acted as a prompt not only for intergenerational learning about eco-technological features but also for learning about their homes and the fluctuations of energy usage. In a sense, it began to unpick the 'taken-for-grantedness' of at least some sustainable urban technologies, although further work would be required to assess the longer-term effects of having such monitoring devices within the home. Indeed, recent work by Snow et al. (2015: 929) highlights a disconnection between 'the processes through which energy is consumed and the ways that families typically receive information about their consumption'. They suggest that more research is needed on family technology use in designing shared eco-feedback systems, acknowledging that each member of the family has valuable knowledge, experience and routines which could be fed into the design of such technologies. More broadly however, Collins (2015: 22) recognises that sustainability within the home 'requires collaborative home-making and shared identities' and thus she advocates a research agenda which includes *both* adults and children in understanding home-based consumption and practice. We concur and, indeed, if the family unit is seen as part of the assemblage of living in sustainable urban places, then, analytically, young people should not be dislocated from their human and nonhuman co-inhabitants.

In bringing this section to a close, we would highlight again that Hettonbury is an exemplar sustainable community, lauded for its commitment to sustainable architecture and eco-technologies both at the community and household scale. The site continues to attract attention from a diverse range of professionals, including housing developers, politicians, architects, urban designers and members of the public, particularly attracted to the visually striking urban design. Here, we have shown that, despite the uniqueness recognised by 'outsiders' to the community, sustainable eco-technologies appear to have become an integral part of the make-up of the community and everyday routines for children and their families — un-remarked upon by young residents who are living in and passing by these every day. In the same vein, Marres (2015) comments on the strong material focus of sustainable urban technologies at the household scale, where insulation, thermostats and solar panels 'enable a set of distinctive ideas of participation to be deployed' (ibid.: 2), which are passive not active. However, despite the taken-for-grantedness of the buildings, architectures and technologies, the chapter progresses to show that the children and young people were, in other ways – again extending beyond the concerns of EfS – acutely involved in and aware of *other* community narratives and discourses around sustainable urban technologies.

## Weirdness, anxieties, rumours and wanting answers

We have argued that sustainable urban technologies, as peculiar forms of eco-material-socialities, prompt a 'coming-alive' of sustainable urbanisms. Everyday routines, 'taken-for-grantedness' and play were important elements of this, but so too were urban myth and rumour. In the few studies of myths and rumours in children's lives, the emphasis has been upon perceptions and stories surrounding social differences and abject 'others' (Alexander, 2008). However, in the context of Hettonbury, urban myths related most frequently to the *materialities* of the built environment. Here we draw on young people's narratives of their everyday experiences to construct the social materialities of sustainable technologies. One of the most common rumours concerned anxieties about the presence of rats and 'poo' in the SUD system:

> They (the SUDS) can be a bit frightening because rats might be in there.
>
> *(Amber, female, aged 9)*

> If the rat goes in that water and dies there will be diseases.
>
> *(Mo, male, aged 9)*

Previously we mentioned the biodiversity potential of these spaces, attracting butterflies, insects and tadpoles. Many young people spoke vividly about the playful potential of SUDS. However, their attitudes soon changed when rats and poo became part of the SUD assemblage – prompting anxiety by young people and parents alike:

> The flood plains I can't play in because of rats . . . down in the SUDS where the pipes come, they scatter out of the pipes . . . we used to play in them but as soon as we heard about the rats . . . it's OK, they just need to sort out the rat infestation and stuff like that.
>
> *(Colette, female, aged 11)*

A second and equally significant set of rumours centred around the perceived 'weirdness' of sustainable urban architectures, with comments particularly reserved for the Code Level 6 homes (Figure 4.4). These were deemed 'weird' and, in terms of their aesthetic qualities, were scarcely considered to be houses in any conventional sense:

> It looks a bit weird . . . there's not really much point.
>
> *(Grace, female, aged 10)*

> They're full of windows – you wouldn't even know it was a house.
>
> *(Carl, male, aged 13)*

> I hate all of them, they look absolutely . . . I think they look really stupid.
>
> *(Izzy, female, aged 14)*

> They could have put a chimney on or something.
>
> *(Neil, male, aged 13)*

Sustainable urban technologies 73

**FIGURE 4.4** 'Weird' features on the Code Level 6 homes in Hettonbury.

Research has shown that what children consider to be a 'house', is typically featured as a two-storey building with symmetrical windows, a door in the middle and a pitched roof (Savills, 2008). In other words, children express a 'clear preference for the familiar' in terms of the more traditional and prevalent British domestic architectures (NHBC, 2008: 45; also Osmani and O'Reilly, 2009). While we have noted elsewhere that the children and young people participating in the NUNC study were significantly positive about 'being eco-friendly' (Horton et al., 2015), there was a distinct limit to this positivity when it came to disrupting their preferences for what they considered 'normal' architectural design of a house, as Imogen (aged 14) said:

> We knew they'd attempted to make it eco because they've put the grass and the roofs in and so, I'm sorry but that looks ridiculous . . . I think you can make houses eco-friendly without making them look like something out of Doctor Who. . . . I think you can just do things like put solar panels on and don't need to have the house green and brown with grass on the roof, it's just OTT (over the top) . . . I think it's just silly, it doesn't look like a real house, it's like a children's toy . . . what I think they're trying to do, I think they're trying to make it look more eco . . . by using colours and the random designs, and it just fails.
>
> *(Imogen, female, aged 14)*

**74** Sustainable urban technologies

Apprehensions, anxieties and worries were widely held and circulated in myths about particular features of the Code Level 6 homes. For instance, several children expressed concerns about the sedum roof and the glazed frontage on the Code Level 6 eco-home. They felt that some features pushed eco-architecture too far, challenging their notions of what a house is meant to look like – and generally failed to conform with what is 'normal', both in terms of what a house is meant to look like and indeed, what grass is meant to look like. Not only was there grass on the roof, but as Neil said:

> The grass [on the roof] isn't even green, it's like brown.
>
> *(Neil, male, aged 13)*

Moreover, several children voiced the opinion that these features potentially would facilitate various 'invasions': from water ingress through the sedum roof, to 'being seen' through the glass frontage:

> I don't think I would love to live in one of them houses because it has got lots of windows all the way around it, so say you are like having a bath or something, someone could go like that [peer] and then say, 'oh, look she is having a bath.
>
> *(Millie, female, aged 10)*

In this sense, the children and young people's views were themselves *more-than-social* (Kraftl, 2013): they were composed of sensibilities, narrative and practices that combined longstanding and widespread assumptions about 'normal' houses with (largely mythical) encounters with companion species such as rats (Taylor et al., 2013) and the materialities of eco-technology. Ultimately, these rumours served to operate in a way that combined a curious fascination with an 'othering' that made rats, solar panels and, even, entire houses appear 'out of place' (Cresswell, 2005). Despite the eco-houses not actually being 'dirty' or 'polluted' in any overt sense (in fact, quite the reverse), through rumours, children nevertheless associated the people who lived in them with discourses of repulsion (compare Stallybrass and White, 1986). There was, for instance, a common assumption that these properties were for 'weird people'. Indeed, some empathised that (young) people living in these houses might feel 'left out':

> They are different, they are kind of weird . . . yeah the yellow bits freak me out . . . they are all a bit cuckoo . . . the people living in them.
>
> *(Colette, female, aged 11)*

> *Dr Who*, they remind me of the ones in *Dr Who* a bit, because of the yellow bits and they look a bit weird as well . . . especially during the night when they have the lights on.
>
> *(Sarah, female, aged 11)*

They're really unusual – everyone would think you were weird.

*(Anne-Marie, female, aged 11)*

Oh god . . . that's a bad area . . . [people] living in these homes would feel left out.

*(Zed, male, aged 11)*

Nevertheless, in parallel with these myths about the 'weirdness' of eco-architectural features, children and young people had many *questions* about eco-architectural features. Indeed, they were keen to understand better the meaning of the sustainable urban form of their community. Rather than dismiss with the analytical or pedagogic frames of EfS, we argue that such concerns could be usefully recombined with the emotional, material, everyday anxieties that we have discussed here. Children and young people's perceptions of eco-technologies were combined with a critical questioning and a sense of uncertainty of their forms and functions. These were, for example, evident in the critical questions they asked about eco-housing, photovoltaic panels and SUDS.

However, children also noted that some areas of the development appeared to be 'more eco' than others. At the same time as expressing concerns about the 'weirdness' of certain features, children questioned the unequal distribution of eco-features and lack of external, visible eco-technologies features on public buildings, such as the school that did not have any solar panels on the roof. In particular, when prompted, children raised a torrent of questions about the Code Level 6 eco-houses, which highlighted their passionate curiosity about the technologies. Questions ranged from asking about concrete functional aspects (e.g. how does eco-technology actually work? How is energy saved?) to wondering about abstract concepts (e.g. why would you put grass on the roof? What are the solar panels are for?). Similarly, children asked about the form and function of the SUD system. As we have shown, these eco-architectural features are a key feature in the everyday lives of young people living in this community as they are passed by, admired and played in on a daily basis. However, there were also questions; young people did not understand how and why the SUDS were filled with water at certain times and what the water could be used for:

Do they like use the flood water?

*(Harriet, female, aged 12)*

Is that one of them drinks things? . . . I don't think they are that useful.

*(Emma, female, aged 12)*

Children also questioned the perceived failure of technologies in Hettonbury. A particular point of tension was the previously mentioned wind turbine. In this instance, in addition to their rather more playful engagements, local planning and policy-making processes significantly shaped young people's encounters with the

**76** Sustainable urban technologies

turbine, and their (often) frustrated questioning about its functioning. Constructed in 2008, the turbine sat motionless, mired in a series of technical and legislative problems. Then, after being turned on in 2011, further technological issues prevented its full-time use. Subsequently, the turbine was dismantled. The questions that arose, triggered by the sedentary turbine were intense, with children and young people questioning why the turbine had been constructed only for it not to work:

> I don't think the windmill does much use because you never see it on . . . my brother was asking, 'why did they build that when that don't work?'.
>
> *(Rachel, female, aged 9)*

In an iterative sense, questions about the technological capacity of the turbine, its form and function were then accompanied and superseded by *rumours* and frustrations about why it was 'never on'. More widely, these underlying dissatisfactions were evident with an array of other technologies in young people's everyday interactions with sustainable urbanisms.

> Now that just appeared one day . . . now they've started to build that community centre . . . I think that's going to power the community centre.
>
> *(Jake, male, aged 11)*

> *Interviewer:* Why do you think it's not working?
>
> *Chakor:* Because the wind isn't strong enough . . . apparently they're going to take them down.
>
> *(Chakor, male, aged 10)*

## Frustrations, failures and the danger of 'abandoning' sustainable urban technologies

In reflecting on the failures of technologies, Hobson (2016: 329) highlights that only 'when things break, the lights black out, does an uncanny effect take hold . . . the predictable acting in unfamiliar ways forces reflection on the social and economic relations embedded in the home'. Indeed, the frustrations that children experienced in their encounters with eco-technologies had a direct impact on their opinions of renewable energy more broadly. Continuing with the example of the wind turbine, as a result of their experiences of never seeing the wind turbine move, they had not only become disillusioned with the turbine, but with wind power *per se*:

> Well it has not been on since it has been there really . . . a waste of time mostly if they have built it and they are not actually putting it on.
>
> *(Chakor, male, aged 10)*

Not only did participants express frustration with *community* eco-technological assets such as the wind turbine, but children were involved in *family*-based narratives

Sustainable urban technologies **77**

around the problems of *home*-based technologies. 'Faulty' eco-technologies were commonly raised by children and their families and had a direct impact on their perceptions of the technology – and of living in a 'sustainable' community more broadly. Technological glitches mentioned by children and their families included faulty heating systems, plumbing issues, failing water harvesting tanks and faulty lights. Reports of broken solar panels were frequently revealed in the accounts of young people; examples ranged from issues with panels on their own homes to community-based narratives (and, indeed, myths) around the incorrect placement of panels on their house. Colette explained the issues that she and her family had been having with their eco-technologies, comparing their experiences with those of her friends:

> Our solar panels don't work and the water don't work, exactly like Rose's and the lights didn't work . . . we have got solar panels . . . they don't work . . . all the water is dripping down into my brother's bedroom.
>
> *(Colette, female, aged 11)*

Faulty systems had significant implications for family life, ranging from 'feeling cold' during the winter months to the emotional turmoil which some families experienced as a result of the functional failures associated with the eco-technologies in their homes. Millie described the emotive scenario that her family faced when their electricity meter was incorrectly wired to neighbouring properties:

*Researcher:* So what's it like to live in a home with eco-features?
*Millie:* Good but bad, the good side because you know you're saving but sometimes it's a bit annoying because it doesn't work.
*Researcher:* So what kind of problems have you had?
*Millie:* Well it, I can't remember what, what it was to do with but my mum's bill come up to lots of money and it, and we was paying for everyone else, she paid it but we was paying for everybody else's around us . . . they're saying that it's not faulty . . . and then my mum will have to go to court if she doesn't pay it but she's not paying it because it's not her bill . . . She started crying because she's like oh I've got two kids, how do you expect me to feel when I've got like no money.

*(Millie, female, aged 10)*

Similarly, one of the parents, when asked if she felt proud to live in a home with eco-features, also commented on their limited functionality and charges she had faced due to technological errors:

> no because they don't work . . . if they did work and they were truthful about the financial implication, then maybe adults would feel better about it but I feel that they eco system things are hidden, too many falsehoods and it is not something I would advocate. If someone said to me, buy a house, and by

**78** Sustainable urban technologies

the way it will cost you £7,000 for solar heating, I would say I would buy the house, but I don't want the heating, thank you.

*(Sarah, female, parent)*

In addition to the faults, frustration was also prompted by the lack of knowledge about how technologies work. There was a chasm of knowledge between the product and the user and between the fabric of the building and its inhabitants. From our research with families living in carbon efficient homes, their lack of knowledge regarding the technologies in their homes was seriously impacting on the potential for energy and financial efficiency. Both children and adults acknowledged that no guidance and information was provided with their homes, as a parent, Emily explains:

No, [guidance] none, whatsoever . . . we weren't told how to use them, nor were we given a demonstration . . . when the water harvesting pump became faulty I didn't know the warning signals or anything . . . and it managed to run up £88 worth of electricity in one week, had I been given a lesson in how to use them I might have known there was something wrong, but we didn't get anything, no leaflets, no nothing.

*(Emily, female, parent)*

Similarly, Rachel described how her family did not know how to work the central heating, meaning that she and her family often felt cold:

I don't really know what they are for . . . my mum knows all about them . . . we have got ten ton of them, the whole front of the roof is like that and the rest of the glass . . . Our house is . . . is freezing, because we don't know how to work the central heating . . . we don't have a clue how to turn it up.

*(Rachel, female, aged 9)*

Finally in this section, it is important to highlight (dis)connections with research on children's families' experiences of sustainable urban technologies in other global contexts. Westerhoff's (2016) Canadian-based research at Vancouver's Olympic Village resonates with our findings at Hettonbury. The Village was designed as a *sustainable urban neighbourhood*, advocating energy-efficient development. Residents interviewed by Westerhoff on the lived experiences of sustainable urban technologies reported problems with their in-house washing, bathing and heating systems. The eco-technologies integrated into the household water systems were a particular concern for residents who expressed disappointment with the low-flow features, which continuously inhibited their daily routines – as one of the participants explained:

its about 2.5–4 minutes of just water running, just to get hot water. So not only are we paying for that water, but it's just a waste of water, literally it's just going down the drain.

*(R19, 28 April 2014, cited in Westerhoff, 2016)*

Sustainable urban technologies **79**

As Westerhoff (2016) comments: 'as with their inability to get hot water quickly, such residents have been frustrated with the inconvenience, cost and discomfort of these novel green technologies'. Frustrations too extended to residents living in newly designed 'sustainable' homes in India (Hadfield-Hill and Zara, 2017), where a range of sustainable features had been integrated into homes and the wider development plan. On the one hand, the developers promoted a 'smart' system of technologies that monitor homes, household devices and ICT. On the other hand, residents expressed frustration that the design and materialities of their homes had not been built with respect to the local monsoon environment. This mother describes the impact on the family home:

> the walls were soaking wet . . . we were in shock because they have not designed the houses according to the second highest rainfall in India . . . [however] they did come and they put some waterproof paint outside.
>
> *(NUI project, female, parent)*

From our research with children and young people and their interactions and experiences of sustainable urban technologies in England, and drawing on (the scant relevant) research on children and families from other contexts, we conclude that living with eco-technologies is not a problem or pain-free experience. Frustrations and anxieties are exchanged within families, but are also more broadly in the communities where they live. Within these communities, we have witnessed – as have other studies – the circulation of stories, myths and rumours about malfunctioning technologies, a 'discourse of (potentially) abandoning' eco-technologies and unexpected side effects such as rising financial costs, the appearance of rats and waste water. From this research, we conclude that children and their families seriously lack not only information and knowledge in the sense of EfS, but the practical/technical support to better understand the sustainable features of their home and community, which, in turn, might ensure that they are better-integrated into the kinds of routines that we discussed earlier in the chapter. In some cases aggravations outweighed the benefits and families renounced – albeit to differing degrees – the potential for eco-technologies to act as a vehicle to effectively living sustainably.

## Conclusion

Our focus has been on young people's often taken-for-granted, sometimes playful, sometimes frustrating interactions with sustainable urbanisms. In incorporating but extending beyond concerns with education (and specifically EfS), we have, in developing our arguments for a more-than-social, interdisciplinary childhood studies, advocated an approach that has addressed how children and their families live with the multiple materialities of eco-technologies. There is now an extensive literature that focuses on children's participation in the design of their neighbourhoods, urban spaces and specific buildings (see for example den

Besten et al., 2008; Cele and van der Burgt, 2015; Malone, 2012; Percy-Smith and Burns, 2013). But what are less frequently articulated are young people's lived experiences of sustainable urbanisms per se – their interactions with, practices and critiques of such technologies and architectures. These interactions are, as we have shown, profoundly important – both in the global picture of unprecedented growth in the use of such 'smart' eco-technologies in new urban developments, and in grappling with the complex and often *ambivalent* reception of such technologies by inhabitants at a local scale. Using a new materialist framework, concerned with the assemblage of children's bodies (Lane and Gorman-Murray, 2016) *with* eco-technological features, we highlighted the often emotional, embodied and intra-active everyday lives of sustainable urbanism, which are recursively produced through myths, rumours and discourses about the 'place' of eco-technologies. *These* 'knowledges' matter in the becoming-lively of eco-architectures (Jacobs et al. 2007; Kraftl 2014).

In sum, we advocate for a more-than-social focus on living with sustainable urban technologies, which goes beyond the child (the family and the community) to understand the importance of materialities to unpack the embodied, sometimes emotional, sometimes mundane and taken-for-granted interactions with, and experiences of, sustainable urban technologies. Such an approach encourages insight into young people's interactions with bricks, glass, sedum roofs, wind turbines and swales – an array of eco-technologies – which to some extent go unnoticed in the goings on of everyday life. However, it is through living with sustainable urban technologies that humans, technologies and materialities develop over time. In an age of sustainable urbanism it has become increasingly important to get closer to the ongoing, more-than-human socialities of living with sustainable urban eco-technologies. It is to these socialities that we turn in greater depth in the next part of the book.

# 5

# SUSTAINABLE MOBILITIES

In Chapters 2 and 3, we identified notions of *mobility* as key facets in the constitution of vitality in new sustainable urban environments. In this chapter we use the lens of children and young people's mobilities to show how design and planning for sustainable mobilities need to draw on both material constellations and lived experiences of movement. Our focus is on the practice of urban *walking* by children. We argue that walkability designs that aim to be inclusive to children's mobilities need to draw upon a wider understanding of their experiences of how safe mobilities are facilitated or hindered by design. We exemplify this argument through a focus on a widely popular street design – the 'shared surface'.

The twentieth century became the century of the car – celebrating convenience, speed, and mass democratisation of private transportation – with detrimental effects on transport infrastructure, carbon emission, traffic congestion and waste. In contrast, political priorities for urban mobilities in the first part of the twenty-first century seem set on visions of the city designed to enhance liveability, neighbourhood connectivity, traffic-calming measures, cycling and pedestrian zones, sustainable public transportation and walkability. As such, selected European cities, such as Copenhagen and Amsterdam (both cities with a long tradition of cycling) are increasingly vaunted as exemplars for how *cycling* and other forms of widely accessible, non-motorised transport could be central to urban planning for a sustainable future.

In Chapter 3, we described how sustainable urbanisms across a diversity of contexts are moving towards walkability as part of wider agendas for liveability and conviviality, as well as in response to efforts to reduce $CO_2$ emissions and improve air quality. In the context of the New Urbanisms, New Citizens research, for example, the communities were conceived within a policy strategy that explicitly

**82** Sustainable mobilities

stated a need to create local transport infrastructures that would *both* encourage more sustainable, efficient forms of mobility for residents *and* encourage walking, cycling and other non-motorised forms of transport. As such, their development was a manifestation of two motive forces, which powerfully underpin (and create a tension) in many contemporary international examples of urban development: a market rationality accommodating the habits and aspirations of nucleated private car-owning households (Walks, 2014) *vis-à-vis* an ostensibly sustainable urbanist policy/planning imperative to shift community transport habits away from automobility towards more environmentally sustainable modes of mobility (Burgess and Jenks, 2002; Farr, 2008). In practice, many sustainable urban developments are, despite the rhetoric, inescapably automobile-centric, being planned in a way which normatively centres private car ownership. For example, our four case study communities were all situated in peripheral, suburban (or rural) locations, built relatively distantly from key secondary schooling, shopping, services and workplaces, and with a limited public transport offer; in all four communities, a large proportion of the designed layout was devoted to roads, parking, driveways, garages, etc.; and each community was, to some extent, bounded by heavily trafficked main arterial roads, which were not easily crossed by pedestrians. Indeed proximity to these roads was figured as a chief selling point and raison d'être of each development.

However, in our case study communities there were also numerous examples of street design interventions such as 'traffic-calming' layouts, speed bumps, speed limits, textures, and supposedly safe spaces for walking and cycling. In particular, to varying degrees, the communities explicitly incorporated elements of 'shared surface' street design. In the following sections, and building upon the discussion in Chapter 3, we historicise shared surface streetscapes, and detail how principles of shared surface design have been incorporated into sustainable urban developments internationally, as well as in our four case studies. We also note that shared surface design has often been strongly discursively underpinned by anxieties about children and young people's profoundly limited and declining mobility in diverse contexts. However, we argue that children and young people's own experiences of community mobility have rarely been acknowledged within this discursive context, and in the context of shared surface street design specifically. Against this grain, we explore the everyday experiences of children and young people in relation to hybrid spaces, comprising children, textured surfaces and vehicles. First we note that, somewhat contra to anxieties about children and young people's *declining* mobility, the children and young people were among the most active pedestrians within the new build urban developments. Our research shows that children and young people's encounters with shared surface spaces were often fraught and anxiety-inducing; and we argue that, in its present articulation, the 'shared surface' did not straightforwardly foster benign and egalitarian relationships between young pedestrians and motorists. More broadly, the analysis contributes to understanding the relationship between the built environment and children's sense of well-being and safety. The final contribution of this chapter is a theoretical one, as we develop our case for an interdisciplinary childhood studies better attuned to the more-than-social facets of childhoods and sustainable urbanisms: that is, that 'traffic movement' (if we can use such a reductive term to characterise the multiple mobilities witnessed in this chapter) involves complex interactions of the human, social, discursive and material. Yet we argue here that these modes of understanding urban mobilities do not merely have theoretical purchase; rather, there is also – more pragmatically – a need to understand, carefully consider and implement both linguistic and material orderings to support children and young people (and other pedestrians) in their safe navigation of sustainable urban streetscapes.

## Contextualising 'shared surfaces'

Over the last three decades, the 'shared surface' design has emerged from a longer, international heritage of planning interventions. Indeed, aspects of the design are core to many sustainable urban development projects concerned with the need to 'democratise' urban streetscapes through designing-in the safe co-presence of motor vehicles, bicycles and pedestrians (Imrie, 2012; Department for Transport, 2011; Moody and Melia, 2013; Childs et al., 2010). The 'shared surface' design aims to 'de-regulate' public space through a 'blurring' of conventional distinctions between road and pavement. Typically, this entails the removal of traditional road markings and instructions such as kerbs, barriers, signage and crossings, which hitherto have been effective to demarcate spaces for cars versus spaces for pedestrians. However, the 'shared surface' design aims to constitute spaces where diverse mobilities co-exist equally, fostering an environment of negotiation, cooperation and care via human-to-human and human-to-material interactions and consideration (Imrie and Street, 2009). In the UK, for example, shared surface design has been a key element of many of the new urban developments constituted within the context of the Sustainable Communities Plan (see Chapter 3), and within a contemporary shift in policy discourses around local and regional transport planning. Notably, the White Paper 'A New Deal for Transport' (DETR, 1998) greatly influenced local transport plans across the UK. It set out a commitment to the development of 'an integrated transport policy' with the aim to improve the provision of public transport and enhance conditions for cycling and walking. Local councils implemented measures to control, restrict and manage car use with only minimal investment in building and expanding the existing road network. Within these contexts, aspects of shared surface design have been widely vaunted as key solutions in relation to the planning and governance of sustainable community transport networks. Thus, in many new sustainable urban developments in the UK (including three of our four case studies), there has been explicit articulation of the value of 'shared surface' principles, and direct citation of precursors such as the Dutch notion of 'Woonerf' (Box 5.1) or UK and European experimentation with 'Homezone' principles (see Box 5.2; see also Chapter 3).

**84** Sustainable mobilities

---

## BOX 5.1 THE WOONERF ('LIVING STREET') MOVEMENT

The concept of 'woonerf' (literally 'living street' or 'residential yard'; plural woon-erven) is widely cited as a pioneering example of community-led neighbourhood traffic management. The term originated in several residential neighbourhoods of Delft in the Netherlands during the 1960s. The founding narrative of 'woonerf' is that residents became tired of speeding traffic cutting through residential streets, and so began to manipulate the materialities of their streetscapes (e.g. removing road surfaces and installing barriers, signs, artworks and vegetation). This movement was defined, theorised and popularised by the Dutch urban planners Niek de Boer (see de Boer, 2005) and Joost Váhl (see Váhl and Giskes, 1990). Through the work of these and other campaigners, the movement was legalised and adopted by the Dutch government in 1976. Thenceforth, any area designated a woonerf is governed by the following regulations:

> Pedestrians may use the full width of the highway within an area . . .; play-ing on the roadway is also permitted. Drivers within a woonerf may not drive faster than . . . walking pace. They must make allowance for the pos-sible presence of pedestrians, including children at play, unmarked objects and irregularities in the road surface, and the alignment of the roadway.
>
> *(Southworth and Ben-Joseph, 2003: 121)*

Between 1976 and 1983, 2,700 woonerf features were built in the Nether-lands. Steinberg (2015; after Ben-Joseph, 1995) identifies four key character-istics of woonerven:

*   Visible entrances: woonerf entrances are distinctly marked by a sign showing children, adult, house and car together (with the car the small-est element).
*   The woonerf is a shared and paved space, intended for all street users.
*   Using physical barriers, such as curves, car traffic is slowed down.
*   The woonerf accommodates landscaping and street furniture.

Although very few woonerven are constructed now, their material-planning legacy remains and, internationally, many sustainable urban streetscape proj-ects continue to use elements of woonerf, and explicitly draw inspiration from the woonerf story.

---

## BOX 5.2 HOMEZONES

The concept of the *homezone* was principally articulated by UK road safety and children's play campaigners during the 1990s. The concept derived from the Dutch notion of 'woonerf' described above and has been both a focus for

Sustainable mobilities **85**

specific pilot urban planning projects and a more widely idealised aspiration within turns to sustainable urbanism (see Ben-Joseph, 1995; Gill, 1997, 2006, 2007; Karsten and Van Vliet, 2006). Biddulph (2001: 1) defines a 'homezone' as

> a residential street where the living environment clearly predominates over any provision for traffic. The design provides space for motor vehicles, but fully accommodates the wider needs of residents. This is achieved by adopting approaches to street design, landscaping and highway engineering that control how vehicles move without restricting the number of vehicular movements.

Specifically, Homezone schemes typically involve features such as:

- . . . parking and landscape features which do not allow vehicles to drive too close to residential properties.
- . . . use of signage, landscaping or street furniture so that these elements are visually integrated and attractive rather than creating visual clutter.
- Wherever possible . . . no distinction between a roadway and a pavement.
- Entrances to a home zone are clear and include a home zone sign so that drivers can readily interpret the difference between the home zone and more traditional streets.
- . . . no lengths of carriageway which allow drivers to believe they have priority and subsequently achieve unacceptable speeds.
- Public lighting . . . to illuminate speed-reducing measures at night.
- Dimensions . . . adequate to provide for slow moving through-traffic, parking and the servicing of buildings.
- . . . adequate parking for both existing and potential new residents within direct vicinity of people's homes.
- Front gardens . . . included or retained where possible.
- . . . [spaces] designed so that the whole environment offers the potential for informal play and related activities that do not disturb the peace of other residents.

*(Biddulph 2001: 2)*

'Shared surface' principles were also implicitly or explicitly reiterated in national policy approaches to transport planning such as *The Future of Transport* (Department for Transport, 2004a) and *Walking and Cycling: An Action Plan* (Department for Transport, 2004b). 'Shared surface' principles figured as key in instigating a conceptual shift in the way streets were planned, designed and used, recognising

**86** Sustainable mobilities

that: 'streets are the arteries of our communities . . . they form vital components of residential areas and greatly affect the overall quality of life for local people' (Department for Transport, 2007: 6).

Giving priority to vehicular movement was recognised for its negative impact on the perception and use of streets; as Ben-Joseph (1995: 505) comments, 'sight distance, curve radius, and width were established for vehicular efficiency, but are incompatible with residential livability'. Policy and planning approaches to neighbourhood transport continue to develop a sense of the importance of creating shared surfaces integrating pedestrians, cyclists and vehicles (Department for Transport, 2007; Arup, 2016; CABE, 2008; Biddulph, 2012), recalling historical understandings of the street as a place not only consigned to travel and transport but also as a civic meeting place and a space for children's play (Karsten, 2005; Opie and Opie, 1969).

In practice, this ongoing valorisation of 'shared surface' principles has resulted in the construction of urban spaces in which 'rights of way' are left obscure by design. Shared surfaces are facilitated through the design features including the introduction of physical features to encourage lower vehicle speeds, removal of obvious vehicle priority markings, and removal of demarcations between surface users (Department for Transport, 2011). This constitutes a street milieu in which many conventional signs and clues to guide users are omitted or ambiguous. The intention is that all street users will observe, make eye contact and thus judge and decide the 'ruling right of way in each case' (Hamilton-Baillie, 2008). Pedestrians are free to cross where they choose. As for motorists, low speeds are encouraged through variable road surfaces and design. Physical distinctions such as kerbs, levelled surfaces and bumps, which ordinarily separate motor traffic (on the roads) from pedestrians (on the pavement), have been removed. The street design is intended to not only *prompt*, but *force* drivers, cyclists and pedestrians to be cautious and thus behave with care in the street (Department for Transport, 2007; CABE, 2008). The removal of the usual visual prompts is intended to signal that the street belongs to people. The Department for Transport (2011) stresses the subtlety of the messages which are conveyed in shared space environments; there is less formal indication, which means that the driver has to interpret pedestrian behaviour and vice versa. Importantly here, there is an emphasis on behaviour change. This recalls debates in a longer-standing urban design literature, influenced primarily by the writings of Jacobs (1961), Alexander et al. (1977) and Lynch (1981), that argued for recognition of the power of the built environment in influencing people's behaviour; control, surveillance and politics are woven into the urban landscapes that are not only to be attractive and functional but also change behaviours and attitudes (Handy et al., 2002; Marmot, 2002; Gehl, 2006).

## Young people's mobilities with/in (sustainable) urban places

As we discussed in Chapter 2, in many parts of the world, discourses of children and young people's 'nature deficit' and caricatures of 'couch kids', 'back-seat generation', 'battery-reared children', 'bubble-wrapped kids', 'toxic childhoods', the 'extinction of the outdoor child', are so powerful as to feel like 'common-sense' universal truths. Likewise, the proliferation of reports of children and young people's spatial confinement (because of traffic risks, parental anxieties, family (auto-)mobilities; sedentary, screen-based popular culture and adultist exclusions of younger people from public spaces) can feel so forceful as to effectively disallow alternative data or interpretations. As we reflect on data from our case studies, we worry that the many discourses surrounding children and young people's immobility might lead to academics and policy-makers overlooking actually existing everyday mobilities and how they matter. As Lester (2015) argues, it is important to look carefully at data about children and young people's mobilities and, especially, to acknowledge the details and nuances. In our experience of research in four case study communities, we feel it is important to recognise that the data do not always neatly correspond with stark caricatures of immobile disengaged children and young people in contemporary urban spaces.

Indeed, rather contrary to assumptions of limited spatial freedoms, children and young people proved to be *intensely* mobile within all four of our case study communities. Or, to be more precise, children and young people were intensely mobile, albeit within sometimes tightly negotiated spatial boundaries. In all four communities, most children and young people were restricted, sometimes profoundly, in terms of where they were allowed to go without adult accompaniment. Almost all children described a 'boundary' beyond which they were not allowed to go without an adult (sometimes only metres from their home) by their parents. However, *within* their stated 'boundary', many children and young people were remarkably and intensely mobile, spending significant periods of their everyday lives on the move.

Within Hettonbury, most children and young people had the kind of bounded-but-extensive everyday pedestrian mobilities outlined above. In interviews, participants were asked to annotate maps to indicate where they were 'allowed to go on their own' (although to clarify, their accounts revealed that for them the question meant 'allowed to go with their friends'). Of the 42 maps (21 male and 21 female participants) produced in Hettonbury all but three featured a clear 'boundary'. In line with previous research into the everyday mobilities of children, we found that the extent of children's mobility was often set by parents (Valentine, 1997). Three typical demarcations were identified (i) close proximity to their home; (ii) particular sections of the community and (iii) the whole community. Five children aged 10–11 were only allowed to stay in immediate proximity to their home. Thirteen children (nine of whom were aged 10) drew a boundary that encircled approximately half of the community. Twenty-one children, aged 10–14, were allowed to go 'everywhere in Hettonbury'. Many parents (and children) perceived the nestled location of Hettonbury between two main arterial routes and surrounding fields as a clear demarcation of where it was safe to be mobile. Eleven participants marked locations outside the community where they were allowed to go on their own: the fields, a lane at the periphery of the development,

**88** Sustainable mobilities

the local petrol station, and crossing the main carriageways. Based on analysis of the mobility patterns and boundaries[1] the participants identified, our analysis calculated the extent of their spatial range, as well as the furthest distance each participant was allowed to travel from home (either alone or with their friends). The mean distance from home in any direction was approx. 320 metres and the mean furthest distance was 650 metres.[2] An equal number of males and females completed the mapping exercise, and both their mean distance and furthest distance was similar to the averages of the whole group and to each other. Children's spatial boundary increased with age as well as with the length of time their family had been living in the community. The mean furthest distance allowed from home rose accordingly: residence under 12 months (500 m), 1–2 years (544 m), 3–4 years (683 m) and over 5 years (765 m). For the majority of children, the move to Hettonbury gave them greater spatial mobility in comparison to where they had lived previously. Rachel exemplified this in her account:

> The streets were main, we lived right on the end of a main road . . . so it was quite dangerous . . . as well for us to play out on the front, but we're allowed to play on the drive in the front garden though . . . we're allowed anywhere in Hettonbury now . . . because it is a much safer area . . . and we've been told we're allowed, anywhere!
>
> *(Rachel, female, aged 9)*

In Rachel's account, a child's spatial mobility was closely connected to parents' sense of safety. At the time of the interview the family had moved to Hettonbury only four weeks earlier, which to Rachel and her siblings became imbued with greater spatial freedom to explore and navigate their new community.

Our argument that the children were also highly mobile (walking and biking) may appear surprising given the concerns described above about children's 'retreat from the street' (Valentine, 1996a). Importantly though, research into children's everyday mobility tends to focus on the range or extent of their mobility rather than its intensity. Our study shows instead that children were intensely mobile *within* a set of spatial boundaries. In our conversations and in the analysis of children's individual GPS maps *walking* emerged as a major theme (see Horton et al., 2014, for a detailed discussion). Walking long distances was a key characteristic of their lives, their friendships and everyday experiences of the community. In a conversation Anne-Marie vividly illustrated the importance of walking:

> Yeah, and, and I like just walking round because it's nice to just like see people . . . well sometimes we're in my friend Millie's house, some, yeah, no not in her house but sometimes near her house, she lives in Hettonbury, no, I don't know where she lives but we, we kind of like, we kind of like just walk any, like anywhere, any route really.
>
> *(Anne-Marie, female, aged 11).*

Such intense mobility characterising young people's outdoor movements was significant and confirmed children as frequent users of the streets. Anne-Marie, who was 11 years old at the time of the study, had lived in the community with her family for two-and-a-half years. In discussion of the map showing her mobility during school term time she pointed out how she and her friends went around their local community, through mews, courtyards, roads, the park, the lanes and fields.

Three extracts from interviews with participants in Hettonbury serve to further characterise some key features of this bounded-but-intense pedestrian mobility. First, Simon's notion of 'walking . . . just walking' illustrated how walking emerged as a key, recurring, taken-for-granted activity for many participants. It was *just* something they did: a (usually fun) activity per se, rather than an instrumental means to an end or destination.

*Interviewer:* Okay, and what did you play . . .?
*Simon:* We played walking . . . just walking around.

*(Simon, male, aged 10)*

Second, despite adherence to parents'/carers' boundaries, this everyday walking could be spatially and temporally extensive. For example, as Felicity and Robert traced their typical everyday mobilities on a map, a sense of the lengthy and time-consuming *walking-within-one's-boundary* emerged: keeping going, keeping going, keeping going . . .

*Felicity:* We come out of there going on this big long walk where it goes all like that, we come along and then we get to the road, we cross over, we've got all the, we keep going until, keep going and keep going.
*Interviewer:* Until when?
*Felicity:* Oh, until we feel like it, then we'll turn round.
*Interviewer:* What's like the longest you've been out for?
*Robert:* A day . . . a whole day. Like from ten-ish to like eight.

*(Felicity, female, aged 12; Robert, male, aged 12)*

Third, as Zed and Oliver suggested, most participants did not contest their parents'/carers' rules about mobility. They typically abided by, and agreed with such rules (e.g. agreeing that it was not sensible to go someplace 'because, you know, dangerous'), but nevertheless managed to walk extensively within their boundaries, often walking for hours at a time, around and around a daily route, to the extent that physical tiredness of limbs resulted.

*Zed:* We're not allowed to get too far from [home] because, you know, dangerous, you never know what's outside.
*Oliver:* [but] you can just go really far.
*Zed:* Yeah, your legs ache, oh they're tired, you feel like your legs are going to drop off and then, you know, get away from you.

| Interviewer: | And how long would you stay out for? |
| Zed: | Oh my God, oh. |
| Oliver: | Two and a half hours. |
| Zed: | No, double that thank you. |
| Oliver: | Probably ... |
| Zed: | Times that by two. |

*(Zed, male, aged 11; Oliver, male, aged 10)*

## Moving within 'shared surface' street designs: The Square, play park, courtyards and mews

We have seen so far that children and young people can often be some of the most frequent everyday pedestrians in urban neighbourhoods. Nonetheless, the findings above might be replicated in (and indeed resonate with) children's experiences in *any* urban setting. There is, then, a need for evidence about their experiences of the *particular* streetscapes of new build sustainable urban communities. Indeed, this requirement for robust research about users' experiences of shared surface street design encompasses but extends beyond children to other social groups. For example, in the context of disability studies, Imrie and Kumar (2011) call for further research to explore the safety implications of shared surface streetscapes for residents with diverse visual impairments. They argue that the unpredictability of shared surface environments presents a challenge, particularly as navigation (for both drivers and pedestrians) is centrally based on the premise that eye contact will be made. They argue that 'the adoption of shared space appears to be occurring despite the absence of clear, unequivocal evidence of how such schemes may operate in practice, and the actual effects on different user groups (ibid.: 2). Indeed, Imrie (2012: 2260) concludes that shared surface streets are potentially 'auto-disabling' environments, which 'fail to capture the complexity of corporeal form and the manifold interactions of bodies-in-space'. Elsewhere, Moody and Melia's (2013) research highlights that traffic flow and vehicle speed may cause pedestrians to feel anxious about using shared surface spaces: their exploratory research in Kent, England, combining video mapping of a shared surface street and a pedestrian survey, indicated that 72 per cent of their respondents expressed worry about using a shared surface and 78 per cent felt that as a pedestrian they had less priority than vehicles in the streets; in particular, parents/carers among the sample expressed anxiety regarding children's use of the shared surface street. Thus they call for further empirical research into resident pedestrians' perceptions and use of shared surfaces and encourage those influencing street design policies to evaluate more critically the evidence which advocates shared surfaces. However, to date, no study has specifically focused upon children and young people's experiences of the kinds of 'shared surface' arrangements which have become widespread within many contemporary sustainable urban developments.

Of our case study communities, Hettonbury had the most extensive, extensive, coherent and distinctive shared surface design. Hettonbury is nestled between two heavily trafficked arterial roads (40 mph dual carriageways), with vehicular access required to reach most key services, shops and amenities. However, within Hettonbury, the road network has been designed to encourage a walkable environment, partly achieved through the construction of communal areas such as a square and play park and through the preservation of fields surrounding the new development. Mews, courtyards and other shared surface streets were identified in the community design as places for children's informal play and were in line with policies and efforts to distribute power in public spaces democratically to all their users (Francis, 1987; Cresswell, 2011).

However, as we will go on to show, in practice the purportedly benevolent character of the shared surface street design is not straightforwardly achieved. Children and young people's mobility and safety in shared surface layouts were formed through a complex set of relationships between motorised vehicles (in particular the car), the built environment and the human (children, young people, parents and others). Inter alia, the shared surface streets in Hettonbury actually proved problematic for children's safety because, although the design is materially different, the absence of a shared *understanding* of the meaning of the streets and their particular patterns – as distinct from other patterned surfaces within the community and those without – is unclear to young street users and car drivers alike.

For the above reasons, we are hesitant to ascribe the intense degree of (albeit often spatially circumscribed) mobility to the shared surface layout of Hettonbury. Indeed, our findings suggest that children and young people had an – at best – ambivalent relationship to the materialities of shared surface streetscapes. Indeed, they frequently reported that the shared surface layout was, itself, a cause of anxiety and a barrier to outdoor mobility. Our analysis focuses on four spaces, namely: The Square the play park, courtyards and mews (see Figures 5.1–5.4). These spaces each revealed children's various encounters with motor vehicles and brought attention to the distinct characteristics of children's everyday movements in, through and around these spaces.

## The Square

The Square is located outside the entrance to Hettonbury's primary school. It is designed as an amphitheatre setting, with blocks of stone providing informal seating surrounded by grass and water fountains (see also Chapter 7). The children's GPS tracks showed that they frequently spent time in The Square. When the researcher asked the participants to identify places 'you like to go to in Hettonbury', twenty-nine participants (69%) identified The Square as a favourite place. The children's GPS tracks revealed two distinct patterns of mobility. First, the children made the journey to spend time in The Square with the specific purpose of meeting with friends. Their movements in The Square were characterised by '*walking around*' or 'just playing': moving around on bikes or skate-boards, walking, running and jumping. Their movements were expansive, covering most of the open space and appear unpredictable, almost erratic in nature, taking multiple directions and turns,

**FIGURE 5.1** Spaces to play in Hettonbury: The Square.

**FIGURE 5.2** Spaces to play in Hettonbury: the park.

**FIGURE 5.3** Spaces to play in Hettonbury: courtyard.

**FIGURE 5.4** Spaces to play in Hettonbury: mews.

**94** Sustainable mobilities

and creating intersecting circular movements and routes. The second mobility pattern is mobility as destination. This is purposeful and focused; for example, walking from home to The Square (to play) and from home to the bus stop/school. For example children walking across The Square on their way to the school-bus stop. This movement appeared logical, purposeful, linear (more-or-less in straight lines) across the space travelled.

The Square was a place that children 'liked to go' and was considered by them as a safe place to be; they pointed to measures such as kerbs and 'no access' poles to The Square which securely separated their activities from the cars. The Square is one of the few areas in the community that has restricted access to vehicles; while vehicles may travel around the perimeter roads, The Square itself is preserved as a pedestrian-only, civic space. As Sayo observed:

> [w]here The Square is, they have like, you know where the school is. They have those bars . . . Where no cars can go there and that's where The Square is, so then obviously no cars . . . because last time when me, Millie, Grace and Annalise in Year Four, we were all on roller skates and then was just skating down and we ended up going on the road but the thing is, [cars] weren't there, so we felt safe and that nothing was going to happen to us.
>
> *(Sayo, female, aged 10)*

Somewhat contrary to the spirit of shared surfaces, then, many participants, like Sayo, indicated that they felt safest in spaces which were explicitly *not* shared, as in The Square when barriers prevented vehicular access.

## The park

The children's playground, known to the children as the 'park', is located centrally in Hettonbury. The park was originally designed for young children below the age of eight. It has a climbing frame with a slide, a swing, a roundabout and a few benches. The park is surrounded by a fence within a second fenced off landscaped area with grass, bushes, trees and gravelled paths. The GPS tracks revealed that the park was used by children and young people of all ages. Twenty-five of the young people who carried a GPS transmitter for a week went to the park; many visited on multiple occasions during the week, after school and at weekends. Thirty-two children (76%) identified the park as a place they 'liked to go to'. Thirty-five children (83%) drew their everyday routes going in and around the park.

The street landscape surrounding the park is a shared surface area constructed from different forms of stones laid in varying patterns. There are no physical barriers such as kerbs or levelled surfaces and there is no signage guiding vehicles and pedestrians. This a different environment from some other parts of the community and surrounding road networks.

Figure 5.5 shows the detail of the material design of this area. The cobbles are laid in a pattern that resembles a crossing point but also appears as an extension to the pavement. As we will go on to show, such tacit integration influenced how children read and crossed the road with ultimate implications for their safety. Whilst young people's use of the space was expansive; playing in the park, walking down the centre of the shared surface streets and crossing at random points – as the street design intended. However, the differentiated surfaces shown in Figure 5.5 did not always foster a safe environment for children's mobility.

## *The courtyards*

In Hettonbury, courtyards are open, shared surface areas with designated green space and seating surrounded by housing on all sides. To date, only one of the courtyards has been equipped with play equipment for children. This courtyard has been designed as a private residential space, with secure access. However, all

**FIGURE 5.5** Differentiated street surfaces around the park in Hettonbury.

**96** Sustainable mobilities

the courtyards are popular among children, including those who are not residents. None of the participants regarded courtyards as unsafe places.

While courtyards were places where children liked to go to meet their friends, ride their bikes, and play, for adult residents the primary function of the courtyards was car parking. On-road parking is limited in Hettonbury. In conversations, children were well aware about the shared nature of the courtyards and found it easy to integrate awareness of cars into their activities. The children explained how they were able to 'prepare' for the presence of a driving car:

> Say if there's a car coming, you can get prepared . . .
>
> *(Rose, female, aged 10)*

> well we'd . . . know when the cars, when the car was coming in because the gates would make a little bit of noise.
>
> *(Anne-Marie, female, aged 11)*

The electronic gates to the courtyards provided effective sound signals that worked as *audio clues* for the children alerting them to an on-coming vehicle while playing. Therefore – as with the park – it appears that shared surface areas that have some degree of enclosure (whether a perimeter fence or housing on all sides) seemed to work more successfully in meeting the aims of 'shared surface' design. This observation was in sharp distinction to other, more 'open' public spaces in the community – including the mews.

### The mews

The mews are designed as shared surface streets. Modelled on the 'mews' found in historical areas of cities such as London, with narrower roads and houses directly abutting the roadway. These passageways function as places for residents to park their vehicles – and as a place where children might wish to play. However, the GPS data showed that children only used the mews as a space they passed through, not pausing to play. Only one young person specifically walked to the mews to spend time there. Children highlighted the mews as places that were unsafe. The parked vehicles and cars driving through the narrow streets inhibited their movements and the games they played:

> we can't normally do much because there's cars round and we don't want to hit them.
>
> *(Rose, female, aged 10)*

To summarise, the four distinct spaces in the community discussed above were highlighted by children as places they particularly liked or disliked, often for reasons concerned with their interaction with cars. The GPS data revealed three distinctive patterns characteristic of children's mobilities in these spaces: (i) the expansive, random forms of games and play, in, between, around and through space; (ii) the passing through when walking or cycling from one point to another; and (iii) a preference for more enclosed spaces with clear boundaries rather than more open thoroughfares where interactions with (generally faster-flowing) vehicular traffic were avoided. Within this context the next section addresses children's perceptions of traffic, safety and road literacy.

## Understanding shared surface design: 'This is a road!'

Child accident prevention takes two main approaches:

1 discursive-based efforts to change individual behaviours through educational initiatives (such as road safety training or intensifying parental supervision); and
2 modifications to the physical environment to make it safer (for example, by altering road layout and installing traffic-calming measures such as 'sleeping policemen').

In the UK, children are taught road and traffic literacy at an early age by parents and at school, including: how to cross a road safely, knowing when to stop, and how to behave around vehicles, including 'reading' street signage. This approach is focused on child behaviour and how the child might best adapt to (or navigate) a given environment to ensure their safety. However, the children participating in the study highlighted how they expected the environment to aid (or not) their behaviour. They alerted adults' attention to the fact that street features they were used to (from where they lived before, and from visits to the local larger town) *were missing* in Hettonbury. They also made suggestions for improvements to street safety through the provision of traffic lights, speed limit signs and zebra crossings.

Millie, aged 11, gave an illustrative description of what is involved in children 'reading' and understanding the urban landscape in her account of crossing the road by the school. She said 'like it says, it's a road!' (but it does not look like a road). Millie added:

> Once yeah, me and Amy we were crossing, and then this [car] came and we had to, we had to run back because the car wasn't slowing. There was no sign saying this is a road.
>
> *(Millie, female, aged 11)*

She explained how she subsequently had used previously acquired knowledge about road environments outside of Hettonbury (including the texture of the street surface and its design) to inform her judgement that this was indeed a road – of course, counter to the very intention of shared surface design.

**98** Sustainable mobilities

An incident that occurred later as part of the primary school's cycling proficiency lessons confirmed Millie's account of the problems of identifying 'what is a road?'. The teacher took children in Year 6 on a cycling tour of Hettonbury. The teacher made a sudden stop on a street and pointed out, saying: 'See, this is not really an ordinary junction, there are no lines'. She went on to explain that at a normal junction there would be a STOP sign and white markings on the road. After the lesson she explained in detail about the problems she faced in teaching children the rules of the roads *within* Hettonbury. The lessons were intended to provide children with the skills and proficiency to cycle confidently to their secondary school *outside* Hettonbury. But, the street designs in Hettonbury 'look nothing like the roads outside the community,' she said.

In many areas of Hettonbury the intention is that children and adults actively negotiate the shared street landscape. Street literacy in such spaces is vital. During the study the field researcher (second author) observed numerous instances of children not understanding and behaving in the way intended by the designers; on occasion this could well have resulted in a serious accident involving a vehicle and a child. The following are three extracts from field notes:

> 5th January. One father grabbed the hood of his son's coat to hold him back as the vehicle passed; another mum shouted, 'wait there, don't move!', to her children who had run off in the distance.

> 9th March. When walking from The Square, I was followed by two boys (aged approx. 4 or 5 years-old), they had come out of the primary school with their parents. They ran down the road behind me. Just as they were level with me a car pulled out of a driveway and had to quickly stop. I told the boys to wait for their Dad and signalled for the car to go as I kept back the two boys . . . the parents were right at the other end of the street. After the car had gone the two boys continued running down the pavement, when they reached the end i.e. the 'road', without any 'look, listen and wait' one of them ran across. I am not entirely sure if he could differentiate between pavement and road, given the lack of road markings.

> 16th April. Two boys crossed from the pavement to the Park, they sped on their bikes over the road; neither of them looked for approaching cars.

The above extracts describe situations where children appeared at risk from cars either because the child or the driver did not move with the assumed care and awareness. Given the 'lack' of material and linguistic prompts in the shared surface streets, children and young people articulated and developed a series of 'clues' to understand and manage their own and others' behaviours in the street. Shared surfaces are *expected* to create a democratic environment where drivers adapt to their surroundings by travelling at low speeds, mindful of the equal priority of pedestrians and cyclists sharing the street. In observations of actual practice, another picture emerged. Incidents recorded in field notes regularly included (i) motorbike users doing 'wheelies', when circling the children's playground, (ii) car drivers using mobile phones while in motion, and (iii) speeding motorists. Similar observations were also highlighted by children. Additionally, an important issue was that many motorists did not *signal* as they were required to do, which the children considered a serious omission. They emphasised how pedestrians (including themselves) need to be aware of (in their words 'prepare for') the direction of a car's movement. Moreover, the research team and the children frequently observed motorists not indicating at junctions, further reducing the 'clues' available to young people as they attempted to navigate streets and vehicular traffic. Ultimately, this is of major concern to children who share the street, and need to move along and make safe decisions. The quotes below are illustrative of children's perceptions:

*Emma (female, aged 12)*    It's not just cars that need to know where you are going, it is us kids too.
*Alice (female, aged 12)*    You can like stand for ages, waiting to see which way they go.
*Harriet (female, aged 12)*    No indication! No indication! [chanting]

*(Emma, female, aged 12; Alice, female, aged 12; Harriet, female, aged 12)*

During the fieldwork, accidents involving children did indeed occur. The accidents occurred after school when the children were playing outside and the secondary school buses had arrived; many children participating in the study witnessed the accident. The quotes here below are some of the graphic and detailed accounts provided by them:

*Sasha:*    ..I don't really feel safe on the roads because two people that I know have got hit by a car now ...
*Alice:*    ... yeah, and then she, as you know there's like cars like parked up all on the side ... she started like ... the road but she couldn't see anything, she stepped out car didn't see her, she got whacked ...
*Harriet:*    Yeah, we heard it, I was ...
*Emma:*    ... we heard it and then we seen her go ...
*Alice:*    ... flying ...
*Harriet:*    Yeah, she went quite high.
*Kaamil:*    ... not safe ... there was like two incidents, this little girl got crushed by a car and they went straight off, then this other girl, I don't know, she got runned [sic.] over ...

*(Sasha, female, aged 10; Alice, female, aged 12; Harriet, female, aged 12; Emma, female, aged 12; Kaamil, male, aged 10)*

The children's accounts confirmed the perception that children in specific situations were unaware about the presence of cars and often found it difficult to

**100** Sustainable mobilities

predict their actual speed. However, the children did express as a general concern over the motion and speed of cars. Rose, a 10-year-old girl, vividly described the area around her primary school, the speed of vehicles and potential risk to children. Rose said:

> . . . when we're coming back from school there's always people who are rushing, because there's . . . like a speed limit of twenty and there's people going at forty miles an hour down the road and we, and we've seen loads of people go . . . really fast down there, loads of times . . . they come rushing down the road and they go round the corner and you (children) have to kind of stay there (at the side of the road) for ages and nobody like stops for you . . . loads of people (cars) go like really fast and they know they shouldn't be but they do.
>
> *(Rose, female, aged 10)*

In the application of 'shared surface' designs in our case studies, there was, we would argue, little emphasis on discursive or textual 'clues' to aid navigation by either pedestrians or vehicle drivers (in the form of signs, symbols, leaflets and other local written and verbal communication). Instead there was an apparent *over-reliance* on material design features (like the different nuances of colour and texture of road materials). Our data suggests that such material orderings of shared surfaces do not communicate clearly enough to their users how different road users should or should not behave, or how they should or should not interact. Children are used to playing on surfaces (such as in the park) where being oblivious to certain patterns on the ground does not impinge on their safety. This is especially so in relation to the different types of materials that created the variegated patterns (such as those found in the park but also in courtyards and mews).

It is also important to remember that – with its 'shared surface' design – Hettonbury stands as a kind of 'island' among standard forms of street design and behavioural assumptions within the local area and beyond. This observation holds not only for Hettonbury but our other four case study areas as well as *any* 'sustainable' urban development, *anywhere*. In the absence of discursive clues that explain this novel streetscape to its users, and which, critically, explain the *difference* between this streetscape and the perceived norm, the physical appearance is not only unfamiliar but it is too ambiguous to be readily understood. The result was that children felt unsafe. They were unsure about how to move about and they feared the unpredictable behaviour of other street users, especially car drivers. The accidents that occurred in Hettonbury, as well as children's daily experiences in the street, underpinned and confirmed this.

In terms of our developing argument towards an interdisciplinary, more-than-social studies, the examples cited in this chapter offer a stark reminder that an atten-tiveness to the more-than-representational does not and should not entail effacing the *representational* (Kraftl, 2006, 2013). The conundrum described above illus-trates how social life is sustained *through* combinations of two ordering processes:

discursively, through vitally important (and in this case often *absent*) talk, texts and symbolic representations; and materially, in orderings that encode purposes and intentions in the design and shaping of the environment. As this study reveals, the children's embodied, everyday engagements with the shared surface streets that so heavily relied on material patterning meant to encourage specific social behaviours in reality constituted a problem. Importantly motorists and (child) pedestrians did not easily understand what the arrangement of the material forms was meant to convey to them. While this may have created some hesitation it also produced misunderstanding and actual danger to children. These findings indicate not only the conceptual importance of attending to the discursive and the material in understanding children's embodied engagements with the world (Hörschelmann and Colls, 2009), but that, in more pragmatic terms, only a new, stronger combination of linguistic discursive and material orderings can effectively communicate and secure safety in the design of shared surface streets.

## Conclusion

Our data suggests that children and young people's mobility within new sustainable communities is characteristically bounded-but-intense. Ethnographic and GPS data produced with children and young people showed that the design of the urban landscape (including shared surfaces) afforded intensive forms of outdoor mobility, thus challenging contemporary assumptions (reviewed at the beginning of this chapter) that children's lives are becoming increasingly sedentary.

Shared spaces are a powerful feature of new urban design; a built form intended to instigate social and political change towards urban democracy. In the shared surface areas pedestrians and vehicles are expected to negotiate safely and efficiently their path through open, unregulated public spaces. However, as we have shown, aspects of the socio-material environment actually created recurrent situations where children were at risk and felt so. Through our research it became evident that street users do not necessarily adapt easily to a changed environment (as it may be presumed by the designers and planners). The creation of physical, shared spaces 'for all' needs to be combined with notions of the educated motorist and 'streetwise' children. Therefore, building upon arguments in the previous chapter, we would further reinforce the point that both academic and policy attention to children, young people and sustainability needs to incorporate, but also move beyond, traditional notions of Education for Sustainability (EfS). In this case, producing educated motorists and 'streetwise' children entails *extending* our understanding of sustainability (and of EfS) to critical learning about how new street designs and behaviours may, in turn, foster forms of conviviality and mobility that are both socially and environmentally sustainable.

Moreover – and again in extending beyond EfS – this chapter has highlighted several implications for the design of sustainable built environments and their 'legibility' – both literal and metaphorical. The built environment has significant influence over how humans read, negotiate and move through space; the patterns

**102** Sustainable mobilities

children, young people and adults create in their everyday lives are controlled and channelled by the materialities of the urban landscape. The material arrangements of the street surface (including different textures, colours and the absence of signage) had an impact on how pedestrians, in particular young people, viewed and used the street. Our findings showed that a strong material design is beneficial and important for the children's experience of safety.

However, it is our conclusion that the creation of convivial and, ultimately, 'sustainable' spaces in the form of shared surface streets with higher levels of safety for all (pedestrians, cyclists, and motor vehicles) needs to *fuse the material and the discursive* in the future design of shared street surfaces. Indeed, given that children are some of the most *intense* users of outdoor spaces (as we have shown), far greater recognition of children's embodied, emotional, material and discursive engagements with shared street-surface design should therefore be central to these future designs. Pragmatically, at least during the 'transition' to sustainable, smart and other 'new' urban designs, we therefore advocate consideration of a *combination* of linguistic communication (such as signage, community awareness campaigns and education to promote safe street behaviour) with more fully developed material arrangements, including for example the use of street furniture such as seats and flower beds and the omission of resident and public parking to improve street visibility of children. Moreover, as cities and communities around the world (and especially in northern Europe) have become testing grounds for new urban street and public space design, how in practice these are being utilised in the everyday is important for the safety and liveability of people. As these spaces develop, both in terms of their culture and their history, we therefore call for further research the lived experiences and patterns of mobility of those who use them – and especially the children and young people who can be some of their most significant users.

## Notes

1  These measurements were taken as follows: measuring the distance of their home to the edge of their boundary (in multiple directions). These figures must be used with caution as they are based on hand drawn boundaries which may not be spatially accurate. However, the children's engagement and knowledge of the intricacies of the map makes us confident of their drawn boundaries.

2  This figure was determined by the scale of the map given to the participants. A number of young people in the oldest age group were allowed further than this distance (i.e. into the local town and on long bike rides).

# 6

# CONSTITUTING COMMUNITIES

## Welcoming, belonging, excluding

As we outlined in Chapter 3, the notion of creating viable, convivial, meaningful, cohesive and well-functioning communities is key to the development of sustainable urbanism (Raco, 2007). Internationally, a wide range of agendas have stressed the importance of constructing new urban spaces that are *more* than bricks, mortar, materials and infrastructure, actively constituting spaces that addresses the social (and cultural) sustainability of community life. In this chapter we explore the constitution of these qualities of community in practice, mindful of the often complex notion of 'community'. We will throw new light on the plurality of community, through a focus on the needs, interests, and contributions of children and young people and the perspectives articulated by policy and planning and other stakeholders, including the young people themselves.

During the early twentieth century, urban planning, internationally, began to link notions of the power of urban design to (trans)form human life. For example, as we discussed in Chapter 3, Howard's (1898) 'Garden City' constituted an early call for urban planners to develop, purposefully, the design and planning of urban environments with a focus on quality of life, well-being and community cohesion. The 'Garden City' offered a vision and practical plan for the development of self-sufficient urban environments designed to preserve the best qualities of the built (the city) and the natural (country) environment (agricultural green belts, open public parks). Garden cities were thus imagined to constitute a healthy context for the flourishing of community life and activities. At the time, this vision formed a stark contrast to an era during which towns and cities had become characterised by crowding, crime and pollution, and new urban housing expansions which had led to the development of a 'dormitory suburbia'(Howard, 1902) lacking essential features of community togetherness, vitality and conviviality. At the time of writing this book, the UK government launched what is essentially a revival of the 'Garden City' for the twenty-first century (DCLG, 2017). The 'Garden Village'

**104** Constituting communities

plan sets out to develop and build a number of new villages and towns across the UK that as discrete communities will provide residents with green spaces, good transport infrastructure, high-quality affordable housing and community facilities. The vision is to support residents and communities in developing 'cooperative forms of living' through 'funding, brokerage, expertise and the offer of new planning freedoms' for locally led developments. The scheme addresses the wider problems of housing, job and facility shortages across the UK in alignment with the sustainable development agenda. This agenda foregrounds the development of urban built environments that set out to simultaneously consider and preserve human, economic and environmental resources and qualities, in efforts to create urban spaces that are *more* than bricks and mortar but actively facilitate the development of community, conviviality and co-habitation among residents.

Similarly, the UK Sustainable Communities Plan (ODPM, 2003a, 2004) charged policy-makers, planners and developers with the delivery of new large-scale housing projects with functional sustainable features such as dwellings, utilities, services, amenities and infrastructures. The built environment was not only to work as services and provision but to scaffold the development of community life in 'harmonious and inclusive' local communities (ODPM, 2004: 19) characterised by diversity, vibrancy and creativity, still conveying a distinctive 'sense of place' and community cohesion (ODPM, 2003a: 5, also ODPM, 2004). In all four NUNC case study communities, the ideal of social sustainability was delivered through the provision of 'mixed housing' that would allow for such pluralistic, yet harmonious communities to develop. Developers were placed under obligation to provide a 'balanced and socially viable' mix of housing types (DETR, 2000b; Social Exclusion Unit, 2000; ODPM, 2003b) comprising units that would provide for a range of different family sizes, ages and incomes (ODPM, 2003a: 5). Each development thus offered houses ranging from 1, 2, 3, 4 to 5 or more bedrooms, marketed to diverse segments of prospective residents (e.g. first-time buyers, young couples, families, or pensioners). The housing stock offered diverse forms of tenure, with each developer obliged to provide a certain percentage of social and affordable housing. Houses thus ranged from a market value of multimillion-pound properties to affordable housing with finance schemes to incentivise shared ownership. The latter housing types were to be 'pepper-potted' within the privately owned. So, for example, no more than three social or affordable housing units should be clustered together and there should be no 'outward design differentiation' between the affordable social housing and market rate housing (DETR, 2000b; Social Exclusion Unit, 2000; ODPM, 2003b).

Although diverse in scale and form, the four case study communities shared a range of planning and design features, which were to foster a sense of living in a viable and flourishing community. In the inception of each of the four case studies, the creation of such exemplary communities was prominent. At Romsworth, 'generating community spirit' was central to the initial planning briefs, which made clear that the development 'must not simply be a modern housing estate', it must 'have full regard to the aspects of social and economic life which combine to create a community'. Similarly, Nannton was designed to constitute a 'tight-knit . . . warm local community where you can get involved in a host of events and projects . . . you will find everything you need when you set up home' and at Tillinglow, residents were promised design features 'that make a house a home and a development a community'. In Hettonbury, early development briefs emphasised the importance of 'promoting best practice in community growth and integration' providing an 'intense core of community' focused upon a 'neighbourhood spine' (street designs), a 'flourishing public realm', 'rich in community resources'.

Historically, public space serves 'three vital functions – [a] meeting place, market place and connection space' (Gehl, 2006). In the new communities two of these functions were prominent: the creation of meeting spaces; and the planning of streets to enhance connectivity. The street designs were created as a public realm that as 'a neighbourhood spine' were inherently 'walkable', with convivial streetscapes encouraging everyday, 'neighbourly' encounters through various forms of 'shared surface' community spaces (see Chapter 5). The designs provided multiple forms of community 'connectivity' within and outside the community borders encompassing accessible route ways within the newly built spaces, access points to extant adjacent built environments, transport links to nearby urban centres, and efficient transit to major regional road and rail hubs. The public space design characteristics also included different hallmarks that were intended to act as focal points for community interactions. Squares, plazas, water features, amphitheatres, bridges, sculptures, lighting features, intersecting paths or ornamental plantings were designed-in to supplement the infrastructure made up of buildings such as community centres, amenities, playgrounds and recreational facilities (see Chapters 7 and 8). These design and environmental features were variously described as 'an essential part of new community life' (Romsworth); as 'civic settings' that will 'animate' the community (Hettonbury); as spaces for 'relaxation and social gatherings' (Nannton); or as sites for communities to engage with nature (Tillinglow). The design and planning characteristics reflected a particular faith in the value of social encounters in the constitution of community and a shared sense of belonging to a place. The designs were predicated upon a series of imagined encounters (between pedestrians and other 'shared surface' users; between the new build communities and neighbouring areas; between people spending time at focal landscape and design feature points; between residents making use of local community centres and amenities; and between inhabitants of diversely sized, tenured and valued housing), which were anticipated to be productive of new kinds of enduring and convivial relations. As such, these newly built environments appear as part and parcel of what has been described as a 'cosmopolitan turn' in contemporary international urban planning, policy and theory, wherein 'the implicit role of shared space in providing the opportunity for encounters between strangers' is valorised (Valentine, 2008: 323; see also Binnie et al., 2005; Rumford, 2008; Beck and Grande, 2010; Houston et al., 2016). Urban theorists value the 'being together of

**106** Constituting communities

strangers' (Young, 1990: 240), 'throwntogetherness' (Massey, 2005: 181), affective encounters (Thrift, 2005; Amin, 2006) and hopeful solidarities (Harvey, 2012) afforded by cosmopolitan urban life. In this chapter, and the next two, we critically interrogate these notions of conviviality, drawing initially on empirical material from the NUNC project (Chapters 6 and 7) and then from international scholarship on play (Chapter 8). In so doing, we both evidence and then – principally in Chapters 8 and 9 – advance our argument for an interdisciplinary childhood studies for sustainable urbanism. In this chapter, we focus first upon how children were (and were not) included in the planning of the four case study communities, before examining how children experienced and constituted both a sense of welcome and inclusion, and tension and exclusion.

## Planning for communities for children

As we will go on to show, planners and policy-makers working in the contexts of large-scale urban sustainable development often seriously underestimate the constitutive role that children and young people may have in the development of *community*. For example, first, in documents and briefs considering the mechanisms involved in developing community cohesion, conviviality and community spirit there is a notable absence of representations of children and young people – as a diverse social group and as residents, in their own right. Conventionally, policies and planning of large-scale communities include children and young people as dependants conflated into the notion of 'family', 'family friendly', 'young families'. This means that the perspectives and experiences of children and young people, including their particular values, interests and needs in the configuration of private housing and public space are not included in any depth. For example, within discourses of the 'viable' community in the four case study communities children and young people had a somewhat ambivalent presence. On the one hand, and in a superficial sense, they were rendered very visible. In the visual imaging of architects' drawings, visions documents, planning briefs and housing developers' brochures, different representations of children were ubiquitously present. Images of children featured (whether as sketches, clip-art icons, or stock photographs) in most of these formative documents. The presence of *young* children in visualisations of the new developments appeared as an iconic representation of the newness and positive growth of the community in synchrony with its young inhabitants. The figural presence of children in visualisations of new developments seemed to market an anticipation – or even a guarantee – that these new spaces would be safe, convivial, happy, affirmative, hopeful, liveable, viable communities. Notably, these representations of children tended to have a very similar form, depicting young children outdoors with parent(s), typically holding hands. In all four case study communities, almost all formative visualisations featured precisely this kind of image. Thus, they conveyed that this would be a positive environment for children to grow up in. The discourses of a viable community ostensibly addressed the needs of children or – as they were often called – 'future generations', 'generations to come', 'future residents', or 'future homeowners'.

Young children were present given the prominence of primary schools and designated play areas in planning briefs and documents. Thus, in all four communities the presence and proximity of a primary school was cited as a key guarantor of a viable community. Indeed, three of the communities were specifically designed to attract a population large enough to require construction of a new primary school. The provision of primary education was headlined in the planning documents as a key 'threshold of community viability'. It was anticipated that schools would 'animate' the local community (Romsworth), 'bring the community to life' via pedestrian journeys to/from school (Hettonbury), provide the opportunity for social networking among parents, carers and children (Nannton) and serve as a venue for community events. In Tillinglow, which had too small a population to necessitate the construction of a new school, the family journeys to and from school were pictured as a key indicator of 'connectivity' and links between the new development and the adjacent neighbourhood.

In all four case study communities, almost all formative visualisations and documentation featured planning and design for young children and their families. Their need for places to settle, to be active and for secondary schooling, including services accommodating their travels to school, did not figure. Although, as we will go on to show (Chapters 7 and 8), the presence of playgrounds, playspaces and gaming areas for children and young people can be seen as focal points for the generation of community vitality, conviviality and viability.

But, beyond the visualisations, designated school and play spaces, and discourses of 'future generations', it is our contention that children and young people were significantly absent from consideration within the planning of the new communities. Initially, we saw no evidence that planners and policy-makers had consulted with children and young people or considered their issues, needs and experiences in any meaningful way. Subsequently, we are happy to acknowledge that some stakeholders did develop some effective, sustainable local processes of consultation, in part through collaborative work with our research project and child participants (see Chapter 7). However, on the whole, the point stands that planners and policy-makers involved in these large-scale construction and community-building projects seemed not have considered (nor sought the means to consider) how children and young people might experience the built environments and public spaces under development. We would also argue that many planners and policy-makers working in contexts of large-scale urban development in the UK at this time seem to significantly underestimate the constitutive role of children and young people. Despite planning conceptions of *community* as a place for all generations, diverse ethnic, socio-economic backgrounds and family forms – the new community developments failed to cater for the diversity of their populations of children and young people. There is an apparent absence of any recognition of childhood as a particular part of the life-course, and of the ways in which children and young

## 108 Constituting communities

people themselves may not only *participate* in the planning and design of sustainable urban places (Tisdall et al., 2006; Percy-Smith and Burns, 2013) but are – in combination with human and nonhuman 'others' – *constitutive of* those places and their very *vitality*.

## Living togetherness

Earlier we described how the 'cosmopolitan turn' in urban theory and planning 'celebrates the potential for the forging of new hybrid cultures and ways of living together, but without actually spelling out how this is being, or might be, achieved in practice' (Valentine, 2008: 323). As Valentine (ibid.) and other critics argue it seems a sometimes uncritical romanticisation of urban encounters has increasingly led to the circulation of urban policy discourses and planning mechanisms which presume that constructing opportunities for such encounters will *necessarily* be productive of affirmative community relations. This is certainly evident in our four case study communities, where discourses and interventions did not seem to acknowledge the possibility that the planned-in encounters between residents *might not* produce a lasting sense of convivial living and community. Or indeed, as we will go on to show, that encounters between strangers in newly built housing developments might leave them unaffected, or might generate lines of social difference and a sense of exclusion. We share Nayak's (2017) concern that urban planning and policy discourses founded upon logics of the cosmopolitan encounter need more careful critical reflection and empirical evidence. For Nayak (ibid.), smoothly 'melodic' ideals of the diverse, yet harmonious cosmopolitan encounter should acknowledge 'cracks', 'warps', awkwardnesses and exclusions that also form part of real life urban encounters. Against this grain, the following sections will consider children and young people's participation in the constitution of community in the planned convivial spaces of the four case studies. We first highlight their often-underestimated and centrally constitutive role in the development of new communities. However, mindful of aforementioned critiques of cosmopolitan urbanisms, we also want to acknowledge the roles of children and young people in constituting somewhat darker – and particularly classed – exclusions within these new 'communities'. Our focus is the development of community and neighbourhood *social sustainability* and the insights that arise from making the experiences and agency of children and young people central. More candidly expressed, and building upon earlier bodies of work on children's urban geographies (Skelton and Gough, 2013), we will show how children literally come to both *make* and *know* their place in *new*, *'sustainable'* urban communities.

## Children as creators of community

The children we worked with in the NUNC project grew up in the new urban environments as these were in the process of *becoming* a community: while houses

Constituting communities **109**

were built, while families moved in, and while (at least some) residents began to create a sense of belonging to the community. Here we focus on two distinct stages of what we would call the process of creating a sense of community, which we here will refer to as the different stages of *welcoming* people and *feeling welcomed*. These stages engaged, as we will go on to show, family members in different ways. The first stage considers acts of *welcoming* and feeling welcomed, including children's acts of generosity. The second stage involves children and their families *coming to know their place* and *develop a sense of belonging* to their community and the place where they live.

## Stage 1: welcome

For families, the journey of moving house begins a long time before they actually move in to their new home. Children and young people described the first stage, as the time during which they begin to understand the family are going to move and it is decided where they are going to live. It was clear from the accounts of children and their parents that children had only a limited part or indeed any decisive say at this stage. Whether it was a matter of the family choosing to move house or their having been forced to move due to various events or circumstances, it was seen by parents as their responsibility. Children explained how they together, as a family, explored the community where they were going to live through virtual excursions on Google Earth, conventional maps and on family visits to the building sites. During this initial phase and first encounters, children were delegated more of a stakeholder role. However, they took on a very significant role during and after 'moving-in', when children often took the lead in getting to know their place, and mapping their physical and social environment through movement. During this phase children's awareness and close observation of the everyday comings and goings of people and vehicles, including removal vans arriving should prove important to the making of community. Children's curiosity and keen detection of the arrival of new neighbours led them to welcome and make essential first introductions. Children in our study described how, in the course of their everyday mobilities, they would notice, greet, wave to, or speak to new residents, as they were moving in. Evidently, it was often the children who were the first to offer gestures of welcome. In our investigation of children's ideas about citizenship and of their perception of their duties and obligations, we as researchers, asked children: whose responsibility should it be to welcome new neighbours? In response, many children concurred with the sentiments of Imogen and Emma:

*Imogen:*  Me, us!!
*Emma:*  Us, kids and adults.

*(Imogen, female, aged 12; Emma, female, aged 12)*

**110** Constituting communities

For example, many participants described (like Hayden, below) how, on noticing newcomers, children would habitually 'say hi' and perhaps 'stop to have a chat'. When children observed a new neighbour moving in and the family included children, they would, on their own or as a small group, go to the house and invite the children out to play or to show them around the community.

> [If] we were out I'd go up to them and like say: Hi, my name's [Lucy]! Do you want to play with us or something?
>
> *(Lucy, female, aged 10)*

> [We] welcome, welcome new neighbours to Romsworth . . . go round to their house and greet them into Romsworth and say 'hi this is Romsworth'. We did it when the neighbours came . . . we all did, all three of us . . . we all go around together really, it's just nice because I know that like the [Stewart] family, they moved in when we (already) lived here and they've got children so we went and talked to the kids and the adults went and talked to the adults. And now we're really good friends with them, the Stewarts.
>
> *(Hayden, male, aged 10)*

> Well one of my neighbours they moved in at the same day and exact same time . . . we were playing football and then she [neighbour] came out and asked to play with us and then we made friends and then my other next door neighbour, all them came out and then we all started playing together.
>
> *(Tom, male, aged 11)*

> The day I moved in he was playing out and he just came up [and] said: Here you are – come over here – and he showed me to his house.
>
> *(Matt, male, aged 10)*

Children's gestures of welcome were evident in all four case study communities. Importantly, as illustrated by Hayden's account, children often initiated contact and then *parents* (or other adults) would *follow*. In this manner, children's acts of welcoming worked as 'social glue' in the communities we studied (after Karsten, 2005). We were struck by the consideration with which children did this: not wishing to call by at times which might be inconvenient, or act in ways that might cause unease. For example, Charlotte, who lived in Hettonbury, emphasised to us that it was important to pick the *right* time to greet new neighbours; that was, in her observation, when the family no longer received removal vans with boxes and furniture.

Interviewer:  Okay, have you met [new neighbours] yet?
Charlotte:  There's this little girl down the lane but we ain't knocked for her yet because they ain't settled in and they've still got moving in to do, so . . . because we keep seeing lorries of stuff coming down.

> *(Charlotte, female, aged 12)*

Charlotte's account illustrates how children performed the 'first responder' role sensitively, yet generously and frequently through the vehicle of play, during the becoming of new communities and times of ongoing influx of new residents. A similar argument can be advanced about play *spaces*, like playgrounds. Playgrounds are, of course, not solely the preserve of children; neither are they necessarily the preserve of activities that always resemble play. However, during the research we witnessed how playgrounds were constitutive of the everyday lives of our case study communities in ways that encompassed but extended beyond children's playing. For parents – and especially mothers – playgrounds were sites of social interaction with other parents (other children and young people). For parents it was their children that brought them to meet, chat, spend time on their mobile (cell) phone. For teenagers and young people, playgrounds were places to be seen, and to watch the comings and goings of community life (Matthews et al., 2000). As noted by play theorists, play can be seen as central to the performative practices of meaning–making in children's everyday lives that have repercussions for the social lives of people of all ages in a community (Gill, 2007), and, as we have shown above, as intrinsically connected to broader negotiations of sociability within the community. One of the central persuasions running through this book is the recognition that children live in families, families make communities and communities create cities (Cortés-Morales and Christensen, 2015). Here, the simple act of 'welcoming others' the invitation of one child to another to come outside 'to play' led parents to initiate contact and as the snowball effect developed, new relationships and ties were formed and reinvigorated through encounters at the playground, waiting to collect children outside school gates, at parent's meetings and at community events and activities. Children and children's activities made possible the connection of families in friendships and neighbourliness to the wider sense of living in a community. We develop these arguments further in Chapter 8, but note here that, critically, all of these acts of welcome and generosity were couched within and produced by children's embodied, emotional, and mobile engagements with, in and as part of their communities. As such, they should not be seen as distinct from, but rather productive of (and produced by) the kinds of experiences that we have recounted so far in this book.

Our findings also build on research undertaken elsewhere. For instance, in Copenhagen, Denmark, Christensen (2003) examined children's active exploration and construction of 'a sense of place', through multi-sensory experiences and bodily movement in and through the local natural, built and social environments. In this way children were observed to engage in constructing (and understanding) their personal biography in/and of particular spatial localities, which is essential to the broader understanding of children's lives and inhabitation of contemporary urban environments (ibid.). Thus, moving into and settling in a new place is formed through a processual relationship between children's everyday mobility and their exploration, understanding and interaction with their wider socio-physical environment (ibid.). However, in developing that work, our key contribution here has been to emphasise how children are the 'first responders' in

**112** Constituting communities

*new* communities as they act as the 'social glue' in welcoming new children *and* adults. Although we turn later to the arguably more 'negative' forms of tension and exclusion that emerged in the NUNC research, our findings offer a rather more positive sense of the kinds of intergenerational relations that may result from children and young people's presence in public spaces than much other work has done (e.g. Matthews et al., 2000; Punch, 2015).

## Stage 2: fostering a sense of 'belonging', building 'local knowledge'

As discussed in Chapter 5, children and young people were remarkably mobile and *intensive* pedestrian users of outdoor spaces in the four case studies. Local walking – whether to/from school, or 'just walking' around with friends – emerged as a key everyday activity for most participants. In marked contrast, their parents, carers and adult neighbours appeared to be considerably less mobile as absent-presences in local public spaces. Of all residents in newly built developments, children and young people were typically the ones out and about, day-to-day, experiencing and encountering natural, built and social spaces of their community (see also Christensen and Mikkelsen, 2009; Benwell, 2013; Horton et al., 2014). Several authors argue that we must pay attention to how emotional, embodied, and 'more-than-social details and socialities of everyday urban mobilities can often challenge prevailing constructions of 'social difference' (e.g. Middleton, 2011; Amin, 2015). It is our contention that our framework for an interdisciplinary childhood studies could be a particularly sensitive tool for teasing out more nuanced understandings of how those 'Others' deemed 'out of place' in public spaces – like children and young people (Cresswell, 2005) – are in fact importantly constitutive of their very liveliness and *vitality*. Here, and pushing further our critiques of the rather negative analyses of children and young people's presence in urban public spaces (Chapter 5), we attend to the significant agentic roles of children and young people in the facilitation of a sense of community and communities-themselves. We do so not only in terms of how children and young people display 'care' for each other, and for other adults (Evans, 2010), but how they 'open out' spaces in their new communities that had not previously been used, often for the benefit of the whole community. We also examine how, recursively, these agentic roles were not only entangled with their urban mobilities, but with their production of 'local knowledges' about their communities, which were also crucial to fostering senses of belonging. Crucially, we detail how – in support of our conceptual framework for an interdisciplinary childhood studies – these kinds of practices and knowledges entailed significant interactions with nonhuman others (especially the *material* 'stuff' found within their communities) and were often highly *emotional* in nature (for instance in 'in jokes' about local people or places). In this section, we focus on the period after the initial 'welcome' – as children and young people became more established members of their communities.

Constituting communities **113**

During our research, we observed that children regularly went out of their way to offer gestures of care and togetherness in the course of their everyday mobilities. Participants' acts of greeting were part of a wider repertoire of gestures of inter- and intra- generational consideration and community-mindedness that were frequently displayed by friendship groups while out and about. In a number of senses, children and young people were often the ones (and often, apparently the *only* ones) who actively were *doing community* within the newly built urban spaces. Local marginalisations of 'antisocial' young people seem particularly unjust given the wide range of caring, considerate, sociable, community-minded practices noted during our study. For example, many participants described habitual gestures of care and responsibility for one another when outdoors with friendship groups. Children and young people took responsibility for each other in a range of touching ways (see also Horton et al., 2014). While walking, for example, they frequently worked collaboratively to keep each other safe: looking out for one another, checking surroundings together, or protecting one another's possessions (see also Nayak, 2003, on children's sense of safety in public spaces). These kinds of small, everyday on-foot encounters were one, immediate way in which children and young people repeatedly fostered and sustained care and sociality in newbuild urban spaces.

> Like when there's a car coming my brother will always warn me because my skateboard's so, so noisy, so my brother has to come out with me and . . . he makes sure that I'm safe if there's a car coming and I make sure he's safe if there's a car coming.
>
> *(Ella, female, aged 10)*

> If I'm with Felicity then I sometimes, one of us goes in [the shop], one of us stays outside. And then we swap over. Yeah, and it's like 'oh hurry up, it's like freezing out here'. [laughs]
>
> *(Liz, female, aged 10)*

> And we always check, like down the alley if we're like just up between the gates then and if we are tempted to go [to nearby shop] we always check to see if we can see any people for about, we check for about two minutes to see if like some people just come out the bushes or something.
>
> *(Emma, female, aged 12)*

In all four case study communities, friendship groups described how they sometimes would take care of younger children, whom they considered particularly vulnerable to bullying or 'getting lost'. Participants described a range of ways in which they extended care and community to younger residents while out

**114** Constituting communities

and about: from chatting and playing together, to keeping them company until parents returned, to actively including them in games or treats like trips to the ice cream van.

| | |
|---|---|
| *Harriett:* | Yeah, but sometimes little kids will come to play with us and then we wouldn't really mind . . . |
| *Interviewer:* | So if there was younger people playing on the play, on the park would you turn around and go away or would you go and play? |
| *Emma:* | Well I always stay in there I wouldn't really leave them on their own . . . if they hadn't, didn't have their parents with them because sometimes like kids get lost. |

*(Harriett, female, aged 12; Emma, female, aged 12)*

| | |
|---|---|
| *Interviewer:* | You were saying how you look out for some of the younger children, can you give some examples of that? |
| *Imogen:* | Well like if we see them sort of around or on the park or something, we'll just sort of talk to them say 'hi how are you?', kind of thing . . . Erm, we look after them. |
| *Henry:* | Yeah, I play with them a lot, they're alright. |
| *Imogen:* | We mix with them, like if I see someone [younger] wandering round I sort of say 'hi' . . . or we'll meet up to do something. |
| *Henry:* | Choice of cones. |
| *Imogen:* | Yeah, we all meet up at the ice cream van. |

*(Imogen, female, aged 14; Henry, male, aged 14)*

Children also described acts of 'looking out' for older teenagers. 'Looking out' for others was a significant example of how children and young people expressed an intra-generational solidarity: solidarity that was stronger than the sentiment of an ambiguous relationship among the younger and older young people. Teenagers were seen as somewhat risky and threatening and children often expressed apprehension towards them. Nevertheless, they were also afforded care, sympathy and generosity by the younger children, who perceived teenagers and young people as particularly vulnerable to being marginalised (see Weller, 2006).

> There's not really much to do for teenagers . . . There's stuff to do [in town] . . . so it's not like immediately where we are but it's sort of around, so there's not really, you get lots of people vandalising like the swings and sort of turn, you know, when they turn the swings up and down, like round? . . . But I feel sorry for them because there is literally nothing to do . . . We will say 'hi' to some of them and look out for them. Like if [brother's] friend is out on his own.

*(Jake, male, aged 10)*

| Darcy: | Sometimes I see teenagers around and about and they sometimes say 'hello' to me, so ... |
| Hydie: | Erm, well if I know them on Facebook or something and they [know] my sister or they were at school ... a year ago or something. Then I will play with them. If they were boys and that ... I've never saw before I would just turn away. |
| Darcy: | But some, we will say 'hello, how are you?' |

*(Darcy, female, aged 12; Hydie, female, aged 10)*

We have argued thus far that children and young people constituted community through their playful, observant, exploratory mobilities and related narratives. However, children and young people also created new 'local knowledges' about their communities. While childhood studies scholars have explored these kinds of knowledges for decades (e.g. Bunge, 1973), we wish here to draw attention to the *newness* of the communities that children were navigating. For, in the four case study communities there was, literally, no roadmap, GPS, or online cartography; it was significant therefore that it was *children and young people* who acquired and shared pioneering knowledges of community routes, short-cuts and features. As a result of their everyday mobilities, children displayed intimate knowledge about the socio-physical details of their community, such as landmarks, 'undiscovered sites', events and happenings and different residents. Children and young people were often literally at the frontiers of the new communities opening up built environments to community usage (for adults as well as children). In Chapter 7, the history of Hettonbury's square offers one substantial example of this *opening up* of community space for wider community. But this was just one of many examples of such practices, the like of which have never before been systematically analysed in academic research with children and young people.

In the above light, we note that our participants recounted many other examples of 'opening up' newly built spaces to community use. For example, many children described how they had been leading in figuring out routes or short-cuts, which had subsequently been used by other residents of all ages. In Tillinglow, Sabina described the discovery of a short-cut to a bus stop and a 'cut through' which later came to serve many residents, as a point of connection between the new development and adjacent neighbourhood:

| Interviewer: | Okay, and when you moved in, because it was new, how did you find your way about? |
| Sabina: | When we first moved in because obviously we couldn't get anywhere. We found a bus stop because we ... we were looking for like a place where the bus was and we found one and it was just like literally round the ... it was like a couple of weeks when we decided to take a walk but we went all the way round for like a week and then we found a shortcut which is where you go over the top of the hill and |

just cut through . . . And like that was the way that we found and then obviously my dad decided to go another way, so we walked to the shop, and we didn't know, we looked it up on Google as well, so my dad tried to find a way and he found that way where we walked in the first place through the bushes and that and then I said we might as well just went go this little other shortcut which is like up a muddy hill. And he thought okay, so we went that way on the way back, on the way back home.

*(Sabina, female, aged 12)*

Children's detailed knowledge of routes and landmarks was also invaluable to the research team in getting to know our way around the communities, as Ava explains during a guided walk:

Alright, we'll just walk half of the place and then turn round and walk back up this way, because if we got the whole way it'll probably take them more than forty minutes, probably take fifty, because then we've got to go up the big hill then turn left, turn right, up another big hill, turn right then up another big hill, turn left, then right, then round the . . . which I don't know which way it is then up another massive hill and walk along the path again and then we've just got to go this way, this way, so just turned round again, then on the way back we'll go past the school.

*(Ava, female, aged 10)*

Through our ethnographic work, we saw and heard instances of participants being asked to supply this kind of everyday pedestrian knowledge by service providers (e.g. postal workers, delivery vans, police community support officers) as they attempted to navigate these often complex, formally uncharted, part-built new developments. The children's discussions of useful pedestrian short-cuts also revealed the great effort that participants had made to facilitate short cuts, as in Natalie's widening of a gap in a fence in Romsworth or Imogen and Izzy's account of the trial and error involved in optimising their route to a shop near Hettonbury.

| | |
|---|---|
| *Florence:* | I cut across the field. Yeah . . . I sort of made a little gap where the fence is . . . so like I come under the fence and I literally just cut across the field. |
| *Imogen:* | We go down there, down there, down there, to there or we go that way. |
| *Izzy:* | Cut through the park . . . |
| *Neil:* | So there's a cut-through between the houses there you can go through? |
| *Imogen:* | We go, we walk along there. |
| *Izzy:* | We go around the back. |

Constituting communities **117**

*Imogen:*  Because we, we took, we thought we'd . . . [walk] by the road and we were so scared because the cars were so near us we, never do that.

*(Florence, female, aged 13; Imogen, female, aged 10;*
*Izzy, female, aged 14; Neil, male, aged 11)*

As we have exemplified here, children and young people in the four case studies proved to be very knowledgeable and observant about their community. Most children demonstrated remarkable 'expert' pedestrian knowledge of life and spaces within the confines of the boundaries parents set for their mobility. To give just two indicative examples, many participants demonstrated a detailed knowledge of local residents' occupations (as gamified in Barbara's 'spies') and the names and homes of local pets.

*Barbara:*  Sometimes we get on the bin and stand on that, [then] we sit on the wall and play 'spies'.
*Interviewer:*  Ooh tell us about spies, how do you play that?
*Barbara:*  Like we watch people walk past . . . and talk about what they do . . . [demonstrates] she lives there . . . she does catalogue deliveries . . . she's a nurse.

*(Barbara, female, aged 16)*

*Interviewer:*  Whose is this cat then?
*Rory:*  That's Jack's cat. [To cat] Come on then. She's cute.
*Interviewer:*  There's lots of cats round here aren't there?
*Rory:*  That one's Jasper. She likes me. She just normally comes to me and just rolls over so I can stroke her . . . [Neighbour], he's got a dog but don't like cats.

*(Rory, male, aged 10)*

In all four communities, we encountered instances where children and young people had been among the first to discover key landscape or architectural features which have come to be key landmarks in residents' sense of place. In Nannton, for example, Oliver's friendship group had discovered, and partly created, a (somewhat precarious!) path to get near a rail viaduct. This afforded new close-up views of beautiful ornate brickwork and a remarkable, startling, site specific acoustic effect when trains passed. By the time of our visit, the path was already well-used by the residents in Nannton.

Okay, you can take, you can walk in it but you won't be able to walk that far in it because there's, but there's lots of things that you can step on, like big massive rocks, really big rocks and there's a big barrier that you can sit on . . . When the train goes past it's really scary, like 'aarrgh!'. It's a lovely bridge. All the brickwork. It was hand-made as well. Well obviously it's hand-made but it's an old, old, old build.

*(Oliver, male, aged 9)*

**118** Constituting communities

Similarly, in Hettonbury, Colette and her friends had discovered interesting weirs and aquatic wildlife (ducks, newts, water boatmen) just beyond the development's perimeter. They shared these with neighbours and friends via 'nature walks' and games of 'hide and look', accessed via makeshift 'stepping stones' they had placed in the watercourse.

> We just like play and we play 'hide and look', well we call it our nature walk so we all like, sometimes . . . done like a nature walk and got loads of little kids to like follow on behind and [we're] like 'if you find something, tell me'.
>
> *(Colette, female, aged 11)*

As both these examples suggest, and exemplifying the 'more-than-social' elements of our conceptual approach (Kraftl, 2013), children and young people could be active in modifying and adapting built environments and marginal spaces – using whatever materials were to hand – to open them up to wider usage. For example, in all four communities, we were shown spaces where friendship groups had used waste building materials to create ramps, climbs, steps, stepping stones or larger-scale dens (also Kraftl et al., 2013). Perhaps the most substantial example of this kind of construction work was in Nannton, where a group of children used rubble, fencing sections and an old sofa to construct a den under one of the arches of the aforementioned railway viaduct.

| | |
|---|---|
| *Chris:* | It's a den underneath [arch] where no-one ever goes, it's like, we used lots of stuff into it, like lots of rocks because there's a bit of water underneath, we used lots of rocks . . . but when we used to go there Blake moved a sofa into it so we used to pretend that we were watching TV . . . |
| *Interviewer:* | You had somewhere comfortable to sit? |
| *Chris:* | Yes, that was his old sofa that's why I was in, and we used to sit on it. |
| *Interviewer:* | I'm intrigued about how you got it there, how did you get it there? |
| *Chris:* | Well it took lots of people to move it. It took me, [three friends] and took us about five minutes just to get out of his house. |
| *Interviewer:* | And then how far is it to walk with it? |
| *Chris:* | Not that far. We had to get it around the fence, through all the bushes, over a little stream, all past, took us about thirty minutes to get it into its place and we put it against the wall, we tried to make it look like a house actually. Down there, it's down there. In the bushes where the arches . . . I can't believe [friend] found such a good place like that though, it's a wicked den. |

*(Chris, male, aged 15)*

Turning from the material to the *emotional*, through their everyday mobilities, children and young people had developed a rich array of narratives and in-jokes

Constituting communities **119**

which intertwined with their local knowledges (also Alexander, 2008). Most interviews featured stories about notable or amusing walks and incidents. We suggest that, these were nostalgically recounted; developments were narrated, enlivened, historicised and thus became part of a wider sense of community.

Jessica:    Do you remember . . . Well one time . . . me and my friend [went] chasing the ice-cream van all the way around the village . . . but he wouldn't stop. Because he didn't see us and he was playing the music too loud! . . . My brother got nearly shot by the farmer . . . because [the farmer] was trying to shoot a bird, he missed . . . and my brother was in the field . . . so he quickly ran out the field because he was worried the farmer was aiming at him rather than at the birds!

Jack:    I heard like . . . I went down to the other side of the field I see the farmer chasing bulls in his tractor. All you heard was 'moo'!

*(Jessica, female, aged 9; Jack, male, aged 9)*

Alice:    Yeah, like a few days ago . . . there was these skateboarders. [laughs]
Harriett:    Oh yeah.
Emma:    Oh yeah, there was skateboarders.
Alice:    And we thought one of them was like.
Harriett:    Following us.
Alice:    Following us so we kept on.
Harriett:    So we legged it up our street and then I went [to] hide behind the bush and then he just carried on walking because where . . .
Emma:    I think he went [to the shop] or something, somewhere . . .
Interviewer:    So he wasn't actually following you?
Alice:    No, no, Harriett was like 'he could be taking, he could be taking the quick way for us'.
        [laughter]
Alice:    And we're like, 'Harriett how could he, he don't even know where we live?!'
Harriett:    Yeah, but he might, he might see.
Emma:    That was a fun day. [laughter]

*(Alice, female, aged 12; Harriett, female, aged 12; Emma, female, aged 12)*

Children and young people's narratives of landmarks and incidents were key, and again pioneering, in the development of senses of community life. Notably, in all four case study developments, narratives of community were accompanied by the emergence of rumours of existential (often exterior) threats, with recurring motifs such as angry farmers, ghosts, and menacing men in white vans.

I was running across the road but there's a little bit that's not safe because I got . . . followed by a man in a big white truck . . . and it had, and it had

**120** Constituting communities

> an orange light on. My mum's mate got chased by the same van and the man, the man has a hood so you can't see his face.
>
> *(Jack, male, aged 9)*

> I probably wouldn't feel that safe [there] because . . . you feel you're in the middle of nowhere because there's just people's houses that you don't know, and . . . then they've got the haunted house and then the dark woods where there's like foxes and badgers and stuff like that and birds.
>
> *(Rose, female, aged 10)*

In some cases, such as 'the haunted house' in Hettonbury, these narratives became central to the popular naming of specific features of the built environment: such that, for example, the name 'the haunted house' is now widely used, by young people and adults alike, when talking about a particular derelict building on the community's edge. Indeed, it was arguably through these kinds of narratives – to which children and young people were central – that these newly built urban spaces came to obtain meaning *as* places and *as* communities. Young people's mobilities and narratives were constitutive of a kind of emergent community liveliness, as they gained new histories and memories, and as meanings solidified around shared acts of naming, experiences, myths, fears and gossip (see Horton et al., 2014). We therefore understand children and young people's pedestrian narratives, humour, adventures and incidents as generative of community-itself, literally and affectively opening up newly built developments to community life and liveliness. These pedestrian narratives – sometimes shared with and repeated by adults, sometimes not – are part and parcel of the vitalities and playful politics discussed in Chapters 7 and 8.

## Constituting exclusions and boundaries

While children and young people's everyday narratives and mobilities were central to the constitution of senses of community, these emergent community vitalities were not *necessarily* affirmative, all-inclusive or always-benign. Notably, most participants said that they would like to have more opportunities to use their detailed knowledge of local space (and issues and opportunities therein) to contribute to decision-making in their local communities: 'if only we were given the chance' as one young person said. As we argue in Chapter 7, children and young people's specialist everyday knowledges of the social and built environments – and their typical willingness to share their insights – represent a major resource, which is far too often not engaged with by planners, policy-makers and stakeholders working in contexts of urban change. This situation is, we would argue, based in conventional divisions between child and adult and more generalised intergenerational tensions. In all four of our case studies it was striking how the emergence of community – within these newly built, and previously uninhabited urban spaces – was simultaneously defined by and productive of social divisions, conventions and norms, anxieties and avoidances. Communal senses of belonging developed – in part – through the constitution of an *outside*, *outsiders*, *others* and *non-normativities*. Initially, these tensions reinforced senses of intergenerational othering – so apparent in childhood studies scholarship for so long – that see children and young people as 'out of place' in their communities. We discuss these forms of intergenerational othering as a preface to our broader arguments about participation and the politics of vitality in Chapter 7, although we signpost here that they are entangled with exclusions based on other forms of social difference. For, as we demonstrate in this section, feelings of exclusion and boundedness were also intersected by other social differences, and especially (perceptions) of social class. Herein – and drawing upon our previous arguments in this book – we develop recent scholarship on children, young people and intersectionality that has highlighted how the everyday, emotional experiences of children and young people in urban spaces are produced by and constitutive of other forms of social difference (for instance, Nayak, 2010, 2015). Critically, and with the overall aim of the book in mind, in this section of the chapter, we tie these kinds of experiences explicitly to the socio-material spaces of four communities specifically designed with *sustainability* as a central premise.

In the NUNC case studies, the emergence of community coincided with the surfacing or hardening of classed (and sometimes ethnic or cultural) antipathies. Crucially – and again, building upon our interdisciplinary conceptual framework – children and young people's everyday mobilities and narratives formed part of the co-constitution of such social geographies. In particular, participants in our research frequently and routinely casted certain residents, buildings, streets and behaviours as *other*, most explicitly in their everyday avoidance of certain parts of each new development.

In all four case study communities, children and young people described how they avoided – and/or were instructed by parents/carers to avoid – walking in particular streets or past certain buildings. Sometimes these avoidances were explicitly related to architectural or built features. In particular, many respondents described avoidant anxieties relating to particular housing types (especially social housing) and particular built forms (especially blocks of 'smaller', 'cheaper', 'more crowded' housing). In spite of the planned 'pepper-potting' of social and affordable housing in these communities, it was notable that children and young people were often acutely aware of distinctions in local housing values and tenures. These distinctions were often materialised in relation to microgeographical differences between neighbouring houses (e.g. doors, door handles, paintwork, dustbin storage, Christmas decorations, garden upkeep, garage size), and discussed with reference to the behaviour and (un)employment of residents. For many participants, the avoidance of 'council houses' was thus a given.

> There's some like paths I don't go down. Apparently there's some council houses and I wouldn't be familiar, I wouldn't really feel that like great if I was walking past the council houses because apparently, you know like how

**122** Constituting communities

people say that not as nice people live in the council houses so I . . . would feel uncomfortable.

*(Felicity, female, aged 12)*

| | |
|---|---|
| *Imogen:* | Hate it, hate it, hate it, hate it because there's nightmare neighbours . . . It's just annoying. |
| *Neil:* | Just a massive big block of apartment things. |
| *Imogen:* | They look like council houses, they look cheap and rubbishy, while these ones look nice . . . |
| *Interviewer:* | So would you go walking round here? |
| *Neil:* | No. |
| *Imogen:* | No. Wouldn't go there without an adult. |
| *Izzy:* | No, you wouldn't. |

*(Imogen, female, aged 14; Neil, male, aged 13; Izzy, female, aged 14)*

Often parental rules prohibited walking past certain properties or down particular streets, and overwhelmingly participants abided by these rules, and generally accepted and co-constituted the logics of risk which underlay them. Indeed, children and young people appeared to readily incorporate parents' discourses of risk into their own talk about the community and seemed to be as reassured by parental rules. Frequently, these co-constituted logics of avoidance were also key in the (re)production of boundaries between 'new' and neighbouring older communities. Despite the attention given to 'viable' community development, in the three case studies which were urban extensions, we would argue that the planning and design of the interface between new and older housing was not particularly conducive to 'viable' community-building *between* communities. In these three developments, the erection of dividing walls and fences, with just a few access points (often via apparently uninviting alleyways or underpasses), constituted a pre-formed barrier and line of difference from the outset.

Children and young people's narratives and mobilities in relation to these boundaries took different forms depending on the socio-economic and built characteristics of the neighbouring communities. In Nannton and Tillinglow, where new housing had been built as an extension to relatively deprived urban neighbourhoods, it was common for participants to avoid contact with the 'old' community, even forgoing their nearby shops, amenities, parks, playspaces, leisure facilities and community spaces. Notably, in describing this avoidance, teenagers from neighbouring communities were taken-for-granted as key threats, given their behaviour, language and dress code. In Tillinglow, for example, participants like Sabina and Amber avoided a nearby shop and park because they worried about being 'stared at' by 'massive gangs' because their clothes did not match with the skirts and footwear supposedly worn by contemporaries from the neighbouring community.

Interviewer: So would you not, would you go to the park in [neighbouring community] or the shop?

Sabina: No.

Amber: Not really no.

Interviewer: No? And why, why wouldn't you go?

Amber: . . . I don't really find, I don't really like going to parks anymore.

Sabina: I'd like . . . just to hang out but always have like these fantasies in my head [of] like have massive gangs . . . I always go and explore sometimes but I never get any further than the end of the street [laughs] because I never go with anyone so it scares me, just in case I get lost and then I'll be lost on my own and no-one's going to help me . . . and sometimes I feel like a bit embarrassed because there's loads of children from the park [and] I don't like the way I look when I'm like . . . because I'm always dressed . . . in baggy clothes . . . because it's comfortable and there's loads of girls that just wear like really short shorts and that, so.

Amber: . . . it's just, like Sabina said, like when people, when loads of people coming round, some of them just stare at you if you're wearing like trainers and stuff like that.

(Sabina, female, aged 12; Amber, female, aged 11)

Other participants, like Rory and Jake, avoided the same shop (which was the only retail outlet within walking distance) because of concerns about litter and the behaviour of local young people and households.

Rory: I don't go there [area near shop in neighbouring community]. It's quite a manky place but, I don't know, there's loads of rubbish chucked over everywhere . . . because all the kids just like fling stuff everywhere.

Jake: Kids do pick other kids rubbish up and play with it.

Rory: Yeah and other people, other people just chuck the [rubbish] bags out instead of [putting them in correct dustbin].

(Rory, male, aged 10; Jake, male, aged 10)

Similarly, in Nannton, children preferred to avoid local parks and shops because of a 'bad mood' occasioned by evidence of smoking and alcohol-consumption. This concern led children like Zia to actively steer clear of local play spaces and feel sad on behalf of contemporaries from the neighbouring community.

I think like what sets a bad mood around [nearby park] is like people are drinking and smoking and you see smashed glass around the park and stuff . . . sometimes when I go to the park . . . I see like shattered glass on the floor, so we have to walk round the other way on the grass [avoiding play area] . . . and sometimes like [around nearby shops] there's a lot of litter and stuff . . . sometimes I step on like boxes and bags and some, the smoking

**124** Constituting communities

boxes which is even worse. And cigarette lighters. Yeah, when I'm walking up to [school] I feel really sad because I see smoking boxes on the floor and that makes me feel like young people are smoking.

*(Zia, female, aged 9)*

Conversely, in Hettonbury, where a proportion of social and affordable housing had been built adjacent to an older development of larger, owner-occupied housing, the older community was sometimes experienced, and avoided, as dauntingly 'posh' and 'nice', with 'massive' housing.

*Fahy:* Houses [in neighbouring older community].
*Emma:* They're massive compared to ours.
*Fahy:* Massive.
*Harriett:* Yeah, they're four, three, four storey.
*Fahy:* They're big, funky, lots of space.
*Emma:* They're nice and posh.

*(Fahy, female, aged 10; Emma, female,*
*aged 12; Harriett, female, aged 12)*

In all three of these case studies, the alleyways and underpasses which connected new and neighbouring older communities were described as particularly uncomfortable spaces.

*Harriett:* [Alleyway connecting new and older communities feels] so unsafe or uncomfortable . . . the, the one that's sort of unlit.
*Emma:* Because there's gangs down there . . . it's really tight and there's loads of trees and bushes and like you're not sure if someone's hiding in trees. So people can hide there.
*Alice:* We don't know if they're hiding or anything, yeah
*Interviewer:* So what gangs, gangs of?
*Harriett:* Like gangs of teenagers.
*Alice:* Teenagers.
*Emma:* Teenagers.
*Alice:* Or in their twenties.
*Emma:* Teenagers to adults.
*Alice:* In their twenties or something, drinking down there.
*Harriett:* Yeah. Yeah and also when we saw the alcohol bottles and stuff, oh yeah, there's a piece of clothing but we didn't go, we didn't go like all the way round so I weren't sure if there was a drunk person there or anything, so we just pegged it.

*(Harriett, female, aged 12; Emma, female,*
*aged 12; Alice, female, aged 12)*

Constituting communities **125**

| | |
|---|---|
| *Sabina:* | I wouldn't [go in underpass] because there's loads of people always sit under it and but it's like bright [perhaps a reference to the bright orange lighting] thingy. |
| *Interviewer:* | Thingy? |
| *Sabina:* | Like. It's quite, I don't know, like oh how to put it? Claustrophobic. Because it's small and it's like there's loads of people in there . . . I always get like, I don't know, it's just like bad. |

*(Sabina, female, aged 12)*

Within each newly built case study, it was striking how particular streets or housing segments came to be cast as 'no go' areas because of their 'roughness'. This notion of 'roughness' was deeply classed – and sometimes racialised – and codified in relation to residents' behaviour, dress, language and, again, housing tenure (also Nayak, 2010). In all four case studies, particular sub-areas attained this reputation, seemingly within a matter of weeks of construction, and were thus avoided by many children and young people. Their narratives in relation to these places combined an attention to aforementioned details of behaviour and housing type with sometimes slightly histrionic projected anxieties about consequences of setting foot in these spaces. In Hettonbury and Romsworth, housing developers' names for particular sub-areas of the community came to be bywords for 'roughness'.

| | |
|---|---|
| *Interviewer:* | So you said that you've heard about [name of area of development], so how have you heard about it? |
| *Amy:* | My mum. |
| *Chloe:* | My, my dad. Because my mum works in the office she gets people coming in and she says they're not the nicest of people to . . . and there's things that have happened down there with the Police and stuff. |
| *Amy:* | I've heard about that from friends as well so. |
| *Chloe:* | So my mum just says stay clear of them . . . it's sort of rough. |

*(Amy, female, aged 13; Chloe, female, aged 13)*

| | |
|---|---|
| *Andrew:* | I wouldn't say I'd feel as safe [in named area of development] . . . because there's lots of teenagers. And like scruffy like, kind of like rough people. |
| *Interviewer:* | . . . So those areas that you've just said are a bit unsafe [including named area of development], how could they make it more safe? |
| *Noah:* | Like blow it up! |

*(Andrew, male, aged 12; Noah, male, aged 11)*

**126** Constituting communities

Similarly, in Nannton and Tillinglow, particularly marginal areas of each development (the 'top' of Nannton; the 'bottom' of Tillinglow) came to be labelled and avoided as 'rough'.

| | |
|---|---|
| *Tilly:* | At the top of Nannton there are some places that are rougher than the rest. It spoils it for the rest of us. |

(Tilly, female, aged 13)

| | |
|---|---|
| *Dylan:* | At the bottom there are some scabby kids. |
| *Interviewer:* | Scabby kids? What do you mean by that? |
| *Dylan:* | Like they have nothing to do so just walk around. |
| *Interviewer:* | Right. But that, you don't get that here? |
| *Ava:* | Sometimes you do but with the houses down at the bottom you do. |
| *Interviewer:* | The houses at the bottom . . . all the time. |

(Dylan, male, aged 10; Ava, female, aged 10)

In all case study communities, these supposedly 'rough' parts of the development became marginalised through children and young people's avoidances, parents'/carers' rules about pedestrian journeys that are 'not allowed', and – most poignantly – participants being told it is 'not a good idea' to pay a visit to schoolfriends living in these areas.

| | |
|---|---|
| *Alistair:* | [Named area of development] is just the worst street, it's where loads of people. |
| *Kevin:* | There's a lot of, there's a lot of people. |
| *Alistair:* | Teenagers live . . . there's lot of swearing. |
| *Kevin:* | It's not one of the nicest places to go. |
| *Alistair:* | No, it is the worst house . . . |
| *Tim:* | I wouldn't walk down there on my own. |
| *Alistair:* | I'm not allowed. |

(Alistair, male, aged 10; Kevin, male,<br>aged 10; Tim, male, aged 10)

| | |
|---|---|
| *Lailah:* | Some, sometimes as well . . . I phone up Dad and say 'Can I go and call on [friend] in [named part of development]?' And he's like 'I don't think that's a good idea, there's stuff there that I don't want you to get involved with . . .' If I see [friend] somewhere [else] we'll play, but I don't usually see her . . . |
| *Camilla:* | Yeah, teenagers hang out in [named part of development]. |

(Lailah, female, aged 9; Camilla, female, aged 9)

In all cases, this notion of 'roughness' was a shorthand for a complex, classed (and also sometimes racialised) often-unspoken series of perceived threats posed by particular modes of lifestyle, behaviour, housekeeping and self-presentation.

Constituting communities **127**

| | |
|---|---|
| *Caroline:* | Oh we don't . . . go down there, it's got like drug dealers. |
| *Ben:* | No, no, it isn't drug dealers, it's just like a rougher bit down there. |
| *Caroline:* | And as well there's this boy in our class . . . and his parents are really like scummy. |
| *Ben:* | That's why we don't go down there, there's rough people down there . . . Jamaican people go down there and they go 'who cares' and they come from like Birmingham. |

*(Caroline, female, aged 10; Ben, male, aged 10)*

The boundaries and contrasts between 'rough' and 'non-rough' spaces within case study communities were not particularly evident to us as researchers and outsiders. However, these distinctions *mattered* acutely to participants in our research, and strongly affected their everyday experiences and mobilities. It is important also to recognise that children and young people's relationships to these spaces were sometimes closely co-constructed with parents'/carers' rule-setting about everyday mobility. Indeed, as in much of the data presented in this chapter, participants seemed to readily incorporate parents'/carers' discourses of risk into their own perceptions about their community (Nayak, 2003; Benwell, 2009). In many cases, participants seemed to be as reassured by these rules of avoidance as were the parents/carers themselves.

| | |
|---|---|
| *Rose:* | [Pointing at map] I don't go there . . . because my mum, because my mum doesn't like me going there . . . I'm not allowed to go [there] on my own. |
| *Fahy:* | No, neither am I. Not down there because . . . the cars just zoom past there . . . so I'm allowed from there round to about there with friends. Probably to just around there, because I'm not really allowed to go down the bottom [of the community] . . . because my mum doesn't really think that I'm safe . . . because there's loads of people just that, they're like, well how to, how can I put it? Well they look like. |
| *Rose:* | Unsafe people. |
| *Fahy:* | Yeah, like they're, they look unsafe . . . |
| *Rose:* | And they look. |
| *Fahy:* | They look really just. |
| *Rose:* | Kind of weird and you kind of, the sort of person that you'd want to keep away from. |

*(Rose, female, aged 10; Fahy, female, aged 10)*

The impacts of this 'keeping away from' were, sadly, all too evident in interviews with those participants who lived in houses or streets cast as 'rough' through these discursive exclusions and pedestrian avoidances.

Up the top . . . they're obviously used to all that posh lifestyle and everything . . . people down here, obviously they don't have as much in like designer clothes, because they can't afford it and stuff and then like when you

**128** Constituting communities

> walk up the top of [community], they've got all their nice cars and every-
> thing and their children are all dressed nice, like in their designer clothes and
> like, they're like 'oh you shouldn't be here' . . . you get the look . . . you get
> the look, you're like that and it comes out of the side of your eye, it's like
> yeah, we know what you're thinking, the way you're dressed . . . then like
> the way you walk.
>
> *(Ellie, female, aged 14)*

## Conclusion: future challenges

In this chapter we have explored the complexity and plurality of community, and
how children and young people are conceptualised and practically incorporated (or
not) in planning what a community is meant to be. We have shown how children
have a central, constitutive role in welcoming neighbours and opening up urban
spaces to community use, engagement and senses of vitality. Children and young
people's everyday narratives, knowledges and mobilities were (and are) key to the
development of such senses of community in new urban spaces. It is notable that
these activities took place *outside*, and often in spite of, planned spaces of 'convivial' community, from which children and young people are often somewhat
marginalised (see Chapter 7). Underpinning these data was also a sense of the
considerable, detailed knowledges that children and young people frequently produce about new urban spaces. However, as we have already argued, adult planners
and decision-makers have rarely engaged with this kind of expertise and specialist
knowledge. A key question arising from this chapter is therefore: how might planners, policy-makers and adult stakeholders develop more opportunities to work
with children and young people and learn from their rich everyday knowledges?
Moreover, (how) can planners and other stakeholders attend to the multimodal,
complex forms in which these knowledges are produced – through emotions,
embodied interactions and engagements with (non)human 'Others'? Children
and young people highlighted that welcoming someone and being welcomed was
important not only as a first step, but as a continuum throughout the process of
getting to know one's place, settling in and forming a sense of belonging. Children
and young people developed and drew upon a wealth of social, local political and
environmental knowledge, which was generated through their everyday mobilities
and embodied, material engagements with and in their local environments. In particular, children and young people highlighted that their insights and knowledge
were often under-used and under-valued – through age-based exclusions regarding
access and equity. Community planners and leaders need to capitalise on the status
and use of 'community public spaces' (e.g. community centres) as intergenerational
spaces. Children and young people's access to and use of such facilities forms part
of wider possible community engagement.

Moreover, as we evidence further in the next chapter, children and young
people also felt marginalised and disillusioned from formal spaces of community
participation and decision-making. In the latter part of the chapter, something of

the darker side of community development was explored, charting children and young people's constitutive roles in fostering boundaries and marginalisations. The rapid emergence of community tensions, fractures and exclusions in newly built communities is cause for concern, and poses a challenge to planned ideals of 'viable' community. It also questions what we posited as the apparently 'affirmative' politics of a 'new wave' of interdisciplinary childhood studies – namely, that more-than-social engagements with the world are striated with relations of power and prejudice, which are neither solved nor obviated by a decentring of the human (see also Taylor et al., 2013). A second key question arising from this chapter is therefore: what practices of planning, design and community development might be helpful in forestalling some of these rapidly emergent social exclusions and divisions in newly built communities? We return to these questions in Chapter 9.

# 7

# VITAL POLITICS

## Children and young people's participation in public space and local decision-making

This chapter explores young people's experiences of political participation in practice, in places which have been designed to ostensibly foster liveability, inclusiveness and conviviality. Similar to other literature which documents children and young people's exclusion at multiple scales (Wood, 2012), we highlight multiple spatial, social and structural barriers to young people's formal involvement in what we argue are predominantly adult agendas. From a policy viewpoint, this is important, as our research has highlighted that *spaces* that have been designed to encourage participation by 'local people' (Raco, 2007) have largely been unsuccessful in engaging children and young people in formal, community-based politics.

Children's relationship to the political agenda is increasingly being recognised and debated in the academic realm (O'Toole, 2003; Kallio and Häkli, 2011a, 2011b; Skelton, 2013; Kallio et al., 2015). We contribute to this body of literature by shedding further light on what might be interpreted as children's micropolitical acts, defined as having a small 'p' – less than formal, somewhat banal and everyday acts of citizenship, which may be contrasted with more formal Political acts – with a big 'P' – such as voting or public demonstration (Kallio and Häkli, 2011a).[1] While we acknowledge the 'thorny problematics' (Philo and Smith, 2013) of how we interpret children and young people's politics – indeed, how we name, categorise and understand these acts – it is important to acknowledge that the examples drawn on in this chapter were made known to us, as adults, through the conversations and interactions we have had with young people in our case study communities. In a traditional sense, informed by much research in Childhood Studies, we show how young people were restricted at multiple scales from participating in neighbourhood Politics. However, building upon discussion in Chapter 6 – and in particular the ways in which children and young

Vital politics **131**

people 'opened out' spaces for the community as a whole – we also provide another framework for thinking about young people's *political* potential, through an insight into ways in which young people were challenged by, contested and participated in the stewardship of their streets, neighbourhoods and communities.

Within broader Political projects, wider than that of the Sustainable Communities policy, and beyond the UK, young people are very much a part of the Political agenda. Young people are simultaneously protected (Wyness, 2000), controlled (Cockburn 1998; Sharkey and Shields, 2008; Neary et al., 2013), positioned as future change-makers and increasingly invited to participate in formal Political structures. Influenced by Article 12 of the United Nations Convention on the Rights of the Child (UNCRC, 1989), young people are encouraged to form views about issues which have a direct impact on their everyday life. In the UK, a Citizenship agenda has emerged, aiming to foster active participation by young people in social, Political and environmental issues (see for example British Youth Council 2014; Youth Citizenship Commission 2014). In practice, what has emerged is a landscape of school councils, youth parliaments, boards and panels (Kallio and Häkli, 2011a; Weller, 2003; Weller, 2007; Skelton, 2013). The youth Political engagement box has been ticked; critically, however, we should ask, who are these panels, councils and boards for? Who is involved and who is being represented (Wood, 2012)? Is this process more than tokenism (Hart, 2008)? How are young people being asked to communicate? Are multiple forms of communication embraced within these forums (Percy-Smith, 2010)? And, what are the *other* ways in which children and young people can contribute to the (political) *lives* of their communities?

The arguments in this chapter are based predominantly upon empirical findings from our NUNC research, before offering broader arguments (both conceptually and in terms of geographical contexts) in the final two chapters. This chapter begins by highlighting the multiple social and spatial exclusions that prevented young people from exerting agency, influencing and participating in broader community political discourses. We demonstrate not only how children's exclusion from public spaces resonates with many previous studies of intergenerational relations, but also how such exclusions offer a starting point for considering the politics of being young in purpose-built, sustainable urban places. However, we then high light other kinds of spaces, moments and encounters, between young people, adult others, spaces and infrastructures which ultimately shaped community relations and experiences. Here young people were not formally recognised as part of the Political project, but through their voices, movements and interactions were very much a part of everyday political matters, and indeed vital urbanisms. Building on arguments developed in the previous chapter, and upon our interdisciplinary framework for childhood studies, we demonstrate that young people's *bodies* were subjected to and productive of both *intergenerational* and *intersectional* power relations which shape their everyday encounters with space and place. Ultimately – and in developing our arguments in the final two chapters of this volume – the chapter develops to

**132** Vital politics

consider the spaces, moments and stories of *young people's political vitality*, through the knowledges, bodies and the emotional relationships which young people have with land, people and ideals of community.

## Social and *spatial* exclusion: anticipating exclusion from formal Political processes?

The first section of this chapter identifies some of the social and spatial exclusions that young people encountered in their experiences of living in Sustainable Communities. The focus of this section is space – community spaces, which may have the potential to facilitate Political participation. Young people's experiences of public space are well documented in the literature; their everyday negotiations of streets, parks and shopping malls (Valentine, 1996a; Matthews et al., 2000; Matthews, 2003; Cahill, 2000) are often underscored by intergenerational encounters. Thus, a Politics of public space is articulated widely in media discourses about 'deviant others' (Hopkins, 2010), with young people often the focus of police attention and consequent spatial and temporal exclusions (Home Office, 2014). Despite well-designed public space being a conduit for mobility and personal well-being (Design Council UK, 2016), spatial and temporal exclusions are grounded in normative, often age-based, adultist assumptions (Langevang, 2008; Stratford, 2016). These assumptions, compounded by increased privatisation of public space, monitoring, surveillance and unregulated 'automated private policing' devices (Little, 2015), significantly shape young people's experience of public space and, for many of them, make for an uncomfortable terrain of experience.

As described in Chapter 5, in the NUNC case study communities, children's everyday 'restless' pedestrian mobilities were often a response to limited or non-existing spaces to settle, sit or 'hang out'. Most children and young people above 8 years old recounted experiences of being 'moved on' from the supposedly convivial spaces such as streets, the playground and play equipment for young children, from green fields, trees and planting (Chapter 6). Thus, it was apparent that some actions by adults appeared as nothing less than overt expressions of anti-social behaviour *towards* children and young people.

Children described many everyday incidents where they had been moved on – or alternatively when they themselves chose to move on – well aware that their 'place' in particular community spaces was one of exclusion. For example, children above 8 years old were frequently denied access to the local playground and play equipment by parents of younger children.

> . . . there was this swing in the park and I'd just got on it, when this mother came along and said that her boy needed to use it – so I just jumped off.
>
> *(Matt, male, aged 10)*

> . . . we just sit in the park sometimes . . . and then we are asked by somebody to move on to somewhere else because the park is just for young children.
>
> *(Amelia, female, aged 11)*

Vital politics  **133**

> If I see a mum with a toddler coming in, I just stop what I am doing and move on to play somewhere else.
>
> *(Remee, female, aged 10)*

We also observed how adult residents, typically without any children of their own, expressed their discontentment. One resident of Hettonbury, for example, having moved in to their new home, only gradually realised that as the community developed and residents moved in, the view across the public green fields – outside their windows and gardens – became occupied by children, their ball games, play, laughter, shouting and excited arguments. They were seemingly unaware that the large green open space that formed 'their view' from the house was indeed public, and thus open to subjugation by the vitality of youth. As a result of the complex, multistakeholder processes and public–private partnerships through which our case study communities – and indeed many 'sustainable' urban forms around the world – were planned, one key feature of our data was the difficulty residents had in knowing what was private and what was part of public space/domain (see also Raco, 2007; Kraftl, 2014). This led some residents, especially adults, to claim control over its usage – relating not only to who was allowed in (or able to claim access to) particular spaces, but also to how people were meant to behave in a particular space. Such claims of control could be exerted in telling children what not to do, for example building dens in a wooded area or actively destroying a snowman built by children in proximity to one's house – still in public space.

Picking up our arguments in Chapter 5, we would argue that street design and signage were also part and parcel of these emerging contestations over public spaces in the communities, since such spaces were not always easily accessible to the interpretation of their younger (and, indeed, older) residents. Sometimes, street designs were likely to bring children into conflict with how the adult street and road users interpreted their use and traffic regulations. Daniel (10) described the almost bizarre encounters he had with adults, making the travel from home to a friend's house an uneasy experience that did not contribute to his understanding of what made up a friendly neighbourhood. The journey involved bicycling on one of the main roads of Nannton. Daniel's parents instructed him to go on the pavement whenever possible as they expected some motorised vehicles on the road. However, Daniel would not be far on his way before he met a neighbour who instructed him that 'you are not allowed on the pavement when you are on your bike. The pavement is for pedestrians – you need to be on the road!' Daniel continued his journey by riding his bicycle on the road. Not far down the road he met another woman who was clearly anxious to see him on the road where there was no bicycle lane. She commanded him to get up on the pavement and promise her to stay on the pavement when continuing his journey. Here, Daniel finished his story. Whether or not he should be on the road was still a mystery to him but nevertheless he accompanied his story with a shrug of his shoulders and a big smile, humoured by the absurdity of the situation he had been in. Like Daniel, other children and young people seemed to accommodate such encounters with the directions and concerns of adult 'strangers'. As these examples illustrate, children

**134** Vital politics

and young people may be left with a sense of not being in place in the community – but as someone (always) out of place.

While we could recount many more similar stories of spatial exclusion, our intention in this part of the chapter is to build upon, rather than simply reiterate, the findings of previous scholarship on young people and public space. As we have argued, we see these kinds of experiences as a preface to understanding the more overtly P/political engagements of children and young people with, in and as their communities. We also want to highlight how such P/political concerns are wrapped up with the mobilities, emotions, embodiments and materialities that we have discussed so far as part of our interdisciplinary approach to childhood studies.

In order to illustrate the link between children and young people's *experiences* of sustainable urban spaces and questions of P/politics, we want to conclude this section by focusing at some length on the example of the community centre in Romsworth. The community centre represented a microcosm of some of the debates about the relative 'publicness' of community spaces in newly built sustainable urban developments. Centrally positioned in the development, and easily accessible by most of our participants, for many residents it was deemed to be a village hub, a fulcrum of the comings and goings of life. Located in close proximity to the children's park, this area was commonly visited on our 'guided walks' with children and young people, signifying the importance of this space. The centre itself included a large hall, various meeting rooms, an office, a bar (open each evening and regularly holding adult-only ticketed events), toilets and changing rooms. The hall was a prime community asset, used for community functions (e.g. the summer fair, pantomime and bonfire night), a weekly meeting space for local groups (i.e. the church, toddlers, Brownies, Scouts, Women's Institute and youth group) and hired by both residents of the village and external parties for private events (i.e. weddings). The building, run and operated by the manager, under the direction of the Residents' Association, was supported by numerous temporary staff.

From the above description – and from the visual clues evident to children and young people in the form of notices advertising all-age events – the community centre appears to constitute an intergenerational community space. However, many young participants' experiences were of exclusion – both implicit and overt. For instance, a traffic light system was implemented by the community centre management to control young people's access to and experience of this space, as one of the staff members explains:

> We had a traffic light system at one stage . . . they'd give you a yellow, which is a first warning then . . . [if] you got a red . . . you were asked to leave.
>
> *(Centre employee, female)*

The space was governed by rules, on prominent display in the community centre; five out of seven were directed towards young people, with our participants most frequently expressing frustration at the rule stating that 'no children will be permitted in the centre unless accompanied by an adult'. This rule is problematic because, ideologically, the centre is a community asset – a community space intended for all. How could residents (of any age) participate in the vision for community if they were excluded from a prime community space?

Discourses of 'rules' and 'regulations' in determining young people's access to space permeated their acceptance of such spatial and temporal exclusion in *political* terms (also Kullman, 2015). One of our participants, Daisy-Mae, was hoping to join a newly formed youth group in the village. In the quote below, she speaks of the community centre allowing the youth group to take place, lending them the space for a limited period for young people's use:

> There is like a youth club, well they have to ask the centre, to go and I think that's very nice of them to lend the centre just for about two hours to have youth clubs.
>
> *(Daisy-Mae, female, aged 10)*

From young people's experiences of accessing this space, its governance is also problematic for practical reasons associated with young people's mobility. The location of the community centre was in close proximity to the children's playground, and young people spoke about needing to use the facilities, conveniently located at the community centre, when they were out playing. Yet, two of our participants, Jane (aged 10) and Ellie (aged 14) both explained their experience of being excluded from this community building:

> I was with my two friends there, we were playing at the park . . . we needed the loo . . . this one person [in the community centre] just asked, who, where are your parents? . . . [they said] oh go quickly you're not welcome in here . . . but it's just, it's sort of a community place.
>
> *(Jane, female, aged 10)*

> As soon as they see you walk in [to the centre], if they don't see you walk in then you're fine, if they see you, or if there's like parents waiting for the ballet out there, they will go and tell this woman, like, I think it's the manager or something.
>
> *(Ellie, female, aged 14)*

Our young participants also expressed frustration around the inflexibility of the rules in terms of their potential for adapting to different circumstances. Liz explained how she and a friend were asked to stand outside in the rain, waiting for her mum, rather than wait in the shelter of the centre:

> . . . once it was raining outside and we, my friend Emily, we were waiting for my mum to come up, instead of walking home and because it was raining we just stayed inside the centre, the door, and then someone came out of the

**136** Vital politics

> bar and said that we had to stand outside and we weren't allowed to stay in
> the centre . . . we had to just stand outside.
>
> *(Liz, female, aged 10)*

It is evident that young people's experiences of spatial exclusion from the centre have significant implications for their experiences of belonging to the community. Beyond this particular example, many young participants spoke about feeling unwelcome and out of place. What is particularly significant about the community centre in Romsworth is that it also represents a microcosm of the contradictory ways in which children and young people are viewed (in P/political terms) in their communities (also Sibley, 1995). Young people's experiences of exclusion from the community centre were contrasted with material and visual prompts which alluded to it being a space for everyone. Our argument in the rest of the chapter is that these kinds of experiences both produce and preface the opportunities for formal, Political engagement by children and young people in sustainable communities, as well as for informal, political action.

## Formal Political participation in Sustainable Communities

As outlined at the beginning of this chapter, young people are increasingly being given opportunities to 'have a say', particularly with respect to formal youth boards and panels. In this part of the chapter – and mindful of the intention that the Sustainable Communities Plan was intended to foster P/political participation of various kinds among residents of new build developments (Chapter 3) – we examine young people's experiences of more-or-less 'formal' Politics of where they lived.

Generally – and this may not surprise many readers – we found that, despite the planning rhetoric, opportunities for children and young people's formal Political participation were few and far between. In part, as a result of the experiences we recounted in the previous section of the chapter, children and young people from Romsworth were particularly attuned to the lack of possibility for their participation in local decision-making. They made numerous references to the fact that they 'live there too' and should have the opportunity to participate, to 'have a say', and to be included in decision-making.

Indeed, with the pace of urban change across geographical contexts and communities (examined in Chapter 3), there are significant opportunities to include diverse actors in the development of sustainable urban places. In the case of the New Urbanisms in India research, once again, there were missed occasions for young people's Political engagement in the planning, design and implementation of building new urban spaces. The data collected from diverse families evidenced lack of formal opportunities for participation (from the initial planning and development design to the ongoing decision-making with regard to the liveability of their local area) despite the willingness from young people and

Vital politics  **137**

their families and despite their prior relationship with the land (Hadfield-Hill and Zara, 2017).

Across our case study sites in the UK, children and young people spoke about three common negative experiences that they had had with adults. First, they expressed frustration that adults thought that 'children don't know anything' – and their opportunities for 'having a say' should be limited. Second, in relation to this, they articulated the perception that if young people were to contribute to decision-making in their local communities 'it wouldn't make a difference'. Third, they offered the perception that 'adults don't care' about young people's issues and that when young people participate, an adult is always needed to facilitate this process. The following quotations highlight some of the frustrations which our young participants had about their experiences of decision-making in their communities. Jim, aged 10, reflected on 'being left out' due to a generational bias, and Imogen and Izzy, both 14, commented on the capacity of adults to make decisions on their behalf:

> But . . . people are older than us and they don't really think that we've got that many ideas so they just leave us out.
>
> *(Jim, male, aged 10)*

> *Imogen:* I think adults presume that they know what kids want . . . and to be honest when they actually don't . . .
>
> *Izzy:* Haven't got a clue.
>
> *(Imogen, female, aged 14; Izzy, female, aged 14)*

Hence, young people's lives were shaped on a local scale by decisions which were made on their behalf by community groups, boards of the Parish Council and members of Residents' Associations, and, as we saw in the previous section, the Romsworth's community centre committee. These were fora for discussion, negotiation and decision-making, where issues, needs and priorities were acted upon. The make-up of such groups was predominantly male and of retirement age. Young voices were generally absent from such spaces, despite issues related to children and young people (i.e. behaviour, spaces to play) being a frequent topic of discussion. The impact of this was significant, as can be shown by going back to the Romsworth example. Here – in the rapidly emerging Political spaces of a newly-built community – it was notable that a small group of adults sat on the boards of numerous community groups, from the Residents' Association to the Parish Council and the centre management group. Two such members, participating in several committees commented on the 'power' that such groups hold and the distribution of 'workload':

> It's actually the fifty plus generation that actually . . . hold the power, the decision-making power.
>
> *(Local resident and committee member, male)*

**138** Vital politics

> The old farts who do most of the 'work' . . . it's interesting you say they
> hadn't even heard of the [name of group], it's like it's the centre of my life.
>
> *(Local resident and member of various committees, male)*

Young people's positionality as temporary community members was articulated by
a youth leader, suggesting that young people did not have a sense of belonging to
place when growing up, and so did not engage in community matters:

> They're not getting involved at all because they look at it as, well we're
> probably going to move on . . . they don't look at it as their community,
> that's mum and dads' community, it's not their community, they'll move.
>
> *(Youth leader, male)*

There was a tension here, between on the one hand, the adult members of relatively powerful community groups who were frustrated that young people did
not want to get involved and, on the other hand, the many young people who
were explicit about wanting opportunities to be more involved in the shaping of
their communities (a tension replicated in many previous studies). Overwhelmingly, young people pushed for a 'joint responsibility' over the organisation of
community events and deciding on the allocation of community funds, as Izzy
and Suzie explain:

> . . . their views are completely, what they, what they would think is needed
> or necessary to our community is completely different to what we think,
> so if the two groups sat down and combined the ideas together we could
> actually have a positive outcome and something that, not exactly what both
> groups want but it'd be a combination of the two.
>
> *(Izzy, female, aged 14)*

> . . . split it up so that everyone's happy . . . it's like pensioners . . . maybe
> they'd want something, so split it up into groups . . . because everyone gets
> what they want then.
>
> *(Suzie, female, aged 12)*

In the preceding quotes, evidently intergenerational conflicts and discourses
of Othering were present in everyday community relations; however, multiple
intersectionalities were bound up in community-based power relations. In addition to the commonly discussed intersectionalities of gender, ethnicity, age and
sexuality, our data revealed other markers which positioned young people as
'Other' (Hopkins and Pain, 2007; Hemming and Madge, 2012). In the example
above, the youth leader positioned young people as *temporary residents* in their
communities; thus, here young people were identified as an 'other', not having
a full stake in the place where they lived. Another committee member indicated
that adults do all of the 'work' – again positioning young people as outside of
'working' livelihoods, negating their possibility to be included, because they

Vital politics **139**

don't 'work' like adults do, and ascribing *performative* qualities to young people that intersected with age (Staunæs, 2003).

Building on this argument, several young people indicated that their bodily size and capacities exemplified young people's experiences of being excluded from formal kinds of Political participation. In talking about his experience of 'Othering', Robert (aged 12) drew parallels in the relationship between Miss Trunchbull and the school girl in the film *Matilda*, where 'adults are big, children are small'. Indeed, many other young people articulate their bodily size as an important performative trait that intersected with their age. Hydie, a participant from Romsworth, emphasised that her small stature was determined not only by being a young person but also by a physical disability, and that, collectively, these bodily traits made her feel an outsider to the community:

> I think little children should be in the community because even though they're really small, they're still a village, we're still a whole community.
>
> *(Hydie, female, aged 10)*

So far we have shown that young people growing up in Sustainable Communities experienced multiple, intersecting spatial and social exclusions that impacted on opportunities to participate in their communities. However, we found that these exclusions were further compounded by structural factors. In Romsworth, there was an attempt to include the perceptions of young people in the design of a community play facility. From an adult perspective, the Parish Council and the Residents' Association were open to hearing young people's views about play provision. However, they were disappointed by the uptake and engagement of young people in this decision-making process. As a consequence, this was articulated as disengagement and apathy from young people (Henn et al., 2016):

> Through a lack of interest if you want from the youth, we've found it difficult to get them [involved] . . . at the moment I've not had much response.
>
> *(Youth leader, male)*

Adults expressed frustration that young people did not turn up to meetings, that they would not attend local councillor surgeries, and that there was no response to their invitation to submit a letter to the Residents' Association:

> If I had a ward surgery or anything like that, you know, you never see any young people.
>
> *(Local councillor, male)*

> Write to me . . . they have said yeah, they'll do it, but never actually get to the stage of putting pen to paper.
>
> *(Youth leader, male)*

**140** Vital politics

However, our research demonstrated significant structural barriers to young people's participation, particularly in terms of methods of communication, that replicate those found in past research (Hart, 2013). Once again, these structural barriers illustrated the rather paradoxical nature of children's position in *both* the civic spaces of their community (including community centres and the like) and formal, Political processes (Skelton, 2013). For instance, remaining with the example of Romsworth, young people were invited by the Parish Council to 'have a say' in the allocation of community funds for play provision, but were invited to the community centre, a space from which, as we have already shown, they were excluded. An 'open meeting' specifically for young people, advertised in the local newsletter, to be held in the bar was organised; however, none of the young people turned up:

> We did a lot of work on their behalf and they couldn't even be bothered to turn up . . . as a result of which the following year we said well we're not going to give out money to the youth.
>
> *(Local resident and committee member, male)*

As a direct result of young people not 'turning up', funds intended for youth provision were re-allocated. Nick, a 14-year-old, articulated his sense of the power which adults have in Romsworth and the subsequent implication for community provision for younger generations:

> I hope in the future that the issues discussed in the [project] workshop will be resolved and that from it the youth of the village will develop a good relationship with the ruling adults . . . maybe even if we're lucky we'll get a bit of a bigger budget and therefore more money towards the youth, it may one day happen.
>
> *(Nick, male, aged 14)*

In this section, we have argued that young people's *spatial* exclusion from community public spaces articulated directly with their experiences of *Political* exclusion from formal decision-making processes. As we have implied, these findings tend to repeat those of previous research on children, young people and participation. However, we would end this section by making two observations, which have policy rather than conceptual purchase. Firstly, that it is important to recognise that – as we have shown in previous chapters – children and young people highlighted many positive aspects to life (as a young resident) in newly built, sustainable urban spaces. Notwithstanding these benefits, it is notable that children and young people *did* experience some of the same problems in terms of formal Political participation *within* sustainable communities as they do without. Clearly, this is in part because Political processes cut across scales of childhood experience (Ansell, 2009), and therefore it might be argued

Vital politics **141**

that much greater thought should be afforded to ensuring that wider Political frameworks are in place that might enable particular, local 'sustainable communities' to truly deliver on promises of greater inclusivity and conviviality for all. Secondly, however, we have indicated a number of contradictions in children and young people's Political participation, which again articulate with their experiences of spatial exclusion. Some of these contradictions are more unique to purpose-built, sustainable communities – especially in their incarnation in the UK through public–private partnerships and complex, multistakeholder forms of planning. Again, these forms of planning have largely been imposed from without – through the premises of neoliberal urban planning that are steadily spreading globally (Chapter 3). However, we would also argue that local communities are not completely powerless here and that they might examine ways to overcome these contradictions – especially in terms of who 'owns' public spaces – if the (laudable) aims of sustainable communities policies in the UK and around the world are to be met. We pick up on these arguments in more detail at the beginning of Chapter 9.

## Spaces, moments and stories of young people's political vitality

In their work on young people's political agency, Staeheli et al. (2013) recognise that children's modes of being and expressing political points of view are often outside the spheres of adult cultures of communication; yet this does not imply that they are apathetical or apolitical (also Jeffrey, 2012). In the next section of the chapter, and building upon our more specific arguments in Chapter 6 about how children and young people 'opened up' spaces for wider community use, we search for moments, practices and spaces of young people's p/Political agency. In developing the book's overarching arguments about *vitality*, we focus on the everyday spaces, moments and stories of young people's *political vitality* and highlight young people's liminal political potential, extending the work of Wood (2015) who prompts us to focus on the spaces in between: the informal and the personal. Here we draw attention to 'children's mundane politics' (Bartos, 2012: 159) to emphasise why these matter in community life and in the building of sustainable urbanisms. We use liminality as an analytical construct to understand the spaces of 'inbetweeness' (van Gennep 1960; Turner 1967) that young people often experience. We start from Kallio and Häkli's (2011b: 22) premise that 'if we accept that children are active members of their communities and societies (beings) and not merely objects of top down socialisation processes (becomings), we should reverse our thinking concerning children's political lives'. In doing this we show how children and young people proffer a non-romanticised politics of vitality, through a focus on their capacity for creating local political, emotional knowledges, and then through an examination of how their bodies shaped (or could shape) spaces.

**142** Vital politics

## *Local political, emotional knowledges*

Young people's familiarity and engagement with local Political issues was overwhelming across the four case study sites. It has been documented elsewhere that young people have street literacy (Cahill 2000; Christensen 2003): and knowledges of the streets they use, of the public spaces they visit and of their broader social and material environment. Elsewhere in this book we have highlighted that the local knowledge that young people acquire about their communities is closely linked to their everyday outdoor mobility and intergenerational encounters, interactions and observations. We found that young people had high levels of spatial awareness of their local area, clearly articulating knowledge about the social fabric of their community, about occupants, households and social connections. Similarly, young people, through the very act of moving, had detailed knowledge of the built environment, knowing the intricacies of the built materialities, acquired through everyday experimental sensorial outdoor experiences.

However, young people's knowledge was more than knowing where people lived or the spatialities of their local area: it was inherently *political* and *emotional*. Young people spoke about issues frequently raised in adult forums of Parish Council and Residents' Association meetings: for example, stalled building developments, controversies surrounding specific plots of land, the provision of community facilities, social tensions, speeding limits and parking. Young people were acutely aware of, were a part of, and felt strongly about, the community discourses of newly built environments.

For example, a frequently-voiced issue among young people in Romsworth related to a particular parcel of land which, on the original plan, was identified as a public house and had since been re-allocated to housing. Nick and Arthur were keen observers of the progress of the negotiations, as they communicated a commonly heard rumour about the number of houses to be built on the playing field:

> Well they were thinking of making, there was talk in the big board of people at [the community] that there's going to be a pub or something but then it fell through.
>
> *(Nick, male, aged 14)*

> There's another rumour about the council building like an extra ten houses on the playing field.
>
> *(Alistair, male, aged 10)*

Other frequently-discussed issues, about which children and young people felt particularly strongly, included the actual process of building a community (also Kraftl et al., 2013). Young people would frequently express their frustration that a road or a path was constantly being pulled up, and then re-laid. Elsewhere, they raised concerns about the lack of facilities for religious worship, littering, bicycle and access provision and access to services and facilities. Ellie, from Romsworth, spoke about the provision of local facilities, and specifically the local cafe. From the quote below, it is evident that she was involved in the construction of this community *narrative* about local people, businesses and perceptions of affordability:

> It's owned by Paul's mum, she went bankrupt, I'm not surprised by the charge of the prices, like what she charged for a sandwich . . . a sandwich was like six pounds . . . for a hot chocolate, a small one was like three pounds, it's like say four of us, like me, my mum, and my little sister and stepdad, if we went in there, it'd cost us the best part of about fifteen quid just for a hot, small, hot chocolate.
>
> *(Ellie, female, aged 14)*

Young people were keen observers that they were often at the crux of adult dialogues in the communities where they live. Extending our discussion above, where the profiles of local groups were of a particular age and gender, the quote from Suzie below shows that she and her friends were well aware that young people's use of space and behaviour was a point of discussion, referring to the adult 'agenda'. She spoke of her frustration regarding this, being the focus of discussion at the same time as being excluded from the table:

> I think once they had a problem with like younger kids playing on the . . . park at the centre because we were messing around on the swing . . . the parents weren't happy because we were playing on the park . . . they just wrote it up on their agenda . . . there's an agenda outside the bar . . . it just annoyed us all really because they don't get to speak to us, they just talk to all the adults.
>
> *(Suzie, female, aged 12)*

Children and young people were emotionally engaged in their communities, in the knowledge they held, and in their detailed observations of (planned) building work. They experienced sustainable urbanism through a web of emotional, material, embodied, affectional relationships with people, land, bricks, mortar, water, grass and mud. It was through young people's entanglements with these urbanisms that forms of vitality – in terms of the knowledges that communities produce about life-itself – were grounded, experienced, exposed and negotiated. We argue that these knowledges are particularly vital because, through them, a range of emotional and affective registers is articulated – from humour to frustration, and from hope to disappointment. These emotional and affective relations are part and parcel of the *becoming-lively* of sustainable urban places – especially (but not only) after the builders have left (Kraftl, 2014).

Here we found young people to have an emotional stake in the process of building sustainable urbanisms – from being excited when new pathways emerged, to frustrations with ongoing upheaval of construction works, and the disappointments of failed promises with regard to community infrastructures. In distinction, though, it is interesting to note that in the rather different geographical

**144** Vital politics

context of India (from the New Urbanisms in India project), many young people were actively involved in the process of building work *per se* (Hadfield-Hill and Zara, 2017). Many families who lived on the land prior to the development were involved in the actual process of building the new urban space, from laying the piped infrastructures, to pouring in the concrete and laying bricks. This had a profound impact on children, particularly those whose parents were construction workers. For many young participants, their families were 'building the vision', through lifting the bricks, carrying the sand and mixing the concrete – physically building – they were intensely physically and emotionally involved in building the vision. Young participants would speak as a family collective. As one young person put it: 'we take part in building these buildings' (participant, aged 11); they were living with the process of building work, literally living on the building site, picking up the bricks, playing with the left-over materials and, with the family, monitoring the progress of the building work and generating local knowledges. On an everyday basis, young people were part and parcel of the urban changes which were happening in their local area. Through these practices, many felt physically and emotionally connected to the building of new urban spaces.

## *Bodies shaping spaces*

Children and young people did not only contribute to their emerging communities through the generation of local knowledge or physical processes of building. Their bodies in public spaces are widely framed as a negative presence in the academic literature, which often results in adults reasserting their dominance and control over such spaces, from children being told to move on in shopping centres to increased surveillance and curfew areas in specific urban spaces. Here, though, and building upon our arguments in the previous chapter we show how children and young people's embodied social action, in Hettonbury, had a positive influence on the reshaping of community. As noted in Chapter 2, Hettonbury's housing plan was designed around a large open public space, locally known as The Square. Located outside the primary school, as part of the 'neighbourhood spine', this area was pedestrianised and landscaped, and in the design brief intended to be a space at the heart of the community for public events and social gatherings. It was planned to be one of the first infrastructures to be delivered, integrating soft and hard landscaping and water, to mirror the SUD journey elsewhere in the development. Indeed, by 2009, when the fieldwork was under way, The Square was complete, with large granite stones positioned in an amphitheatre setting, established trees planted and the water feature embedded in a sprinkler system. However, despite being complete, it was fenced off for many months. From conversations with developers, builders and members of the Residents' Association it emerged that this space was intended as a 'gift' to the community and on completion of the rest of the development, this space would be opened for use. However, the downturn in the economy and the knock-on consequences for the housing sector had a significant influence on progress with large swathes of construction stalled

Vital politics **145**

and indeed terminated. So, for many months during 2009 and 2010, the space remained boarded and unused until, however, holes started to appear. Young people were appropriating this space – panels were being lifted and squeezed through, opening up access to a large open space for playing and socialising. Children and young people began to use The Square for skateboarding, cycling and hanging out, using advertising hoardings and builders' materials to construct elaborate ramps and obstacles. It was as a result of young people's continued use of this space – through their material, embodied engagements – that the Residents' Association began a concerted conversation with the developers regarding the removal of the boards. Instigated by young people's everyday use of a liminal space, the Residents' Association was able to negotiate an earlier opening of the space with the developers and the development agency. Through these informal political actions – through their appropriation of a liminal space in a way that most adults would in fact frown upon – children and young people's embodied presence led to changes within the more formal Political spaces of interaction between the Residents' Association and development agency and, ultimately, to the earlier opening of The Square for the entire community.

Reflecting on research from the New Urbanisms in India project, there were numerous examples of young people's bodies shaping community relations and acting as a political tool to assert their claim on the space. The site of research attracted a significant number of tourists at the weekends and during festivals and holidays: people would travel to this place as a destination – to experience the clean air, the well-designed urban form, and 'escape' the chaos which characterises much of urban India. However, young people living in this new space, often children whose families were marginalised in the process of urban development (but who had lived in the area for generations), would make their bodies known in certain 'tourist' hotspots. These spaces included the bridge, a popular viewing point, and the promenade, a 'walkable' environment with eateries and shops, were two such spaces. Young people spoke about visiting these spaces for two primary reasons: first to 'practise their English' with the predominately middle-class Indian tourists; and second, to share their knowledge and local experiences in anticipation that tourists would have a positive experience of the place. Young people's embodied, emotional connection with place and the positioning of their bodies in certain places, at certain times, (i) asserted their claim on the space, in that it was their development, their space, and (ii) contributed to the liveliness of place – in this case in terms of the many visitors who come each year (Hadfield-Hill and Zara, 2017).

In our UK research, young people spoke about asserting their bodies, through both physical and non-physical collective action, to campaign for change in their local communities. The first example comes from Romsworth and highlights young people's knowledge of community histories, land legacies and responsibilities, but also their political *potential* in the conversations they had about community issues. In the quote below, Amy described the historical context to land acquisition in the community, in that the land owner was committed to the creation of a 'community' in terms of access to services and facilities, participation and dialogue. However, she goes on to describe growing tensions between the landowners' original vision and

**146** Vital politics

the subsequent changes being made by the developers. She explained that it was the residents' responsibility, both adults and young people, to protest against these changes to the development, to (literally) sit or lie on the land and make themselves heard in ways that – more-or-less resemble form of political protest (Jeffrey, 2013), albeit as conditional, 'implicit' forms of activism (Zembylas, 2013). Amy said that she would be keen to be a part of this collective action, for the benefit of the community:

> [Landowner] did not want to sell the land but his dad did and so it was like . . . he said he was like he wanted it to be a lovely place and he didn't want it to be made for money, he wanted it to be made so that they were going to use the land . . . it was his responsibility and he did his best but now I think it's our responsibility to like speak up and like, I think we should protest lie sit down on the land their building on . . . I would like if enough people did it then I would.
>
> *(Amy, female, aged 13)*

## Conclusion

This chapter has provided an insight into young people's experiences of the P/politics of sustainable urbanisms. Although it has, to some extent, repeated some of the findings of previous research on children and young people's 'place' in urban public spaces, and on their participation in formal Political processes, it is important to remember that the findings presented here are set within the context of places which have been designed from the outset to be participatory, inclusive and convivial. Through an investigation into young people's movements, interactions and voices in diverse community settings, we demonstrated that multiple political barriers to young people's participation still exist, notwithstanding the laudable aims of the UK's Sustainable Communities Plan and others like it around the world. Social and *spatial* barriers limited young people's involvement in what were their communities, often in ways that were inherently and problematically contradictory. From the spatial exclusion which young people experienced in terms of prime community assets such as Romsworth's community centre, to their voices and bodies being absent from community dialogues and their experiences of structural exclusion based on dominant cultures of communication, children and young people were prevented from formally participating in community dialogues, negotiations and discourses.

While it is important to highlight the above kinds of exclusions, it is also crucial to highlight children and young people's vital political action: the spaces, moments and encounters between young people, adult others, spaces and infrastructures which shape community relations and experiences. It is these everyday, often banal acts that can be read as political, as they have the potential to shape the experiences of adults and young people in often unnoticed but profound ways. In India, for example, young people were part and parcel of the narrative of wanting the new urban development to succeed – by young people positioning their bodies in certain spaces, at certain times, they were part of reproducing the story of urban change, claiming that this was their place too (Hadfield-Hill and Zara, 2017).

We demonstrated that the local, everyday knowledges which young people accrued through their community-based mobilities and interactions were vital for the ongoing development of the social, physical and cultural infrastructures of their community. In particular, we argued that these knowledges are deeply emotional, affective and affecting, and therefore key elements in the becoming-lively of newly built, sustainable communities in registers beyond the representational (Horton and Kraftl, 2006a). Together with their use of space, young people clearly demonstrated p/Political potential; their bodies shaping spaces, leading to positive reshaping and use of community assets, and leading in turn to Political change in decision-making and advocacy at a local scale. We draw in part on these arguments in Chapter 8, where we make a broader, conceptual case for critical examination of the spaces between childhood and play. In Chapter 9 we examine further the policy implications of our findings in the present chapter.

## Note

1 Note that, in this chapter, when referring to both formal Political and informal political acts, we use the term 'P/political' as shorthand, as do several other scholars (e.g. Skelton, 2013).

# 8

# MAKING SPACE FOR VITALITY IN SUSTAINABLE URBANISMS

## Childhood and play

### Introduction

In this penultimate chapter we argue that notions of 'sustainability' need to be accompanied or even supplanted by notions of multiple versions of 'life' in sustainable urban places. Our argument introduces the final frame of the book: *play*. So far we have shown how children and young people are continually engaged in processes of world-making (Chapters 4 and 5), contributing to and building (senses of) community and neighbourliness (Chapter 6) and active citizenship (Chapter 7) – all activities that are central to the liveliness of sustainable urban places. In this chapter we will extend our discussion of sustainable urbanism to show how planning for 'liveability' and 'conviviality' are always-already entangled with vital materialisms and diverse ways of doing life. In this way we wish to extend what it means to think, plan and practise 'sustainable' modes of urban life.

Our principal argument is that to make space for vitality in sustainable urbanisms greater attention needs to be given to the analytical space *between* childhood and play. In response to recent theories of the ludic that attempt – to some degree – to disconnect childhood and play – we ask what happens if we hold childhood and play in productive tension, but do not conceive them as essentially coupled or dualistically related. Play(ing) is not the distinct realm of children, yet children may have something distinctive to contribute to playful spaces that could be full of more diverse forms of life – vitalities. We contend that such vitalities emerge in multiple, contingent co-minglings between children and play – subjectivities and events that are cut across by and produced through social difference, everyday practices and manifold nonhuman Others. The space between is not merely a hyphen connecting two terms ('child's-play') but a space of eruption/disruption (Lobo, 2016), filled with multiple Others and excessive of that relation: it extends beyond a magic circle that circumscribes any 'natural' association of child/play

(Henricks, 2015; Ryall et al., 2013). Our analyses further develop, combine and extend beyond the theoretical notions that we introduced in Chapter 2, in theorising for an interdisciplinary childhood studies: mobilities, othering, emotion/affect, embodiment and the nonhuman.

The chapter begins with a brief schematic introduction to the diverse ways in which 'play' has been conceived and expands on the argument for de-naturalising and re-imagining the relationship between childhood and play. The chapter proceeds to discuss four thematics that *involve* childhood/play: everyday social relations; nonhuman agency; social difference; the politics of vitality. Primarily, the chapter makes a *conceptual* case for understanding the often *ambiguous* energies that emerge from the space between childhood and play as vitalising. In doing so, we introduce the final, and crucial, component in our broader arguments about the place of vitalities in sustainable urban design. To make this case, we combine reflections on preceding chapters with empirical material from the New Urbanisms, New Citizens (NUNC) project and the New Urbanisms in India research together with carefully-chosen examples from around the world.

## Characterising play (and childhood)

Despite its perceived frivolities, play has for centuries been a serious subject for academic debate. Play's attraction has been widespread, spawning research among philosophers, social scientists, psychologists (and latterly neuroscientists), educationalists and the arts and humanities – not to mention diverse practitioners concerned with the role of play in promulgating public health, well-being, economic competitiveness and learning/skills acquisition. Therefore, we will not attempt to provide any singular or all-encompassing definition of play. Rather, we distil some key characteristics of play that guide the rest of this chapter. We note – as does Henricks (2015) – that there are multiple ways to schematise play and that any attempt to do so must be critically cognisant of the social and geographical positioning of its originators. With this caveat in mind, Henricks (ibid.) outlines several ways to characterise play, from which four are particularly pertinent:

1   *Action.* Play is conceived as 'a distinctive pattern of *consciously guided* behaviour, undertaken by an *individual*' (Henricks, 2015: 24, original emphasis). Play is associated with action (not quiescence), and with a range of bodily comportments and dispositions – having fun, running, jumping, fighting, experimenting, etcetera. This approach is common to psychologists of play and often tied to developmental models (such as Piaget's). It is, therefore, often the model of play most solidly associated with children and their becoming-adult (Cook, 2016). While such approaches might indicate 'universal' play traits, Henricks argues that such an approach is replete with mythologies of individualism and (ostensibly middle-class) values found in the Minority Global North.

**150** Childhood and play

2    *Interaction.* Henricks's critique of play as 'individual action' implies that play does not happen in a vacuum. Rather, play involves engagement, action and reaction, 'assuming a distinctive stance toward the world's patterns and processes' (Henricks, 2015: 25). In more recent, posthuman-inspired scholarship (discussed at greater length below and in Chapter 2), play involves multiple nonhuman actants, and is figured as 'an emergent co-production of entangled bodies, affects, objects, space and histories in ways *that make life better* for the time of playing' (Lester and Russell, 2014: 241, emphasis added). In the rest of this chapter, we assess some of the implications of recognising multiple forms of social and more-than-social difference that are entangled in children's play, in and of sustainable urban places.

3    *Activity.* Whereas interaction is a (more-than-)social characteristic of play, Henricks (2015: 26) argues that play may also mimic or mock cultural values. Thus, play entails not only communication but cooperation: in turn-taking, for instance, 'play is a form *of* and *for* human conduct': 'eventfulness'. In this chapter, we use these observations about play-as-activity to foreground the everyday micro-politics of play in children's lives.

4    *Disposition.* Henricks asks what it is that makes an event enjoyable – what makes it *playful.* He argues that play needs to be felt and declared as such, requiring not only a cultural but psychological commitment, or energy, or 'vision' *to play* (Henricks, 2015: 28). In the more recent parlances of nonrepresentational and related theories, playing is generative of a kind of *affect*, which constitutes a push in the world (Woodyer, 2012; see also Thrift, 2004; Harker, 2005). Play is autotelic and intrinsic (Rautio, 2013; Ryall et al., 2013): it is a form of power that is not only imposed from without the immersive feeling of playing, but also constituted from within. Play also feels affirmative and it is for *this* reason that play is so closely aligned with theories of vitalism (see Chapter 2). As Woodyer (2012: 319) summarises: the ability of play to bring us together (affectively, materially, bodily) 'is achieved by our being affected. In this sense, the proximity of play is self-perpetuating as the vitality emerging from it encourages one to be more responsive to others'. Play is therefore potentially generative of certain kinds of *generosity*, which we explore later in this chapter.

In Henricks's categorisation, there is, aside from the first component, little that is particular to *children* about play. Indeed, many contemporary play theorists deconstruct the assumed relationship between childhood and play. They seek to 'disrupt and unsettle both ideas of discrete boundaries for play and many of the romanticized visions of play . . . as the activity of children' (MacLean et al., 2015: 5). This disruptive urge has two implications for this chapter. First, we would note a rich and longstanding (although not large) vein of scholarship-practice around play and the city – what Stevens (2007) terms the *ludic city*. Drawing on Caillois's (2001) fourfold characterisation of play as competition, chance, simulation and vertigo, Stevens considers possibilities for building-in play into city spaces. Although his is a

Childhood and play **151**

rather specific conceptualisation of play, he discusses how particular kinds of urban spaces may be enlivened through play – such as paths, intersections, boundaries and thresholds. Play also figures highly in accounts of alternative/experimental uses of urban space – from skateboarding (Borden, 2001) to parkour (Mould, 2009) to yarn-bombing (Price, 2015). We explore some of these examples later, in order to extend analyses from the New Urbanisms, New Citizens project. However, we would also make two critical observations about this work: one, it only *gestures* to how play might be linked to *sustainability*; two, whether deliberately or not, it tends not to consider *children's* play in the city. Given children's unique positioning especially within public urban life (Chapter 2), there could be much to be gained from integrating studies of urban play with an interdisciplinary approach to childhood studies.

Despite these contentions, we make a second observation about attempts to disrupt the child/play dyad. That is, we would not advocate a simple (re)turn to investigating children's playing in the city. Neither do we call for a re-interrogation of child/play because of some sense that children are 'missing' from accounts of parkour or yarn-bombing. In a powerful piece, Cook (2016) argues that the de-essentialisation of childhood that forms the fundament of sociological studies of childhood has been somewhat undermined by a (re)essentialisation of play. Within childhood studies scholarship, there has been an incessant (and necessary) questioning of the meaning of childhood, but not of *play* (also Woodyer, 2012). Thus, in a world full of fears about standardised testing and children growing up too fast, '[c]hildren's play and playful exploration [still] promise to provide the font of salvation and the content of an imagined civilisation to come . . . indeed, the creative, assertive and disruptive child in many ways constitutes the ideal child . . . of childhood studies' (Cook, 2016: 4–5). These generally normative assumptions about play allow a *certain kind of essentialised child* to re-enter the imaginings of NSSC, via the back-door. This darling child of NSSC is the middle-class, Minority Global North child, whose figure haunts both the UNCRC and policy-making for children in so many other contexts (Ansell et al., 2012).

One response to Cook's argument would be to avoid eliding children and play altogether, and to engage in studies of urban-based play that do not start with children's experiences. But as we argued above, if children play too, then it is insufficient to consider these kinds of playful practices in isolation from how children play with/in cities. Here, though, we might reach some kind of impasse: how can we make a case for (re)turning to children's urban play without recourse to essentialist arguments about how and why *children* play? What's the difference between adults' play in the city and children's?

Our response is to offer a critical, creative and affirmative re-theorisation of the *space between childhood and play*. Doing so starts with the observation – so central to childhood studies – that children's play is not universal or natural in nature. Rather, children's urban experiences – including play – are often framed in ways that are different from adults'. This is as a result of socially constructed norms, images, laws and institutions that frequently marginalise children, as we discussed

**152** Childhood and play

in Chapter 2. Meanwhile, in different ways, in diverse social and geographical contexts, children grapple not only with these adult-constructed frames, but with the often complex and multiple roles and responsibilities they take on (Evans, 2012). These experiences are framed by competing and intensifying efforts to institutionalise childhoods through schooling and other interventions (e.g. Conroy, 2010). Finally, we are beginning to recognise, through emerging fields of biosocial theorising, that children's bodies and brains are – in interaction with the various social praxes listed above – different from, (usually) smaller than, and 'Other' to, those of adults (Jones, 2008; Lee and Motzkau, 2011).

For these reasons, we seek to (re)turn to the space between childhood and play. That space is not simply an essentialising, hyphenated relation (it's not *just* 'child's-play'). It is a space that articulates with, that is produced through, and that is experienced with, all the other concerns noted in the previous paragraph. One problem with eliding childhood and play is that those two terms are held together in simplistic, dualistic relation. It is our committed intent to expand, complicate, and even smash that dualism, by recognising that there is always something *more* (Horton and Kraftl, 2006a) entailed in the relationship between childhood and play. On one hand, this is because both childhoods and play are articulated with/in all of the other concerns noted in the previous paragraph. As Bosco (2010) so beautifully exemplifies, play does not happen out of turn with work, activism, care, or, in the present case, attempts to build sustainable urban places. Play is thoroughly and differentially enmeshed within those concerns, in the flux of everyday life. Therefore, and on the other hand, we return to one of our guiding conceptual arguments, underpinned by 'new wave' theorising and vital materialisms. That is, we are most interested in moving towards a more-than-social, but also thoroughly *ambiguous*, analysis of how children's lives – and children's play – are enveloped by, entangled in, and productive of, sustainable urbanisms. This is a non-dualistic, non-dialectical, generative and, we hope, generous (Woodyer, 2012; Stratford, 2016) conceptualisation of the space between childhood and play. Critically, children belong to one of the demographic groups most vulnerable to climate change *and* at the same time they are seen as future key agents in attempts to foster resilience against its effects (UNICEF, 2011, 2014).

In order to achieve this second goal, we draw in this chapter upon an eclectic bunch of scholars writing on play and/or childhood, but all of whom have (broadly conceived) sympathies for 'new wave' approaches to materiality and nature. In order to further dismantle and complicate the essentialist dyad of child/play, *we also need to recognise the nonhuman forces 'at play'*. These literatures offer an important theoretical step through which to complicate and question the relationship between childhood and play (Cook, 2016). In particular, they enable us to view childhood and play as contingent, emergent and evental: as constantly entangling and disentangling modes of life. Yet we challenge and develop even those approaches because they do not, generally, attend to the questions we have set out above: to the diverse ways in which the exigencies of the playful moment are enfolded into the other concerns of children's lives

Childhood and play **153**

(following Mitchell and Elwood, 2012). We need to go somewhat further to assess how childhood and play *matter* (Horton, 2010; Kraftl, 2013). The remainder of this chapter sets out how we might begin to understand how childhood and play *matter* to the creation of sustainable, *vital* urban places. The additive, complicating, ambiguous, creative and generous spirit that we seek to engender is signified by the titles of the thematic sections. We ask: what can be achieved by thinking through 'playing and childhood and . . .'?

## Playing and childhood and . . . everyday social relations

A central aim of this book has been to examine children's experiences of living in sustainable urban places. Throughout, *play* has been a sometimes hidden, sometimes clear concern – both for the children and young people themselves, and for our analyses. For instance, in Chapter 5, children's experiences of 'just walking' pre-empted or accompanied moments of playfulness, and in their engagement with (and around) the wind turbine in the snow, in turn prefaced their political (with a small 'p') interactions with sustainable urban technologies. Similarly, in Chapter 6, some of the ways in which children constituted their own status as active citizens in the lives of their new communities unfolded through play. For example, the story of The Square in Hettonbury offered a key moment where play was meshed into and a cipher for a whole bundle of important discourses and practices that mattered, profoundly, in the unfolding and bifurcating vitalities of a growing urban place. There were many other examples where play of all kinds was embedded into the everyday lives of our case study communities, and, as we illustrate in this chapter, in other urban places around the world.

In particular, we seek to draw together the ways in which childhood and play are entangled within and co-constitutive of the mundane and routine everyday practices, mobilities and lives of families and communities (see Chapters 4–6; see also Christensen, 2004b; Horton and Kraftl, 2006a). In further reflecting on children, play and everyday routines, two extracts from our ethnographic fieldwork notes are illustrative.

> The two children seem to be quite close friends and much of their outdoor mobility was centred around visiting each other's houses and playing together. Previously . . . concern had been raised at school, due to the amount of time she was spending caring for her brother. One of the first things that she said to me was that her mother is now a lot better; she also said that her dad is home at the moment.
>
> *(Field notes, Hettonbury)*

> A teacher stood at the entrance to the gate monitoring the children leaving with parents. I was surprised to see two young children were standing outside of the school gate, initially the older boy was holding tight onto his little sisters jacket. I wondered why they, like all the other children did not wait inside the playground. After a while of waiting, the older brother relaxed

**154** Childhood and play

slightly, loosening his grip on her jacket and laying down his satchel whilst he made a snowball. Their mum, after five minutes or so, shouted at them from a distance, telling them it was time to go home.

*(Field notes, Hettonbury)*

In the first extract, opportunities to play are intimately connected with a girl's caring responsibilities. In the second, play emerges tentatively, implicitly, without fuss, and with some trepidation. As the older boy and his sister nervously considered playing, they were surrounded by groups of other, more boisterous children, throwing snowballs at each other and their parents. This was play in a fragile, uncertain state: the moment at which everyday routine spills over into play, or slowly gathers enough momentum that the participants and, in this case, those observing, can agree that what they are doing may be called 'play'. In this moment, as Huizinga (1955) has it in his classic *Homo Ludens*, play takes place through consensus – through bringing a very subtle, modest, little world into being. Contra Huizinga, however, we do not interpret moments of playing as de facto opposed to or demarcated from the flow of everyday life. Play is not figured in these examples as a 'magic circle', although particularly intensive or noteworthy forms of playfulness may erupt within or interrupt moments that initially formed part of the routine 'waiting to be collected from school'.

Indeed, here we can also reflect on resonant examples from India, where, as Dyson (2014) argues, work and play are often inseparable in the lives of children. In the following examples, taken from the New Urbanism in India data (Hadfield-Hill and Zara, 2017), we can see how everyday routines of collecting water and washing clothes are spaces of playful activity in the lives of the children. In the first quote, the young person describes collecting water from the tanker. As part of her daily household chores, she describes a moment where play happens, as a collective, with friends, with the cows and with the water itself. In the second quote, the young person speaks of her family washing their clothes in the lake, a space and time where she speaks of playing with friends and nonhuman Others, in this case fish:

We take two pots, one pot and we fill water and take it and come. It is easy for us because we have filled water from our childhood. That is why. We feel very nice bringing water, we play and enjoy. [We collect water] for taking bath, for washing clothes, for our cow, to drink her, to wash her.

*(Sangita, NUI project, female, aged 11)*

We go, ma'am, to wash clothes . . . we catch friends no, my one friend comes with me, she and I catch the fish.

*(Priya, NUI project, female, aged 11)*

Tellingly, some of the younger teenagers in our NUNC study sometimes struggled with the word 'play' in our interviews with them – unsure whether what they told us about time spent outdoors, about their mobilities, constituted 'playing out' or 'hanging out' or something else. Importantly, such difficulties in discerning the difference between 'playing' and 'living' are not unique to a particular moment in the life course when younger children become younger teenagers (compare Weller, 2006). Rather, they are a microcosm of the broader point that playing and living are co-produced, co-mingled and co-constitutive (Woodyer, 2012; MacLean et al., 2015): *playing-living*.

## Playing and childhood and . . . public space

Our argument develops through a focus on the controversial issues surrounding *access* to 'play' *spaces*, if playing-living are considered in the ways we outlined at the end of the previous section. It is here that – as in previous chapters – questions of politics and power intersect with and co-produce the embodied, emotional, material elements of children's urban experiences (and, in turn, of sustainable urban 'vitalities'). In the UK context, community playgrounds were spaces which could overwhelmingly be physically accessed by all, although not surprisingly, many young people recounted the temporal and social constraints of being and feeling out of place (see Chapter 6). However, research in India found that playgrounds built into new urban developments were privatised (Hadfield-Hill and Zara, 2017). The privatisation of play has further exacerbated inequalities for children and young people, between those who can afford to pay to play, in formal playgrounds and spaces, and those who cannot (Figure 8.1). Many quotes from young participants expressed

**FIGURE 8.1** Who can afford to play? Example from India.

**156** Childhood and play

frustration that they could not play in this space, or to use the water to cool down in the summer months:

> They can enjoy, they can play, those who are rich, [but] we can't. Those who have money, they can enjoy, they can swim in this dam, they can play. Everything.
>
> *(Ranu, NUI project, female, aged 11)*

However, it was speaking with young people whose families could not afford to pay to use the children's water equipment that showed the diverse sense of what play can mean for young people. Play for some participants was not paddling, being with friends, feeling the water spray on their faces, running around and through the deep puddles of water; for them it was *watching* – watching other children play – that constituted their playful activity (Hadfield-Hill and Zara, 2017). In the quote below, a 14-year-old participant speaks of the times when he is playing: he goes to the water park, a space which he cannot afford to access, but nevertheless he describes how he is watching other children play and will wait for them to come. These are not his friends, he does not know these young people, but he enjoys watching them play:

> . . . then we went [there], in that water, just play and I stand, I wait here for peoples to come.
>
> *(Anil, NUI project, Male, aged 14).*

Elsewhere, as Langevang (2008) observes in her study of young men's 'bases' in Accra, Ghana, playing-living is not confined to playgrounds; it is articulated through, and articulates, the vitalities of public spaces in a far wider sense. Langevang focuses on young men in Ghana who are experiencing mass unemployment as a result of global economic changes. With hours of enforced leisure time, and without paid work to anchor their identities, young men carve out spaces – in neglected courtyards, buildings and street corners – where they hang out, play football, and watch the world go by. Although seen as a threat by other users of public spaces, these 'bases' form key spaces wherein young men can assert new, collective masculine identities. Yet these bases and the activities therein go beyond identity: they presage new modes of living and of engaging with urban life, in direct response to the very social, economic and environmental challenges that have spawned movements for sustainable urbanism:

> young men create personal bonds, socialize, and discuss and practise masculine identities . . . they produce a space through which they endeavour to satisfy their social and material needs and to find meaning in a changing urban environment.
>
> *(Langevang, 2008: 239)*

Childhood and play **157**

In the New Urbanism, New Citizens project, we also observed the banal, everyday comings and goings of life in the public spaces of our four communities. Unlike Langevang, however, we attended to the co-presence of young people and adults, and to a range of more diverse activities – some of which appeared (at least to us) to foment as 'play':

> In The Square this afternoon there were numerous young people playing in the water fountains [see Figure 8.2]. There were a mix of ages, the oldest was probably eleven and the youngest approximately five. Some of the children were out playing in their swimming costumes. At one point a disabled man in an electric wheelchair came through the [civic space] with his dog; his dog drank from the fountains. There was a man sunbathing and reading his book, he was lying on the grass. There was also one mother, watching her two younger children. Most of the young people were playing at the [civic space] without adult supervision. After a while two boys bought a football to the [civic space], they were playing with it in the sprinklers. There was also a group of girls, they were chatting to one another, fully clothed but completely soaking. They were hanging their hair over the fountain, just like in the Vidal Sassoon advert! The pool areas were once again filled with rubbish.
>
> *(Field notes, Hettonbury)*

This vignette is indicative of our argument that the elements of playing-living are inextricably entwined. There are small instances where *children's play* emerges as a distinct facet of this snapshot of urban life (in the water fountains). But there are other moments when it is more difficult to tell whether what is happening is 'playing', 'relaxing', 'leisure', 'hanging out', 'passing through', or simply 'being'. Did the man with his wheelchair and dog enter the civic space simply because they were passing through, or because they wanted to briefly experience the apparently playful atmosphere of that moment? Were the older girls hanging their hair into the water engaging in 'play' – or were they playing with or parodying the imageries of shampoo adverts? How, as we ask in the next section of the chapter, were the nonhuman agents 'at play' in constituting this moment: the dog; the water; the rubbish in the fountains; the football?

Conversely, it must be acknowledged that this was a distinct *moment* in the life of Hettonbury. This was a snapshot characterised by a certain *vitality*: exuberant, playful and, apparently, affirmative. Yet in both conceptual and applied terms, we do not wish to over-exaggerate the importance of these moments, even if they do neatly encapsulate the co-constitution of playing-living. For there are certain things that we do know about Hettonbury: this civic space looks very different in the winter time, and again when children are at school; adults and children are co-present in apparent harmony here, yet there are many tensions between adults and young people (Chapter 6); and this very civic space – The Square – has been at the centre of a range of controversies (Chapter 7). There are also things we do not

**158** Childhood and play

**FIGURE 8.2** Running through the fountains in Hettonbury.

know about this particular moment, and which might colour any rose-tinted view of this being some kind of 'exemplar' of a sustainable urban life: the pool areas, filled with rubbish, perhaps diminish the aesthetic of this moment (but perhaps the other actors in this scene don't care); the groups of children and adults may be co-present, but that does not necessarily mean that they are 'getting along' harmoniously (but perhaps they are); some of the children appear to be playing, but maybe they would not have agreed (but perhaps they would).

In other words, play – and playing-living – highlight a set of ambivalences and *ambiguities* about urban life. We use this latter term – ambiguity – quite deliberately, since it chimes with a relatively longstanding theoretical concern about play:

> Play, as a unique form of adaptive variability, instigates an imagined but equilibrial reality within which disequilibrial exigencies can be paradoxically simulated and give rise to the pleasurable effects of excitement and optimism.
>
> *(Sutton-Smith (1999: 253), cited in Henricks (2015: 38))*

Play is caught within and expressive of various kinds of ambiguity (Sutton-Smith, 2009): between the cruelty of practical jokes and the joy of collective game-playing; between affirmation of the status quo and rebellion; between the ludic moment and the longer-term, social, health, political, even evolutionary import of play; between the individual and the social; between the consequential and the inconsequential (Henricks, 2015; MacLean et al., 2015). Therefore, 'whilst the field of play studies has promoted the idea that play is an unmitigated good' (Henricks, 2015: 110), we seek in this chapter to introduce and retain a sense of ambiguity about play and (especially) any simplistic association with childhood. The example of The Square is illustrative of this ambiguity: playing (and living) may be entrained in affirmative, progressive, vital moments such as the ones we described above; but there are always-already residual questions, concerns, or anxieties. In this rest of this chapter, we extend well beyond Sutton-Smith's use of the term to explore a range of ambiguities in the spaces between childhood and play.

## Playing and childhood and . . . nonhuman agency

As we discussed in Chapter 2, a key tenet of the 'new wave' of childhood studies has been an emphasis upon the more-than-social production of childhood, with and as nonhuman agents. Within this emergent approach, contemporary play theorists have played a crucial (yet undervalued) role. As Lester (2015) puts it, drawing on a range of posthumanist philosophers, a crucial task for play scholars (and by extension, childhood studies scholars) is to denaturalise the triad childhood–play–nature (compare Cook, 2016). He argues that we must move beyond a doxa in which the perceived 'vulnerabilities' and 'deficiencies' of children, play and nature are glibly identified in order to justify various therapeutic interventions.

Instead, we must introduce a kind of openness or uncertainty – what we term later in the chapter a kind of 'looseness' – that can help expound the ways in which 'heterogeneous and messy components of life can get on and go together' (Lester, 2015: 64).

In the above light, throughout the book (again, for instance, in Chapter 4, through the example of play happening in the snow around the wind turbine), we have exemplified and developed our argument for an interdisciplinary childhood studies that is better attuned to the more-than-human. But such an attunement prompts questions about how play *matters* (Horton, 2012) and, specifically, about the nonhuman matters that co-constitute the ambiguous spaces between and beyond childhood and play. For instance, another – perhaps also unusual – facet of everyday life at the four case studies from the NUNC project was that, for several years, residents had to live with building work. In part as a result of the global economic downturn from 2008 onwards, construction work was a prolonged process, lasting more than a decade in two of the communities. Thus, children recounted various ways in which 'living on a building site' had formed part of their everyday

**160** Childhood and play

lives for as long as they remembered (for detailed discussion, see Kraftl et al., 2013). However, an important subset of their experiences related to their play on building sites and with the various material remnants of building work.

Some young people accessed building sites and unfinished areas of the community, even though these were generally fenced off to prevent public access. In one example, Zed and Daniel told us about a parcel of land they had named 'Mud Hill':

> You know what Mud Hill is don't you? Well it's a bit wicked, Mud Hill, we made it in, last year, about a couple, five months ago, basically we, okay, we come out of our houses, my house, oh where is my house? Come out my house, yeah, I go to Daniel's on my bike, he comes out, we drive through here . . .
>
> *(Zed, male, aged 11)*

> . . . we have to stand up (on our bikes) and you lean back so . . . [demonstrates]
>
> *(Daniel, male, aged 10)*

'Mud Hill' itself is a weedy slope that was created by the builders' bulldozers when razing land for future development. When Zed and Daniel talk of 'making it', they ostensibly mean that, through months of repeated use, their bikes have – in an example akin to the footprints in the snow – smoothed trails in the mud where they enjoy riding. Significantly, this example sits at the confluence of meaning and mattering, representation and nonrepresentation. It speaks of the embodied encounters of Zed, Daniel and other children with the messy, muddy, heterogeneous materialities of a building site (compare Christensen and Mikkelsen, 2008; Lester, 2015). Indeed, Daniel's narrative tailed off as he became lost for words as to how to describe his performative engagement with the hill, leaning back to show the researcher how he rode. Simultaneously, however, this narrative is a microcosm of the processes of meaning-making that are so central to the life (or, to the becoming-lively) of newly built, sustainable communities. As we have already shown, the process of *naming* is fundamental to the process of belonging (Chapter 6), and emerges not only in the planning of a new community by professionals, but in the spaces between childhood and play.

In the last part of the chapter, we consider how such processes may be constitutive of a presumptive generosity in which the space between childhood and play is central. In the previous chapter, we described how young people had used the various artefacts of building work to create an informal skate park. We highlighted the ambiguous but ultimately affirmative effect of such interactions for the community. Yet we encountered other examples of children playing with the materialities of building work.

> The area outside the playground is currently under construction, the builders are in the process of re-setting the pebbled path which runs around the

Childhood and play **161**

perimeter. There were two little girls (aged approx. 5) squatting down by the outer playground fence, playing with the sand which had been left by the builders. After a while they moved on with several other small children to play in the large SUD, located in the outer playground. They were squatting in it, placing stones etc., into the pipes of the swale.

*(Field notes, Hettonbury)*

This vignette indicates some of the perhaps less spectacular ways in which children engaged with left-over building materials. Following Gibson's (2014) work on ecological affordances, the sand appears to hold an attraction (both visual and haptic) that engages these 5-year-old girls to play (also Kyttä, 2004). The sand affords multiple capacities for play, in particular for what Pellegrini and Smith (1998: 578) term 'rhythmic stereotypes': forms of play that engage (young) children with the physical environment and that bear intrinsic value through the 'satisfaction of making the body work' (Christensen and Mikkelsen, 2008; Henricks, 2015: 148). Relatedly (although under a different ontology), we might see these as one of a series of what Rautio (2013: 394) terms 'autotelic practices': apparently human traits that are intrinsic to themselves, but that extend beyond the individuated agency of a human being. For instance, Rautio seeks to move the debate from *why* children carry stones in their pockets to *how* they do so, thus thinking through the capacities of the 'child-with-stones' or, the 'child-with-sand' (ibid.: 396). For Hultman and Lenz Taguchi (2010), who briefly touch upon the question of a child playing with sand, the children and the sand are mutually intra-active – different, but not clearly divided. The children will probably be covered by the sand when they move on to the SUDS; it will be in their clothes; they may even swallow some and it will become part of them for a while.

Through this example, we are directed to a 'congregational understanding' of agency (Bennett, 2010: 20–21), where a world – in this case 'child's-play' – is constituted by encounters, assemblages and ad hoc groupings: by the *multiple* constituents in the space between childhood and play, which render that space always-already *more-than-dualistic*. Childhood and play are accompanied by and constituted through the path, the sand, the pebbles, the fence, the builders, the children and, then, the children move on to new encounters: with the SUDS, with water snails, plants, slopes and other children (see other examples in Chapter 4). As Rautio (2013) asserts, these are momental encounters: they are meaningless (really, what else *can* we say about children playing with some sand?). Yet, can we carve out an alternative sense of (perhaps mon*u*mental) responsibility for these kinds of encounters – a space for new dispositions such as foolishness, silliness, *play-ful-ness* – that seemingly provides the sense of 'push' (Thrift, 2000) in many of the moments recounted thus far in this chapter?

These encounters and assemblages have shown different ways in which children, young people, sand, stones and left-over building materials have constituted largely positive, affective, playful activity. However, in spaces of new urban development, places which are in the making, with half-finished buildings, piles

**162** Childhood and play

of bricks, sand, mortar, open patches of land, diggers and other machinery it is important to highlight the messy, frustrating and sometimes dangerous affordances which these assemblages may have. In new communities in the UK for instance, children and their families alike would express frustration with the mud, the dust and the ongoing messiness of their local area. Children would speak of the ongoing muddiness that would stick to their shoes 'like glue', and the unfinished curbs and potholes which would cause damage to car and bike tyres and human bodies (twisted ankles). Similarly in India, children also spoke of playing with left-over construction materials and the ongoing mess which living in a site of urban change caused. In such spaces, particularly in the UK context, there are site warnings, danger signs and high fences, partitioning bodies from the ongoing building work and materialities – reminding observers also of the dangers of such human and non-human encounters (Figure 8.3). Yet, soon after the fieldwork in India (Hadfield-Hill and Zara, 2017), the research team heard the devastating news of the death of a young boy, who had been playing with an exposed wire – a stark reminder of the risks associated with certain assemblages of human and nonhuman materialities (see also Chapter 5).

Finally, it is important to attend to the significance of nonhuman animals in children's playful activity. Indeed, across our research both in the UK and Indian contexts, young people frequently spoke about the importance of nonhuman

**FIGURE 8.3** Partitioning bodies from the messy (and potentially dangerous) materialities.

animals in their description of play, their everyday encounters and often as a third party with another human friend. In Hettonbury, the SUDS were magnets of biodiversity, with butterflies, snails, frogspawn frequently being an important part of playful activity. Children, often with friends, would spend time in the SUDS watching, speaking to, collecting, prodding and touching these nonhuman Others. On guided walks, the researchers would be taken to these spaces, would squat down alongside the participants to take part, for a short while in these playful moments.

Young participants in India were also entangled in a web of nonhuman animal interactions, from speaking about insect parties on their balconies, to listening to the birds talking with one another, playing with rabbits and walking with dogs – nonhuman Others were a significant actor in the lives of the children (Hadfield-Hill and Zara, 2017). In the following particularly lucid accounts, first, a young participant tells the researcher about the birds which speak to him and remind him about certain activities and second, a participant speaks of the playful activity with his friend, nonhuman Others (puppies, chickens, small dogs), milk, water and chappati:

*Interviewer:* Has any other bird spoken to you?
*Amit:* Red-wattled lapwing.
*Interviewer:* Red-wattled lapwing. What did it say?
*Amit:* . . . the other day our father told us that . . . we would build . . . er, take a scooter. That too my father had forgotten. Then one time when I went to the jungle . . . I was climbing the branch. There [the bird] it told me immediately.

*(Amit, NUI project, male, aged 11)*

. . . there are small dogs, puppies, chickens that we play with that only. We take them and we play with them. Give them milk, water, chappati to them. Then I feel better.

*(Shreya, NUI project, female, aged 12)*

In the final section of this chapter we ask: what are the opportunities for learning from such apparently mundane, sometimes fleeting moments, a 'deeper understanding of what humans are growing as part of, and in relation to' (Rautio, 2013: 401)? These are surely crucial questions for the generation of truly *sustainable* places.

## Playing and childhood and . . . social difference

In Chapters 6 and 7, we built up a detailed picture of how particular forms of social difference cut across children's experiences of life in sustainable urban communities. There, we argued that children's (and adults') negotiations of social difference were a crucial component of the ongoing *sustainability* of 'sustainable' urbanisms. In whatever context, sustainable urbanisms can only succeed

**164** Childhood and play

if social differences such as class or age are given careful consideration, since it is only then that residents will form a sense of community in which people feel they belong, and where they have a stake in community life (Raco, 2016). In so doing, we have developed an argument about the centrality of intersectionality and intergenerationality to an interdisciplinary childhood studies for sustainable urbanisms (Chapter 2).

In this section, rather than repeat the analyses presented previously, we develop a specific set of arguments that we introduced above: the idea that play is an interactive (i.e. social) practice rather than merely active (i.e. individual) (Hendricks, 2015); the sense that play is constitutive of everyday social lives – but that, in distinction to the rather utopian vignette set on a summer's day in The Square in Hettonbury, play is not an unequivocally positive activity; the inclination that play is not only intrinsic but that the more-than-social, for-the-moment spatialities of play may *matter* in manifold ways; and, as we have been at pains to highlight, the assertion that play is fundamentally ambiguous – not least in terms of how it is articulated through and articulates social difference. In developing these arguments, we analyse indicative moments from the NUNC project, before discussing examples from elsewhere in the UK, and from Denmark.

Our first series of indicative moments relates to a range of intergenerational tensions between children and adults, which were entangled with the 'play' of children of different ages. In both Hettonbury and Romsworth, young people who were playing or hanging out were moved on (or made to feel they should move on) by adults who contested their use of urban public spaces.

> They [younger children] go in there [a small wooded space] all the, like all the time, you can't get them out of there and they're always, they're like, they build swings in there and they make their dens but then there's this really funny bloke, he moved . . . here and, and he came and told them off and was like that's private land you're not allowed to play in here. And we were all, like, 'Weren't you a kid once?'
>
> *(Daniel, male, aged 10, Hettonbury)*

Lily:        I don't know, it's really strange, I don't know. It's [Romsworth] just got different rules I guess and people have just adapted to them rules while you're in the village. Like, when, if I go into [a nearby village] then yeah, I would hang around the shop and stuff, it's just different ways, I dunno.

Interviewer:  And are those rules, has anyone ever said those things to you?

Lily:        No, it's just expected. It's an understanding, innit? You kind of expect it. And it's like, people wouldn't want to see us hang around the shop. That's why we go on the field. 'Cause they, they like, I guess they think we're trying to cause trouble and stuff that we're not. Stereotypical really.

*(Lily, female, aged 16, Romsworth)*

Childhood and play **165**

These are fairly typical experiences of intergenerational tension in public spaces that detained early children's geographies scholarship (e.g. Matthews et al., 1999, 2000). Crucially, social differences are not only internal to play – for instance, in disagreements about what constitutes mimicry rather than mockery (MacLean et al., 2015). Instead, or in addition, play – in public spaces – is one of several key elements of everyday life that may constitute social tensions. There is a clear ambiguity here, which Daniel identifies all-too-readily: that children are doing exactly what many proponents of the 'nature-deficit disorder' thesis (Louv, 2005) would have them do – they are playing, alone, in patches of woodland. Yet, young people occupy a 'liminal' (or ambiguous) space wherein those activities are also cast as problematic. However, the very *newness* of these spaces – and the intention to build-in sociability and 'liveability' – cast a different light on such experiences. In terms of their newness, there is a lack of shared community history about where children (today's adult residents) played in the past, and therefore no real agreement on where – other than the playgrounds – children 'should' play. In terms of their planned infrastructures, as we discussed in Chapters 6 and 7, the planning processes and ownership structures have been so complex that few residents are certain about which spaces are 'public', which are 'private', and which fall somewhere in between. At the very least, it is important to recognise that *intergenerational tensions* between children and adults *matter* (to both children and adults) and are therefore a key axis of difference that needs to be addressed in sustainable urban planning. Furthermore, *play* is once again a key point of articulation for such tensions.

A second series of indicative moments relates less to age than to class. As we outlined in previous chapters, there have been significant tensions both within the community (between owner-occupiers and those who live in social housing) and between the new community and the older suburban housing estate that abuts it. The two following field notes report in part on conversations with a local policy community support officer in Hettonbury (referred to as 'he' in the extracts):

> He commented that there is a 'very different feel to parts of the community, especially in [Corner Way].' There are 'smaller streets and pavements . . . your neighbours are in your face . . . there is no green space . . . and there is nowhere for children to play.' He pointed to [a particular] area of the development and commented, 'the landscaping and everything is much nicer over there. With regard to this last comment, he suggested that the [Corner Way] section of the development feels very much isolated and separate because developers pulled out of building around The Square.
>
> *(Field notes, Hettonbury)*

> One area of [Corner Way] is a magnet for young people, an open courtyard, ideal for playing in. However, this backs onto the older community. There have been some problems with the divide between the old and the new. People from the new development were climbing over the walls as a cut

**166** Childhood and play

> through to the petrol garage, instead of walking all the way around. To stop this 'the developer made the wall higher.' He also said, referring to those who live in the older estate, 'a lot of them have come round to it . . . before they were very stand-off ish.'
>
> *(Field notes, Hettonbury)*

Once again, playing and living are ineluctably entwined. Yet playing is not a secondary concern in this process. Rather, it is a key point of articulation for a cutting series of reflections about how the very *design* of Hettonbury seems to mark out class differences. Although the first extract (with reference to 'nowhere to play') takes a narrower definition of play than we do here, the point is that public spaces in this part of the community do not appear to be child-friendly and add to a sense of isolation. In the second extract, the courtyard space that is 'ideal for playing in' is also located at a flashpoint between the old and new communities.

In the above examples, play is entrained in, and should heighten our attention to, two considerations that form keystones for any *socially* sustainable urban place (Chapter 3). In terms of the first example, the status of play is used to raise a wider critique about the *density* of new urban places, where in the UK there has been a clear emphasis upon increasing housing density and reducing space for gardens and car parking. In terms of the second, a popular playspace is proximate to the boundary between old and new communities. We know from our research that there is only one pedestrian connection between the two communities and, therefore, that *connectivity* between neighbourhoods (whether of different or similar ages) is a key consideration – both for avoiding social tensions and for ensuring the walkability of urban spaces.

We finish this section by reflecting briefly on two examples taken from elsewhere in the world. Firstly, we explore how notions of the 'ludic city' (Stevens, 2007) and 'loose spaces' (Ameel and Tani, 2012) might be re-interpreted in terms of the more formal design of sustainable urban spaces. Moreover, it is here that children – and especially older young people – re-enter the equation. Like other authors (Borden, 2001; Mould, 2009), Ameel and Tani (2012) offer a critical analysis of alternative practices of urban movement, such as skateboarding and parkour. They argue that parkour practitioners in Helsinki, Finland, 'loosen' the spaces of the city by (re)negotiating assumptions, rules and rights in and about urban public spaces. In contrast to 'tight spaces' – with only one well-defined use – this loosening takes place through the experimental, contingent, embodied, creative and playful encounters that parkour practitioners have with the material and built environment of the city. This behaviour, Ameel and Tani argue, can cause questioning, confusion and bewilderment among onlookers and, like Situationist and other arts of urban exploration before that (Pinder, 2011), may cause some city dwellers to engage in a reappraisal of their preconceptions about the utility of urban space. Ameel and Tani note that in their study it was generally *children* who were most accommodating of and tolerant towards parkour practitioners in city spaces.

Reflecting on the arguments about the child/play dyad with which we began this chapter, there is a crucial point here. That is, that play does not have to originate *from* children at all, but that – for a diversity of reasons – children and young people appear to be accepting of alternative and potentially progressive forms of play – whether the laughter of ethnically diverse social groups (Bennett et al., 2017) or the performance of parkour. Of course, we should not assume that children and young people are *essentially* more accepting of social difference than adults – indeed, some studies have shown the reverse (e.g. Valentine et al., 2015). Therefore, we should be continually vigilant in our critical considerations of the spaces between childhood and play.

Nevertheless, Ameel and Tani's work begins to open out questions as to how we might re-imagine the space between *childhood* (in this case, becoming child-like) and *play* in sustainable city spaces. In these ways, one might engage further forms of social difference that exceed identity categories such as age, class or ethnicity but, rather, are encapsulated by performances or subcultural groupings. Such an engagement might not mean designing *for* skateboarding or parkour or any particular 'alternative' urban practice *per se*. Rather, as Stratford (2016: 355) puts it in her critical engagement with street skating in Australia and the USA: '[i]t is absolutely feasible to build into the fabric of cities' enclaves and armatures more diversely playful spaces and "sacrificial zones" . . . capable of wearing use and possible abuse with dignity without compromising their non-ludic purpose' (citing Rawlinson and Guaralda, 2011: 22). As Stratford explains, to design in such a way as to *welcome*, rather than explicitly exclude, skateboarders and other alternative urban practitioners, might actually offer a radically different starting point for more inclusive and sustainable cities.

We return to the implications of Stratford's work in the final part of this chapter. In closing this section, however, we turn to an example of an attempt to design in a way that ties together the various strands of play and difference discussed above. We focus on an architectural practice – SNE Architects, from Denmark – whose work has the potential to open out spaces between and beyond childhood and play in some radical ways, yet whose work also has important ramifications for sustainable urban design.

SNE Architects (www.snearchitects.com) was founded in 2006 by architect Søren Nordal Enevoldsen. Enevoldsen is heavily influenced by his ongoing and active engagement as a skateboarder. His architectural practice therefore pays keen attention to the qualities of surfaces, textures, gradients and other affordances – even though he never designs spaces that are *just* 'for' skateboarders and other urban sports (Stratford, 2016). Enevoldsen aims to create beautiful places, but – in indirect accordance with the idea of 'loose spaces' – places that challenge preconceptions about how we interact with urban contexts. His aim is to 'create spaces in which play and movement take place side-by-side with rest and adventures', 'creating social sustainability [through being] confronted with the unexpected and "the others"' (SNE Architects, undated). SNE's vision of *social* sustainability is, then,

**168** Childhood and play

driven by but not exclusively centred on play: there is an ambivalence between play and rest, stasis and movement.

SNE's work in outdoor public spaces in Denmark is noteworthy because it combines a particular vision of social sustainability with one of environmental sustainability. Their design for Rabalderparken in Roskilde is exemplary in this regard (SNE Architects, 2012). The park is a large outdoor urban space comprising a series of drainage channels and reservoirs, which manage runoff from rainwater. The main purpose of this system is to deal with excess water during a potential flood event. The channels and ponds have also been designed with smooth surfaces and multiple gradients, with the intention of attracting skaters, skateboarders, BMX-ers and others during the (prolonged) periods when the system is dry. Although starting from these two principles (water management and urban sport), the park is designed to do far more:

> The overall theme of the park is a celebration of free movement and the flow of water. In addition to the skate and BMX facilities, a range of fitness equipment, trampolines etc. has been installed, as well as paths for running, parkour equipment and many other designated activities. But the park is also [a] place for quiet rest, recreation and slow activities such as walking the dog. The city park is a *generous space*, where activity and recreational needs meet.
>
> *(SNE Architects, 2012; emphasis added)*

While we would be careful not to position the Rabalderparken as an exemplar to simply be mimicked in other contexts (even within Roskilde itself), it nevertheless provides an excellent illustration of how the themes that we have explored in this section of the chapter might be woven together. It is a purposely designed 'loose space', which begins with an ethos of play, but in which (particular kinds of especially spectacular) urban play form but *part* of a rich tableau of possible uses. Although an attractive space for children, and designed with them in mind, it is a multi-generational space that offers an alternative way of engaging with social difference (through the ambivalence of play/rest). Moreover, social and environmental notions of sustainability are combined into the formal design of an urban space. We pick up SNE's explicit reference to 'generosity' in the final part of this chapter, in which we focus on the (possible) politics of vitality.

## Playing and childhood and . . . the politics of vitality?

In this final section, we revisit questions of politics that detained us in previous chapters. As in earlier sections of this chapter, we consider how (micro-)political challenges enter into and produce the space between *play* and *childhood*. In doing so, we raise further questions about the *vitalities* of urban spaces, anticipating the broader arguments in Chapter 9. We consider three ways in which play is entangled

Childhood and play **169**

with/in politics: play and micro-politics; play and resistance; play and presumptive generosity. We draw briefly on material from the NUNC project but supplement that with examples from elsewhere.

Our first observation – which is ostensibly a reminder of arguments elsewhere in the book – is that play is entangled with and constitutive of the 'ordinary' *micro-politics* of urban life (Kallio and Häkli, 2011b, 2013). We have reported on manifold forms of citizenship, participation and politicised critique in which children were engaged. In Chapter 4, we highlighted ways in which children were acutely aware of developers' 'promises', and their tangible disappointment at delays, malfunctions and failures. In Chapters 6 and 7, we highlighted some of the power relations and politics through which children and young people made a contribution to the lives of their growing communities. Following the argument we introduced in Chapter 4, our relatively straightforward assumption is that these kinds of reflections and critiques do not only emerge from conversations with parents or EfS at school. Rather, they *also* emerge in and through children's play: through their everyday acts of 'just walking' (Chapter 5); through playing in the SUDS and with other aspects of sustainable technology (Chapter 4); and through the everyday interactions with social difference that we discussed in this chapter and Chapters 6 and 7. Such critiques are neither solely the property of children nor uniquely emergent from play. Instead, they emerge from the manifold, complex and emergent spaces *between* childhood and play.

Our second observation is that such micro-political acts sometimes spill over into moments that may appear to constitute '*resistance*', subversion, or dissonance (for useful critical discussions of the relationship between play and activism, see Routledge, 2012; Price, 2015). One example derives from the playground in Hettonbury:

> Initially there were five boys and one girl playing in the inner playground (some still dressed in their school uniform). The boys were playing football and the girl was standing watching. They kept kicking the ball out of the playground, either into the outer area, or onto the street. To retrieve the ball they would leap over the fencing, rather than enter and exit via the gate.
>
> *(Field notes, Hettonbury)*

Like this vignette, such acts may be virtually hidden or 'implicit' – their political significance and efficacy questionable (Horton and Kraftl, 2009b). As Zembylas summarises:

> These modest forms of activism may not leave much (representational) trace but extend the field of activism and open more possibilities for schools to get involved with pragmatic everyday actions that make a contribution to social justice causes rather than assuming that activism is only about the grandiose and the iconic.
>
> *(Zembylas, 2013: 85)*

**170** Childhood and play

The vignette above provides just one of literally thousands of examples of banal, everyday moments that 'matter' somehow, and which we may or may not classify as 'political'. This activity (repeated over and over again) was one of many small acts of apparent transgression that simply constituted the flux of children's lives: we doubt whether the children hopping the fence were thinking 'resistance' when they went to retrieve their ball. When children told us – smirks on faces – that they shared the gateway security codes to enter each other's courtyards so that they could play there, we would not be completely persuaded that they were thinking 'subversion' at the time. When, as we discussed in Chapter 7, groups of teenagers 'broke in' to The Square in Hettonbury before it opened, we could not be certain that they were thinking 'dissonance' or intending that The Square be opened for the entire community. In the four NUNC communities – as in many other contexts – children were engaged in ongoing, usually low-level power struggles, tensions, acts of mockery, transgression, cheekiness, silliness and more.

Many of these acts may appear 'playful' or a component of children's play (Henricks, 2015). Yet they signal a particular kind of ambivalence and ambiguity about theorisations of power and resistance that are apparently so minor that they are (almost) unremarkable, especially in contrast with other, more overt and spectacular forms of youth agency and protest (e.g. Juris and Pleyers, 2009). Therefore, we are caught in a further trap here in our very efforts to name – albeit tentatively – these apparently nonrepresentational, everyday acts. As Philo and Smith (2013: 142) argue, the politics (with a small 'p') of nonrepresentational children's geographies, apparently beyond adult purview, may be doomed to being a 'much-filtered projection of adult concerns'. Rather, 'maybe the "political" charge for adults concerned with children . . . is precisely to ensure the possibilities for children . . . to remain outwith "politics"' (ibid.).

Our response to this (insightful) charge is twofold. On one hand, we agree, although observe that in partitioning off politics from childhood – even in some circumstances – that gap may be back-filled by the kinds of universalising, essentialising constructions of childhood (and especially of their playfulness) that we discussed in opening this chapter. On the other, we would deploy the ambiguity of play to introduce a twist to Philo and Smith's argument. We would argue that the political charge is to ensure possibilities for opening out politics – and, especially, politics of vitality – in the spaces *between* childhood and play. In order to illustrate this argument, we take two examples – not from the NUNC project but from the United States and Mexico. Neither example is expressly concerned with sustainable urbanism, but each bears some important implications for how we might conceive sustainable urban vitalities.

The first example is taken from the US–Mexican border, where Bosco (2010) focuses on what we might for shorthand term the 'agency' of children who have crossed into the United States with their mothers. Clearly, such acts of cross-border migration can be perilous, and in that context, Bosco identifies a range of entwined activities, undertaken by children, which are usually considered

Childhood and play **171**

separately: 'play', 'work' and 'activism'. Instead, he cites several examples of where these three kinds of performance – and far more besides – combine in children's everyday lives. Children support their mothers in a range of ways: because they speak English and Spanish, they facilitate interactions with representatives at banks, government offices and other institutions; they are involved in 'car washes, rummage sales, neighbourhood clean-ups' and other activities that provide financial aid to migrant advocacy groups (Bosco, 2010: 387); and they attend and help organise celebrations and festivals. Bosco argues that children frequently engage in such activities *playfully*, or through their play, not necessarily always 'knowing' that they are doing activism, even if they are. He concludes: 'children engage with [activism and advocacy networks], both as play and as work, both as socializing and as a way to get to know other children and, knowingly or not, as part of their mothers' local political work, which becomes fused and inseparable from the children's' (ibid.: 388). In the spaces *between* and *surrounding* childhood and play, work and activism (re)combine in particular ways that – whether implicitly or not – enable children to support their families as they attempt to forge new lives in the United States. This space is, then, fundamental to attempts to carve out livelihoods – to carve out a *vital* space for lives lived on the edge.

The second example is taken from Mexico City. Crossa's (2013) work does not focus on children *per se* (although they are part of the picture): instead, she focuses on a group of artists and artisans located in Coyoacan, a neighbourhood of the city. They had been displaced as a result of attempts to 'reclaim' public spaces by Mexico City's governing authority, which made two of the most popular public squares inaccessible – not only to the artists and artisans but to tourists who had previously visited the area. This policy led to forms of resistance that mobilised 'the relationship between play, space and protest' (ibid.: 827). Akin to the concept of 'implicit activisms' (Horton and Kraftl, 2009b), Crossa argues that the groups of artisans had not originally planned to create a social movement: rather, through creating an 'alternative' (and generally youthful) culture they developed a kind of subtle, tentative oppositional consciousness that they had not even been aware of until the threat of eviction. Thereafter, this consciousness was expressed in the form of a celebratory market, which took place on one of the construction sites where previously popular public spaces were being redeveloped. The market and an associated exhibition lasted for 8 months, during which time the artists and artisans lived on site – combining their exhibition activities (banners, artwork, videos, photos) with the demands of everyday life (collaboratively feeding and looking after each other) and *play*, through a series of playful artistic workshops that engaged visitors to the area – including children. Their activities crossed play, laughter and theatrical forms of resistance with the everyday social and economic demands of artisanal life (they also supported themselves financially through the market). Crossa's analysis is significant because – in tandem with Bosco's work and

**172** Childhood and play

other examples cited in this chapter – it highlights that the space between childhood and play is a cavernous, complex and contested one. Importantly, it is one in which many of the concerns of city life – *of equitable, just and, essentially, sustainable city lives* – are played out. Children and/or play may recede into the background, but understood in the non-dualistic, non-essentialised, non-romanticised ways we argued for at the beginning of this chapter, they nevertheless provide key lynchpins for articulating richer and more diverse senses of *what matters* in the production of sustainable urban vitalities.

Going beyond the narrow confines of resistance-thinking, our argument is that the space between childhood and play is one in which the vitalities of life – and, particularly, *sustainable urban lives* – might be reimagined, potentially for the better. A final example in support of this argument is taken from one of the authors' previous research projects. The vignette presented below took place within and just outside a 'sustainable' public housing project in Vienna, Austria (published in Kraftl, 2010). The Hundertwasserhaus is a social housing block designed by the Austrian artist–architect Friedensreich Hundertwasser. It is an example of ecological architecture that acts as a 'symbol' (Jensen, 2002): it has grass roofs with tree planting, wavy, colourful walls and residents are (to a limited extent) allowed to reach out of their windows to paint whatever they like. However, the house does not incorporate many of the technologies that one would expect to see in contemporary eco-houses (Pickerill, 2015). Outside the Haus, there is a pedestrianised public area with trees, uneven paving and small, bulbous 'hills' that are intended to disrupt people's visual and haptic engagements with the space. Since its construction in 1986, the Haus has become a major tourist attraction in Vienna.

One of the authors of this book spent time outside the Haus and interviewed many of the residents. He was repeatedly struck by how residents characterised specific moments of their time at the Haus as 'paradise' or 'spiritual' or 'utopian' (Kraftl, 2010) – in particular during *playful* interactions with tourists in the public space outside the building. In one example, John recounts the first few weeks of life as a resident. The second extract – taken from the author's field notes – recounts one of many moments where children and other users of the public space outside the Haus engaged with the space playfully (and which were recounted in John's memories).[1]

> I've got to tell you about this, when we moved in, we had a flat in the other side of the building. And it was a really brilliant time, and, it was in high summer. We had a flat with a terrace – a big terrace – with cherry trees, yeah? And that was the time, we moved in in July and got married in August, yeah? And it was a heilige[2] time! And this new flat, in this extraordinary house . . . We experienced it, it felt like the whole environment was part of it . . . there was loads of work . . . but it was totally beautiful, the whole thing in the new house. . . . And I must add to that, we had a window to the north, where the tourists are, watching the children (and the adults!) running

Childhood and play **173**

up and down the hills[3] and just spending time being a bit silly. And as we had so much time, we sat there and talked with the tourists down on the street, yeah? And it was all probably a bit more than we expected.

*(John, male, aged 30, Hundertwasserhaus, Vienna)*

A young woman with a little girl comes around the . . . corner, child, holding one hand, dressed in bright pink, camera in the other. The girl gets excited upon seeing the house, constantly looking up, running onto one of the 'hills' in the pavement. The mother looks at me, smiling. . . . Another tourist catches my eye – as I turn back . . . the mother takes a picture of the girl. Then they wander up the steps of the café, stay on the terrace a few minutes, come back down, and disappear under the arch.

*(Field notes, Hundertwasserhaus, Vienna)*

There are many possible ways to interpret the (admittedly rather different) experiences of young people in the NUNC project and residents and tourists at the Hundertwasserhaus. Yet they are tied together by empirical observations about *welcome* and *encounter*, and by the posthuman, postfeminist notion of presumptive generosity: 'of rendering oneself more open to . . . other selves and bodies and [being] more willing and able to enter into productive assemblages with them' (Bennett, 2001: 131). In Hettonbury, out of the complex, everyday multitude that constitutes play emerged small-scale but important act of welcome (Chapters 6 and 7). At the Hundertwasserhaus, out of the complex assemblage of moving in, high summer, the cherry trees, the 'extraordinary house', and the sheer, weighty *presence* of thousands of tourists outside, came a banal but nevertheless remarkable act of hospitality, as John and his partner chose to engage with tourists who have become (for some residents) an intense annoyance.

Building on our arguments in previous sections, we contend that such moments of presumptive generosity emerge out of the complex socio-material encounters generated by play – especially, but not only, when children are engaged. These arguments relate to a gathering body of city-thinking. They relate to critical musings on how we might design 'looser' (Ameel and Tani, 2012) or more 'generous' spaces that act as 'sacrificial zones' that are nonetheless socially *and* materially resilient enough to bear diverse forms of play (Stratford, 2016). They also relate to attempts to think through 'light-touch' forms of planning for 'playful encounters' (Lobo, 2016). These forms of planning may take their inspiration from spaces like the ad hoc market in Coyoacan, Mexico City, or the public space outside the Hundertwasserhaus. Or, as in Lobo's (ibid.) example, they may take the form of an open-air cafe in Darwin, Australia, at which settler Europeans and Indigenous (Aborigine) Australians can interact through informal, playful encounters – sharing tables, sharing stories, sharing jokes, and sharing experiences of what it means to sit in the shade of a particular species of tree endemic to that region. For Lobo (ibid.: 166), '[s]uch vitality, intensity, and eruptive energy is productive if it encourages responsiveness and speculative thought, rather than

**174** Childhood and play

moralising judgements about how we might live with difference'. The cafe is a 'loose' space whose human and nonhuman participants are patrolled with a light touch: a playful encounter between settler Europeans, Indigenous Australians, and a lizard leads to an encounter between Northern and Southern ways of life, 'affirming the vitality of different ways or forms of life and the vibrancy of matter' (ibid.: 172). For Amin (2015), the above might all constitute ways of imagining cities as 'animated spaces' – as might the diverse examples he chooses of 'smart' city software, witchcraft in Kinshasa, and much else besides. Herein, cities are not simply sites of civic formation, based upon the simplistic interactions of apparently individuated human subjects. Rather, we might (re)imagine and (re)trace the city as eventful, and more-than-human – 'the urban landscape as sentient in its own right, as a hum of interacting humans and nonhumans that exceeds and performs its occupants' (ibid.: 239), wherein the space between childhood and play could be a particularly forceful constituent.

But what are the implications of these theoretical notes for *designing* sustainable cities? Returning to Elaine Stratford's work (and that of SNE Architects in Denmark) – it may mean creating spaces that invite skaters – but also invite play by all manner of urban others, too. It may mean a reduction in the spatial dominance of the car, as a way to foster elements of playfulness and conviviality (Chapter 5). It may mean engaging with more diverse political agendas (of the human and nonhuman) about what it means to be mobile or static, playful or not, in the city. It may mean attention to people from diverse age groups (perhaps especially children). And it may mean recognising that all of these things may not only mean a more tangible sense of *social* sustainability, but *environmental* sustainability and justice too – perhaps acting as trigger points to reduce carbon emissions or energy use through looser (but not necessarily less 'smart') design. None of these suggestions are necessarily 'anti-design' or 'anti-technology', but geared towards a radical shift in terms of how we conceive and move through cities, recognising that, as per some of the earliest definitions of *sustainability*, '"giving up" is not always about loss but about opening spaces for new ways of being' (Stratford, 2016: 355).

## Conclusion

We have – as we promised in Chapter 2 – ended this chapter with an affirmative, yet critical, stance that neither romanticises nor dismisses play, but seeks to forge a space both somewhere between and somewhere else. Ours is not an uncritical endorsement of the examples cited in this chapter as forms of 'blueprint' from which more sustainable cities might emerge; nor is in an unreserved celebration of the spaces – the cafes, markets, drainage channels, urban squares – that have illustrated our arguments. We recognise that these spaces have their own problems, power relations and exclusions; and that some of these examples represent rarefied or ephemeral 'moments' – perhaps of euphoria or escape.

However, we want to retain the affirmative mindset that has underpinned this chapter because it speaks of both the importance and ambiguity of play as a

Childhood and play **175**

constituent of potentially more vital, sustainable urban spaces. What we are advocating, then, is – as part of a theory of sustainable urban vitality in constant conversation with an interdisciplinary childhood studies – a *critical affirmation* of a more playful set of dispositions to urban life, understood specifically through the space(s) between childhood and play.

We have critically considered how the ambiguous, contested, complex, more-than-social spaces between childhood and play might open up new conceptualisations in the generation of sustainable urban *vitalities*. Specifically, this conceptualisation comprised four components, each ambiguous, and each prompted by the suffix 'playing and childhood and . . .'. First, a sense that play is constituted by and constitutive of everyday social relations – of other concerns, like identity. Second, a sensitivity to the more-than-human entanglements at play *in play*, and their relatedness to questions of responsibility – for a community, or for a more sustainable future. Thirdly, an acknowledgement of play as simultaneously wrapped up as a means of expression for, and a possible solution to, social differences and tensions. Finally, in bringing these disparate themes together, play (and childhood) presages important and novel forms of political disposition – of resistance, subversion, dissonance and activism – that might sometimes be stunningly banal, but nevertheless might *matter*, profoundly.

In closing, we note that play retains its uncertain status – and that that is why any generative theory of sustainable urban vitality cannot be focused on play alone. Yet, if we reconfigure play as an emergent co-production of scales, bodies, affects, objects, spaces and histories (Lester and Russell, 2014), it may be possible to create spaces that are more inclusive and that foster health and well-being for human *and* nonhuman inhabitants. This should be (part of) the aim for creating more vital urban places, wherein, rather than targeting individuals, 'attention is given to the *conditions* that constitute health-enabling spaces [that] intra-actively and indeterminately produce moments of care and reciprocity', through play (ibid.: 255). If, 'for the time of playing, life is simply more vibrant' (ibid.), then ours is an argument for a careful, critical but affirmative consideration of what children's play might mean for a broader theory of urban vitality.

It is neither play, nor childhood, nor some reductive dualistic conception of the two that matters here. Rather, *in the spaces between (and beyond) play and childhood*, we gain a heightened sense of what it might mean to foster sustainable urban vitalities. A focus on the spaces between play and childhood might enable collectives of academics, politicians, professional practitioners and communities to raise powerful questions, and tell more compelling stories, about how we seek to raise children in and live with a thoroughly entangled world, without losing a sense of how that world is patterned by exclusions, boundaries and stoppage points to the flux of life-itself (Taylor et al., 2013). The *vital* encompasses challenges of survival, livelihood, lifestyle, resilience, activism, (more-than-)social justice, enjoyment, laughter, (more-than-)social difference, the everyday mundane and the extraordinary, a sense of well-being, and so much more. We have highlighted in this chapter how play matters, to all of these challenges.

**176** Childhood and play

## Notes

1 The interview quotation and field note are lightly edited versions of extracts appearing in Kraftl (2010).
2 The original interview was undertaken in German. The German translation of 'heilige' is rather complex: it can mean holy (in the Christian sense), spiritual or moving. Colloquially, it can also be used to denote a time or place of euphoric intensity or heightened pleasure.
3 Hills is a literal translation of 'Hügeln' – referring to the undulating rises and valleys in the pavement outside the Haus.

# 9

# CONCLUSION

## Towards a theory of children and sustainable urban vitalities

### Engaging with children and young people in sustainable urban spaces

Through this book we have evidenced how an international turn towards 'sustainable' modes of urban planning and development continues to constitute new types of urban space and new experiences of childhood and youth, and – consequently – profoundly important new questions for researchers, practitioners, policy-makers, planners and professionals working in diverse urban contexts. The array of case studies featured in this book provides some indication of the remarkably pervasive, enduring and internationalised concept of sustainable urbanism, which has underpinned so many sites of urban change and expansion over the last three decades. As we noted in Chapter 3, canonical antecedents and exemplars of sustainable urbanism are widely cited (see, for example, case studies on UK Garden Cities and New Towns, or the iconic urban spaces of Curitiba and Malmö), policy/planning discourses and models envisioning sustainable urban development are internationally hailed (see, for example, case studies on the Freiburg Charter and the Egan wheel), and more recently large-scale infrastructure projects in the Majority World are being badged as smart and sustainable, promoting liveability and urban well-being (see the case study on Indian Smart Cities).

However, we have argued that, although much existing scholarship has studied policy discourses and planning visions of sustainable urbanism, surprisingly little attention has been paid to the diverse *actually-existing* urban spaces, communities and experiences constituted via policies and visions of sustainable urbanism. Most markedly, we have critiqued the remarkable lack of attention that has, to date, been paid to children and young people's everyday presences, mobilities, experiences and participations within these actually existing spaces of sustainable urbanism. Given the proliferation of policies and articulations of sustainable urbanism,

**178** Conclusion

we can ask questions such as: how are new urban spaces which are promoting walkability and safe transit zones impacting on children and young people's safe outdoor mobility? How do children, young people and their families experience diversity in mixed-housing tenure developments? How is social sustainability being promoted and advocated – what possibilities do children and young people have to participate in decision-making in their communities? Given the investment in sustainable urbanism in diverse contexts around the world, children are growing up in these new spaces and their affectual, embodied relations are *part* of the process of community-building and the lived experience of sustainable urbanisms.

Against this grain, our interdisciplinary New Urbanisms, New Citizens project entailed a four-year programme of careful mixed-method ethnographic research, with 175 people aged 9–16 living in four contrasting sustainable urban developments in south-east England. As we outlined in our Introduction, these case studies were diverse in terms of their size, conceptualisation, populations and planning histories. However, in common with most sustainable urban spaces, both in the UK and elsewhere (see Chapter 3), they shared particular characteristic material, infrastructural, architectural and planned features. Indeed, we have observed that sustainable urban spaces are, in practice, characterised by some very specific and globally widespread (albeit locally interpreted and patterned) in-built planning interventions relating to *sustainable urban architectures*, urban *mobility and connectivity*, and community *participation, liveability and conviviality*. Spatial interventions of this kind were focal concerns of Chapters 4–8, where we have evidenced a recurring constitutive tension between the intended aims of sustainable planning interventions and the (often unanticipated) ways in which newly built sustainable urban spaces are experienced and lived with in practice.

Throughout our analyses, and although we have attended to adult and non-human 'Others', we have emphasised the importance of focusing upon the experiences, emotions, mobilities, play and political agency of *children and young people*. Through a range of empirical insights, taken from the NUNC project and beyond, we have sought to develop and exemplify an interdisciplinary conceptual framework for childhood studies that can, in turn, respond to the challenges of building sustainable urban places (this framework is summarised in the last part of this chapter). For example, Chapter 4 showed how the incorporation of sustainable architectural features into large-scale housing developments has generally normalised some 'environmentally friendly' technologies and behaviours among resident families, but has also generated a series of troubling rumours, misapprehensions and 'urban myths'. Similarly, Chapter 5 evidenced how planning interventions intended to foster neighbourhood walkability did appear to afford considerable outdoor play and mobilities in the four communities, but nevertheless also constituted some profound anxieties and tensions among children and young people and their families. In Chapters 6 and 7 we evidenced attempts to manufacture spaces of sustainable urban *vitality*; to some extent these spaces did constitute opportunities for neighbourly and intergenerational senses of belonging and citizenship but also afforded a range of social, spatial and deeply felt exclusions, *particularly* among children and young people. In Chapter 8, we advanced an argument for deeper attention to play – not as some romanticised activity that is the sole preserve of children, but as something conjoined to childhood and youthful experiences in myriad ways that are productive of urban vitalities.

Running through the empirical and conceptual discussions in Chapters 4–8 is a strong, recurring sense of the ambivalent, contradictory – and ultimately effectively marginalised – presence of children and young people within the planning and formal politics of new sustainable urban developments. On one hand, we have noted how policy discourses and planning visualisations often prominently feature (very particular) representations of children and families in the constitutive visioning of sustainability, transport and liveability within new urban communities. On the other hand, across each chapter, we have evidenced how children and young people are often rendered invisible and marginal in the practical planning and regulation of new sustainable urban spaces: through the formal and familial policing of pedestrian mobilities; through their unanswered questions about the eco-architectural materialities which constituted their communities; through the exclusionary operations of designated community spaces; through the typically limited provision of play, leisure or social spaces for older children (above 8 years old); and, above all, through the typically profoundly limited extant opportunities for children and young people to participate in formal processes of neighbourhood planning and decision-making.

This latter point is especially important. An axiomatic finding of our study is that children and young people have a huge amount of local knowledge of – and are profoundly important in constituting everyday, embodied, emotionally charged socialities and vitalities within – new urban spaces; but unfortunately these knowledges and capacities are often seriously underestimated by planners and policy-makers working in the contexts of large-scale urban sustainable development. A great joy of working in the case study communities has been to witness diverse children and young people's generosity in sharing their rich, detailed, opinionated and insightful observations, stories and knowledges of these newly built urban spaces. At the same time, it has been greatly disappointing and even sad to fully appreciate just how rarely their wealth of intimate experiences and expertise on their own lives (including the built, natural and social relationships in their community) is meaningfully engaged with by local, regional or national stakeholders in sustainable urban development. In too many instances (and across most of the themes discussed in this book) we found that planners, local policy-makers, residence associations and other professionals seemed not to have significantly explored how children and young people's local expertise might be useful – indeed, integral – to the development of sustainable urbanisms. Research considering children and young people's participation in community decision-making (Hart, 2013; Matthews, 2001; den Besten et al., 2008; Percy-Smith and Thomas, 2008) in diverse contexts has repeatedly found that urban planners and policy-makers frequently feel that they do not know where or how to begin in undertaking this kind of engagement. As one concluding resource, we offer Box 9.1 – a set

**180** Conclusion

of practical, evidence-based prompts which we hope will prompt further work to engage children and young people in affirmative participatory work in relation to sustainable urban spaces.

---

**BOX 9.1 EVIDENCE-BASED PROMPTS FOR FUTURE PARTICIPATORY WORK WITH CHILDREN AND YOUNG PEOPLE IN THE PLANNING, DESIGN AND BUILDING OF SUSTAINABLE URBAN SPACES**

**Involving children and young people in urban policy and planning**

- How might those who are responsible for the design and development of new urban places create time and space to engage with, and learn from, children and young people?
- How might each of us, whether, planner, architect, teacher, parent or researcher, collaborate to facilitate this kind of engagement?
- How can those responsible for the design and implementation of sustainable urban technologies capitalise on the curiosity and 'buzz' surrounding eco-friendly forms of design and architecture in new communities?
- How can teachers, youth workers and others facilitate learning about sustainable urban architectures, through the creation of new learning resources (e.g. through school visits and lesson plans, or interpretative leaflets and boards) or public engagement activities (e.g. through visits to community centres, youth groups, residents' associations)?
- How can diverse groups of people (both children and adults) become involved in teaching, learning and information sharing about new technologies? What roles do we have in providing: more accessible guidance regarding the usage of innovative technologies and features; timely updates about ongoing issues with architectural and technological innovations; information countering common misconceptions and urban myths; procedures to attend to residents' complaints and concerns about new technologies?

**Involving children and young people in transport and mobility planning**

- How could children and young people be more involved in trialling, monitoring and maintaining of transport and mobility planning schemes?

Conclusion **181**

- How might education and engagement activities around innovative street or 'shared surface' layouts be more effective in developing the 'street literacy' of: local residents, especially parents/carers (e.g. through information leaflets, posters, communication via residents' associations); drivers (e.g. through signage clarifying expectations and speed limits); and children and young people (e.g. through visits to local schools).

## Fostering community development with children and young people

- What kinds of community building projects are feasible in new urban developments? What opportunities might be supported through partnerships with local voluntary organisations or education providers? How might diverse groups of people (across all ages) be involved in the setting up, running, maintenance and delivery of community infrastructures?
- How can community infrastructures be visualised and planned in the initial development plans? Is there potential to 'leave space' for the new community to shape their own community infrastructures?
- How might activities such as community arts or archaeological projects, community clubs and activities, or events (e.g. opening of a community centre, an annual fête) be supported, and how might children and young people's involvement be facilitated?
- How might community building projects be made more inclusive (e.g. to all ages and parts of the community)?
- What practices of planning, design and community development might be helpful in developing community connectivity and forestalling social exclusions and divisions in newly built communities?
- What roles do teachers and schools have in being 'the glue' that holds the community together in the initial stages of community development?

## Making community decision-making more accessible for children and young people

- How can future residents be involved from the outset in the designing and planning of community spaces?
- How might community leaders be open to the views and experiences of young people living in their community? What resources might be needed to facilitate these engagements?
- How can we best communicate with children and young people using language and forms of communicative practices that are not necessarily based on meetings – and verbal communication only?

- How can formal spaces of community politics and decision-making be made more welcoming, accessible and engaging for children and young people?

### Developing play/ful and liveable spaces with children and young people

- How can children and young people be involved in shaping play/ful spaces in the new development?
- How might spaces be 'left over' for creative, unstructured play by children, young people and adults?
- How might play spaces be accessible for all, considering design, cost, mobility and geography?
- How could designers, architects and planners be open to the possibility of playful encounters with nonhuman Others?

## New urbanisms, new childhoods, new questions: an interdisciplinary framework for childhood studies and sustainable urbanisms

Our sustained encounter with 175 children and young people living in new urban spaces – and with a range of diverse global case studies – has enabled us to articulate some much broader challenges for multidisciplinary studies of childhood and youth, particularly, but not only, within the contexts of sustainable urban design. Most immediately, our experiences have led us to call for more careful, interdisciplinary research, scholarship and practice with children and young people in diverse new urban spaces (Christensen et al., 2011; Hadfield-Hill, 2013; Horton et al., 2013, 2014; Kraftl et al., 2013; Kraftl, 2014). While urban childhoods have been a long-standing concern of multidisciplinary childhood studies or NSSC (Ward, 1978; Christensen and O'Brien, 2003; Hörschelmann and van Blerk, 2013; Skelton and Gough, 2013), we argue that there remains an urgent need for research with children and young people in changing and shifting urban spaces, particularly given the unprecedented proliferation of newly built, rapidly expanding, regenerated or socially-materially-economically reconfigured urban spaces in so many global contexts (Hadfield-Hill, 2016).

At the time of writing, the UK government announced the development and delivery of fourteen new Garden Villages encompassing 48,000 homes – with emphasis not only on the delivery of much needed housing provision, but the creation of communities (DCLG, 2017). At the same time, but on a larger scale, ninety cities in India have been selected for Smart City investment (Government of India, 2017), whether it be the redevelopment of existing city spaces, the development of greenfield sites or pan-city approaches. In these contexts and others, including the Chinese Sustainable Cities Programme (UN-Habitat, 2009) and an array of European urban development programmes (Lafferty, 2001; HCA, 2009), new spaces, new infrastructures, new communities are being formed – shaping millions of children and young people's everyday experiences. This international context of sustainable urbanism is presaging processes, spaces, politics, discourses, emotions and materialities – ultimately, urban *vitalities* – that are being imagined and often replicated across contexts. This context affords new possibilities for young people's lives, but also challenges – possibilities and challenges which cross-cut childhood into the family, community and wider urban life. As we have noted through the preceding chapters, these programmes are proving significant in the contemporary social-political discursive construction of childhood and youth, constituting a particular, pervasive, normative sense of children and young people's mobilities, behaviours and citizenship. Given that – as we have shown – children and young people are some of the predominant users of and contributors to urban public lives, it is striking that, all too often, the processes of sustainable urban planning and policy-making seem to marginalise and limit children and young people's formal participation in community development, while also (often counter-intentionally) constituting spaces of unanticipated *vitality*, agency and community life. Through this book we have sought to foreground these latter spaces, evidencing children and young people's important roles, capacities and knowledges in relation to the social-materialities of new urban communities. This foregrounding constitutes a demand to recognise, value and engage with children and young people's everyday expertise in future research and practice relating to sustainable urban spaces.

Beyond this immediate thematic and empirical demand, we suggest that the preceding chapters should open out some wider challenges for *theorisations* of childhood, youth and sustainable urbanism. The everyday urban inhabitations, mobilities, knowledges, emotions, materialities, narratives and participations witnessed through this book seem to us to speak directly, and critically, to key lines of debate with what some are terming a 'new wave' of childhood studies scholarship, introduced in Chapter 2. As outlined in our introductory chapters, work within this context has characteristically been framed by engagements with new materialist, nonrepresentational and posthumanist theorisations of: mobility; othering, intersectionality and intergenerationality; emotion/affect; embodiment; and materialities, biopolitics and nonhuman natures. In closing the book, and in drawing together the arguments that we have developed throughout the previous eight chapters, we offer a critical re-engagement with these lines of theoretical work, returning to our five framing questions (Chapter 2). In each case, we argue that these questions are critically recast and extended via careful, interdisciplinary engagements with children and young people, as in the New Urbanisms, New Citizens project. Collectively, we suggest that these interlinked reflections – bringing children and young people's everyday narratives into conversation with scholarly theorisations of movements, (social) differences, embodiments, feelings, materialities and nonhuman natures – should constitute the basis for more careful, sustained, critical interdisciplinary engagements with children and young

**184** Conclusion

people's *vitalities* in diverse settings – but particularly in the context of globalising movements towards sustainable urban design.

## Mobile vitalities: in what ways can we conceive of mobilities as core to the vitalities of sustainable urbanism?

In Chapter 5 we noted that contemporary academic, policy and popular discourses in Europe and North America have normatively framed children and young people's mobilities in terms of anxieties about *im*mobility, and in terms of individualised 'independent' mobilities. However, our encounters with children and young people during the New Urbanisms, New Citizens project and elsewhere have prompted us to think critically about these prevalent individualised and anxiety-ridden assumptions (Christensen and Mikkelsen, 2009; Horton et al., 2014). It is true that, in our four case study communities, family lives were principally auto-mobile, and children and young people's pedestrian mobilities were profoundly regulated and restricted. However, despite this, we find that our data are *full* of mobilities. Everyday mobilities – of different types, durations and scales – were absolutely core to our participants' narratives in practically every aspect of the project. However, these discussions were both implicitly and explicitly about mobility describing their goings-on, their playful activities, their routines and interactions with human and nonhuman Others. In Chapter 4, for example, we showed how young people recounted routines with eco-technologies in their homes and communities, walking past Code Level 6 houses on the way to school, using the swales of the SUD system to leap, jump, set challenges and be the stage for games with friends and siblings, or seeking out favourite spots to search for insects or tadpoles and to interact with the biodiversity of life – their mobile bodies co-present with the materialities of these technologies. Similarly, in discussions of community life (Chapter 6), citizenship (Chapter 7) or play (Chapter 8), many participants detailed their daily pedestrian practices and the gestures of generosity or exclusion done or experienced through walking-itself. There were examples of where walking brought people together with friends crafting routes to collect one another on their way to school for example, but other times and spaces where walking further perpetuated social divides and feelings of exclusion – with participants anxious about walking in certain areas of the development in fear of the 'Other' and feeling 'out of place'.

Reflecting upon these data, our challenges for ('new wave'), interdisciplinary childhood studies are threefold. First, how can multidisciplinary scholarship move beyond a normative presumption of, and an uncritical reproduction of anxious discourses about childhood immobility? How might we acknowledge and engage with the manifold mobilities that evidently do exist and matter, even in spaces where children's independent mobility is tightly regulated? Second, how can multidisciplinary scholarship move beyond an often-unquestioned focus upon children and young people's *independent* mobilities, to productively acknowledge the complex constellations of people, things, technologies, animals and more which constitute everyday urban vitalities? As we have shown, people and things move and are made mobile by each other, sometimes for each other and often against each other; the consequences of the affectual relations between bodies, objects, things, nonhuman Others are diverse, and P/political in both formal and informal senses (Chapter 7). Each moment of our lives, when walking to school, when playing out, when just-walking, happens in a time and space where mobile Others have the power to affect and be affected. Young people in our research spoke about the diverse ways they were affected by the mobilities of human and nonhuman Others, whether it be the dragonfly which had just landed on the retention pond, the snow lying around a wind turbine, the flick of a curtain in a neighbour's house or a glance from another young person. How we unpack and make sense of these entwined mobilities is important in our framing of a diversity of life in new sustainable communities. Thus, our third challenge for future scholarship in childhood studies lies in asking: how are urban planning and policy-making processes productive of distinctive mobilities and *themselves-mobile*? In considering young people's lives it is important to understand how the global transference of sustainable urbanism is facilitating or challenging what it means to be mobile – indeed, how childhood is represented and experienced in spaces which encourage different forms of mobility.

## Vital intersectionalities: how might we re-theorise processes of othering and, especially intersectionality and intergenerationality, in order to respond to the challenge of vital thinking?

As we discussed in Chapter 2, the intellectual currents of 'new wave' childhood studies effectively constitute a rethinking of assumptions about 'identity'. Certainly, the combinative critiques of new materialist, nonrepresentational and posthumanist theories *can* be read as a fundamental critique of traditional, prior, anthropocentric identity categories. These lines of argument *could*, therefore, constitute an unsettling of normative labels for identity (gender, age, class, ethnicity, disability) and terms, like 'intergenerationality' and 'intersectionality', which posit a neat, rather additive relation between them. In theory, then, 'new wave' thinking offers a series of prompts for engaging with children and young people without necessarily having recourse to limited, problematic normative identity labels.

Like many multidisciplinary scholars swept up in this intellectual context, we have been excited by this potential for 'new wave' childhood studies to allow new, affirmative, potentially emancipatory ways of rethinking childhood and youth. However, our work with children and young people during the New Urbanisms, New Citizens project has made us rather more hesitant and critical of this kind of claim. In short, we have come to worry about the *politics* of some new materialist, nonrepresentational and posthumanist thinking; or, to be more precise, we increasingly wonder about the usefulness of 'new wave' thinking for addressing the obdurately persistent exclusionary politics predicated upon normative identity

**186** Conclusion

categories. In our case study communities, we were troubled by how quickly tensions and exclusions emerged – especially based upon age, social class and housing type – within new communities (see particularly Chapters 6–8). Within these newly built, and optimistically visioned, sustainable urban spaces, it was striking how many children and young people quickly came to (re)produce social norms, divisions, anxieties and avoidances along these lines, with explicit reference to classed and aged identity labels. Within weeks and months of being built and residents moving in, places, people and even material objects and infrastructures soon became Othered – primarily based on classed reproductions of difference. Such derogatory narratives quickly circulated among children *and* adults; particularly worrying were references to war-torn personifications of place and the 'upper' parts of places (geographically) being safer and 'nicer' than those at the 'bottom'. These divisions were vividly felt and narrated, especially by those children and young people cast as *other* or outside the community norm.

Reflecting upon these exclusions, our challenges for 'new wave' childhood studies are again threefold. First, building upon the analyses developed in this book, how might new materialist, nonrepresentational and posthumanist theories acknowledge – and develop concepts and vocabularies for critically understanding – the exclusionary, and often deeply hurtful, social geographies which continue to structure how many children, young people, and indeed their families lives? Second, how should scholarship based upon longstanding concepts such as intergenerationality and intersectionality be expanded to accommodate the compelling challenges of 'new wave' thinking in childhood studies? Third, how might 'new wave' childhood studies and social theorisations of identity, intersectionality and exclusion be brought into more generous, productive conversations with one another? This book has offered a starting point in response to all three questions: however, we would argue that additional, novel methodological approaches and interdisciplinary conversations are required to further develop these lines of inquiry.

## Emotional/affective vitalities: set against the engineering, data-based, planning and architectural knowledges required to construct sustainable urban places, what is the role of emotion and affect?

Diverse lines of 'new wave' thinking in multidisciplinary childhood studies are underpinned by an attunement to emotions and affects. Through our work – both as individuals and as a collective – we have been drawn to theorisations of emotion and affect in order to acknowledge the characteristic, but often effaced, emotional-affective complexities of children and young people's everyday lives (Christensen, 2000, 2004a; Horton and Kraftl, 2006a; Hadfield-Hill and Horton, 2014; Kraftl, 2013). Certainly, when we reflect upon our research in Hettonbury, Nannton, Romsworth and Tillinglow our data and memories *hum* with feeling. Practically every research encounter, in every part of the project, involved the narration of some kind of emotional-affective orientation to these newly built urban spaces. Some of these narratives could be coded as extremely positive or affirmative; other narratives were interpreted by us as more negative and troubling. Some of the disclosed emotions were vivid, full-on and exuberant; others were milder, modest and of a lower key. Some of our research encounters allowed us to participate in truly joyful collectivities; other moments left us feeling dismayed, discouraged, frustrated and sometimes sad. All of these ambivalent, multifarious feelings are constitutive of the vitalities of sustainable urban life, and, in part, our intention has been – through close ethnographic research with children, young people and their families – to simply pay greater attention to these vitalities.

We therefore find new wave scholarship hugely helpful in constituting spaces and vocabularies for discussing emotions/affects in/of research and in/of everyday spaces. However, through this book, and somewhat contra to much new wave scholarship, we have sought to do more than simply acknowledge that children and young people's everyday lives in new communities are emotional/affective, or that urban spaces are similarly full of emotions/affects. Rather, we have reflected, in different ways, upon the constitutive significance of emotions/affects *for sustainable, 'liveable' urbanisms* themselves. Most notably, we have explored a range of situations where everyday emotional/affective vitalities jarred with, or exceeded, the intentions of urban planners and policy-makers. For example, in Chapter 4, we evidenced how schemes to build sustainable technological features into domestic architectures had constituted a range of unintended affectivities, ranging from profound frustration to playfulness and community pride. Or, in Chapter 6 we reported how the planning of civic spaces to foster convivial cosmopolitanism constituted feelings ranging from joys of community generosity to anxious, upsetting avoidances of certain 'rough' areas of each new-built space. Indeed, in Chapter 7, in focusing on citizenship and participation, we found on the one hand young people's affectual energies to be woven into the making of communities – whilst on the other, the social and *spatial* exclusion which they experienced in the formal, ongoing community-building project was frustrating and often resulted in emotive experiences of exclusion and disappointment. Meanwhile, the case study of Hettonbury's square and other public spaces (Chapters 7 and 8) demonstrated how children and young people's playful practices can constitute transformative affective vitalities in ways that were unforeseen by urban planners and policy-makers.

These kinds of emotional/affective vitalities prompt three further challenges for 'new wave' childhood studies. First, how might new wave scholarship create opportunities and techniques for communicating emotions/affects in contexts (such as urban planning and policy-making) which have overwhelmingly and habitually prioritised other kinds of data? In short, how might we convey to urban planners and policy-makers that the kinds of narratives foregrounded in this book *matter*, profoundly, in the constitution of new urban spaces? Second, relatedly, how can we ensure that emotions/affects do not get 'lost in translation' in data analysis or the presentation of findings to diverse audiences? Our attempts to grapple with

**188** Conclusion

(the representation of) such feelings have, we would argue, been partial: we have sought, in our view successfully, to use multiple methods and forms of presentation (ethnographic vignettes, quotations, GPS data, photographs); but, as Taylor et al. (2013) demonstrate, there remains much work to be done to consider the ontological and political assumptions that underpin our efforts to witness emotions, affects and materialities in children's lives. Third, how might we engage with the set of feelings that emerged most pressingly in our research encounters: the sense that children and young people wanted *more* from adult stakeholders? As we have discussed, this kind of feeling was expressed eloquently and urgently by many participants in our project: in their desire to learn more, and understand about the workings of eco-architectures; in their acute feelings of disappointment at the apparently failed promises of planners and policy-makers; and, particularly, in their heartfelt wishes for opportunities to be more involved in community decision-making. For us, this deeply-felt set of emotions is centrally important: how might new wave scholarship *do more*, to collaborate with planners, policy-makers and other stakeholders to work more generously and productively with this set demands and desires?

## Bodily vitalities: how are the bodies of children and young people (con)figured in sustainable urbanisms?

In Chapters 3 and 6 we noted how, in one particular sense, children and young people's bodies figured prominently in the visioning of sustainable urbanisms. Certainly, in policy discourses, planning documents and advertising visualities, children's (playing, carefree, accompanied, hand-holding, well-behaved) bodies typically featured as iconic symbols of hope, futurity and viable new community. However, we have also argued that children and young people's everyday bodily presences and encounters with/in urban spaces have often been effaced within much extant literature on sustainable urbanism. The preceding chapters can, therefore, be read as an attempt to *re-embody* sustainable urbanisms, through an acknowledgement of children and young people's embodiments within particular, newly-built sites.

Reflecting on our project, we are struck by the intimacy of participants' everyday bodily encounters with urban materialities, and the detail with which these intimacies were narrated. In Chapter 5, for example, we explored some of the intimate, domestic bodily encounters which constituted experiences and opinions of eco-technologies, evidencing how these kinds of technologies were often initially perceived as 'weird', but quickly came to be part of habitual daily practices, whether individual, familial or friendship-based. Similarly, in Chapters 7 and 8 we foregrounded some bodily practices of play, and the p/Political potentials of young people's bodies, as they produced the everyday lives and socialities of new, sustainable communities. We thus evidenced how relatively microgeographical bodily practices can constitute a reshaping and rethinking of community assets, even while children's bodies are adversely affected by the construction and regulation of sustainable urban places. This potentiality is also evident in Chapter 6 through the discussion of bodily gestures of greeting (or exclusion): a process which is entwined in social politics, a politics of space, a politics of power, and, ultimately, a politics of community-building.

Throughout each chapter, despite some findings that resonate with previous research on children's engagements with/in urban public spaces, we have shown how children and young people in Hettonbury, Nannton, Romsworth and Tillinglow were extraordinarily connected to their local built environments: most appreciably through intimate daily practices of feeling, touching, observing and living with nonhuman eco-architectural forms. New wave scholarship within multidisciplinary childhood studies provides an important set of concepts for discussing bodies and embodiment, which have animated our work through this project. However, our specific focal concern with the *embodiment of sustainable urbanisms* prompts two related challenges for future scholarship inspired by the 'new wave' of childhood studies. First – given the complexity, multiplicity, intimacy and detail of children and young people's bodily encounters with everyday environments – where to begin? Or, perhaps, where to focus and at what focal distance? That is – if one accepts that everyday lives are always already embodied, and everyday spaces comprise multiple perspectives, embodiments, energies, processes and materialities – how should we decide *which* embodiments and perspectives to foreground? Ironically, we have come to feel that the radical complexity opened up by new wave thinking should require scholars to state their aims and focus with greater clarity. If all is complexly embodied, the decision about which bodies to foreground (and how to do so) becomes a personal, political and ethical question: which embodiments seem to matter to you, and why? Indeed, in asking about which bodies to foreground, we need to be open to Other bodies. Here we have focused on the bodies of children and young people, and upon their engagements with the discourses, emotions/affects and materialities of purpose-built, avowedly 'sustainable' urban spaces; but, what of the bodies of their parents?; of the disabled body which they see on their walk to school each morning?; indeed what about the bodies of other nonhuman Others that we have only partially witnessed – the cats which in some times and spaces seem to dominate the streets; the bodies of the frogs and insects which have found homes in the new SUD systems or the bodies of the bats and other protected species which have been relocated as part and parcel of the political legislation of some developments? How do we choose which bodies to focus on, give 'voice' to (Kraftl, 2013) and foreground in our unpacking of sustainable urban development?

A second challenge relates to the communication of processual and embodied complexity: if we accept that everyday embodiments are more complex than can be exhaustively described, how should we approach the task of communicating bodily complexities in our research contexts? In one sense, the opportunity to develop a sense of this complexity through the overlapping, interrelated analyses that we have developed in Chapters 4–8 has provided the physical and literal space to communicate this complexity. However, for us, this challenge

**190** Conclusion

has crystallised when planners and policy-makers have asked us (not unreasonably!) to summarise what 'feedback' or 'recommendations' children and young people gave about the case study communities. Although we have done so (with Box 9.1 above representing one such attempt), it sometimes seems difficult and reductive to derive this kind of finding from the sheer complexity, plurality and detail of participants accounts of bodily encounters with urban spaces. Through our work, we have tackled this concern by almost training ourselves to speak and write parallel languages for communication with professional stakeholders (via findings reports and briefing notes) and for academic peers (via peer-reviewed papers and conference presentations). But, again, we worry that too much gets 'lost in translation': so, how might the rich embodied complexities of new wave scholarship be communicated to audiences and publics outwith this theoretical 'in crowd'?

## Sustainable urbanisms as assemblages of more-than-human materialities: how can we take (more) seriously the theoretical, ethical and political challenge to attend to human entanglements with nonhuman materialities and natures, in the specific contexts of sustainable urbanisms?

New materialist, nonrepresentational and posthumanist lines of theory push us to acknowledge complex, contingent, always-processual relationalities that constitute any space (e.g. Rautio, 2013; Taylor et al., 2013; Kullman, 2015). Through this book, and through engagements with these theorisations, we have developed an argument that understandings of sustainable urbanism should be radically expanded to recognise the complex social-material assemblages which constitute them (also Hinchliffe and Whatmore, 2006; Houston et al., 2017; Franklin, 2017) and, specifically, in which *children and young people* are entangled. As we have shown in the preceding chapters, children in sustainable urban places around the world encountered, and lived with, sustainable urbanisms via a web of emotional, material, embodied, affectual relationships with people, technologies, multispecies co-presences, land, bricks, mortar, water, grass, mud, technologies, policy discourses, planners' promises, and much else besides. In Hettonbury, Nannton, Romsworth and Tillinglow, children and young people's talk and action was full of evocations of this kind of complexity. For example, bringing into focus nonhuman eco-architectural materialities was an important aspect of Chapter 4, recognising a co-agentic relationship between the human and nonhuman in co-constituting what makes urban vitalisms in practice – in the case of play around the wind turbine, bringing together into loose affiliation an eco-technology, a person's feet and the physical properties of snow. Similarly, Chapter 6 evidenced the importance of understanding mobility as always related to emotion, materialities and nonhuman co-presences, while Chapter 8 highlighted the centrality of interactions with diverse natures in constituting experiences of play and place. Indeed, there we also drew on data from India where children's interactions with diverse materialities

Conclusion **191**

were not always positive (Hadfield-Hill and Zara, 2017); a reminder that there are risks as well as opportunities associated with certain assemblages of human and nonhuman materialities, and that sustainable urban 'vitalities' need not always be affirmative, to all people, in all places.

Through the preceding chapters, we have evidenced how emergent more-than-social relationalities of new build urban spaces have sometimes fulfilled, sometimes exceeded, and sometimes confounded or contradicted the designed intentions of urban planners and policy-makers. We have explored how children and young people's lives were co-constituted in, through and with the everyday lives of sustainable urbanism; and we have come to recognise that this expanded understanding of relationalities poses some central questions for many chief social-scientific accounts of urban childhood and youth, and for the principles and presumptions of 'sustainable' urbanism itself.

In particular, and in closing, we would highlight four key questions for future scholarship, policy and professional practice. First, building upon the analyses developed in this book, what (further) kinds of new concepts, conversations and forms of research are required to develop radically expanded understandings of childhood *and* (sustainable) urbanism, including a far greater degree of more-than-human complexity? We have drawn attention to the particularities of being a child or young person, in the UK and elsewhere, living and growing up in purpose-built, sustainable urban contexts. But to what extent are those lessons transferable to other childhoods, to other social groups, and to other geographical contexts, and what (further) kinds of concepts and forms of research are required to advance such comparative agendas?

Second, what methods, topics or discussions would be useful starting points for these kinds of expanded apprehensions of childhoods (and) urbanities? For example, what kinds of methods or foci would enable greater understanding of the coming-into-being of relationalities and vitalities in newly built urban spaces? Moreover, how might it be possible for multidisciplinary childhood studies researchers to collaborate with one another, and with diverse planners and policy-makers, and beyond, to engage with this coming-into-being in not only interdisciplinary but *transdisciplinary* scholarship?

Third, how might it be possible to move beyond rather reductive, normative ways of framing questions about 'nature' or the 'environment' (as in the tethering of research about children and the environment to education for sustainability), to ask how *else* children and nature relate (also Taylor, 2013; Horton et al., 2015; Malone, 2016; Hordyk et al., 2015), and to situate children and young people as creative and inventive participants, in a world co-constituted by both humans and nonhumans (a task that we began in earnest in Chapter 4)?

Finally, if we acknowledge the radical inter-relatedness of all childhoods and urbanisms, what is the politics of this position, and where does it leave us? Again, we argue this this is ultimately an ethical-political question for each of us: in a world of relationalities and connections, where should we begin, or what should we do next (Bennett, 2010)? We would, it should be clear from this final chapter,

**192** Conclusion

advocate for further research and political engagement with *children and young people*, as long as they are not divorced from their intimate relationships with human and nonhuman others. Others would seek (rightly) to focus their research and/or policy efforts elsewhere. Nevertheless, the onus is on us – as academics, policy-makers and professional practitioners, in collaboration with appropriate, *diverse*, intergenerational, intersecting 'publics' – to make transparent, critically informed choices about which of countless relationalities matter, where, and when. Only then might we imagine, plan and build sustainable urban places that are characterised by the kinds of vitalities that the diverse inhabitants of sustainable urban places – human and nonhuman – might need and want.

# REFERENCES

Academy of Urbanism. (2012) *Freiburg Charter: Requirements on Urban Development and Planning for the Future.* Freiburg: Freiburg Office for Town Planning.

Aitken, S. C. (2001) *Geographies of Young People: The Morally Contested Spaces of Identity.* London: Routledge.

Alanen, L. (2005) Childhood as generational condition. *Childhood: Critical Concepts in Sociology* 3: 286.

Alanen, L. and Mayall, B. (2001) *Conceptualizing Child–Adult Relations.* London: Routledge.

Alexander, A. (2009) *Britain's New Towns: Garden Cities to Sustainable Communities.* London: Routledge.

Alexander, C. (2008) Safety, fear and belonging: the everyday realities of the formation of a civic identity in Fenham, Newcastle upon Tyne. *ACME* 7(2): 173–198.

Alexander, C., Ishikawa, S., Silverstein, M., Jacobson, M., Fiksdahl-King, I. and Angel, S. (1977) *A Pattern Language.* Oxford: Oxford University Press.

Ameel, L. and Tani, S. (2012) Parkour: creating loose spaces? *Geografiska Annaler: Series B, Human Geography* 94(1): 17–30.

Amin, A. (2006) The good city. *Urban Studies* 43: 1009–1023.

Amin, A. (2012) *Land of Strangers.* Cambridge: Polity.

Amin, A. (2015) Animated space. *Public Culture* 27(2): 239–258.

Anderson, B. (2009) Affective Atmospheres. *Emotion. Space and Society* 2: 77–81.

Ansell, N. (2009) Childhood and the politics of scale: descaling children's geographies? *Progress in Human Geography* 33(2): 190–209.

Ansell, N., Hadju, F., Robson, E., van Blerk, L. and Marandet, E. (2012) Youth policy, neoliberalism and transnational governmentality: a case study of Lesotho and Malawi. In P. Kraftl, J. Horton and F. Tucker (eds), *Critical Geographies of Childhood and Youth,* 43–60. Bristol: Policy Press.

Arup. (2016) *Cities Alive: Towards a Walking World.* London: AR University Press.

Barad, K. (2007). *Meeting the Universe Halfway: Quantum Physics and the Entanglement of Matter and Meaning.* Durham NC: Duke University Press.

Barker, J. (2003) Passengers or political actors? Children's participation in transport policy and the micro political geographies of the family. *Space and Polity* 7(2): 135–151.

Barker, J. (2009) Driven to distraction? Children's experiences of car travel. *Mobilities* 4: 59–76.

**194** References

Barker, J., Alldred, P., Watts, M. and Dodman, H. (2010) Pupils or prisoners? Institutional geographies and internal exclusion in UK secondary schools. *Area* 42(3): 378–386.

Barratt Homes. (2013) Hanham Hall. Retrieved on 11 July 2017 from www.barratthomes.co.uk/new-homes/south-gloucestershire/H439401-Hanham-Hall/?WT.mc_id=.

Bartos, A. E. (2012) Children caring for their worlds: the politics of care and childhood. *Political Geography* 31: 157–166.

Beck, U. (1992) *Risk Society: Towards a New Modernity*. London: SAGE Publications.

Beck, U. and Grande, E. (2010) Varieties of second modernity: the cosmopolitan turn in social and political theory and research. *British Journal of Sociology* 61: 409–443.

Bell, S. and Lane, A. (2009) Creating sustainable communities: a means to enhance social mobility. *Local Economy* 8: 646–657.

Ben-Joseph, E. (1995) Changing the residential street scene: adapting the shared street (Woonerf) concept to the suburban environment. *Journal of the American Planning Association* 61(4): 504–515.

Bennett, J. (2001) *The Enchantment of Modern Life: Attachments, Crossings, and Ethics*. Princeton, NJ: Princeton University Press.

Bennett, J. (2010) *Vibrant Matter*. Durham, NC: Duke University Press.

Bennett, K., Cochrane, A., Mohan, G. and Neal, S. (2017) Negotiating the educational spaces of urban multiculture: skills, competencies and college life. *Urban Studies* 54(10): 2305–2321.

Benwell, M. C. (2009) 'Race' or race: reflections on (self-) censorship and avoidance in research with children. *Children's Geographies* 7: 229–233.

Benwell, M. (2013) Rethinking conceptualisations of adult-imposed restriction and children's experiences of autonomy in outdoor space. *Children's Geographies* 11: 28–43.

Biddulph, M. (2001) *Home Zones: A Planning and Design Handbook*. York: Joseph Rowntree Foundation.

Biddulph, M. (2012) Street design and street use: comparing traffic calmed and home zone streets. *Journal of Urban Design* 17(2): 213–232.

Binnie, J., Holloway, J., Millington, S. and Young, C. (2005) *Cosmopolitan Urbanism*. London: Routledge.

Birkeland, J. (2012) Design blindness in sustainable development: from closed to open systems design thinking. *Journal of Urban Design* 17: 163–187.

Blaut, J. M., McCleary, G. F. and Blaut, A. S. (1970) Environmental mapping in young children. *Environment and Behaviour* 2(3): 335–350.

Blazek, M. and Kraftl, P. (2015) Introduction: children's emotions in policy and practice. In M. Blazek and P. Kraftl (eds), *Children's Emotions in Policy and Practice: Mapping and Making Spaces of Childhood and Youth*, 1–13. Basingstoke: Palgrave.

Blazek, M. and Windram-Geddes, M. (2013) Editorial: thinking and doing children's emotional geographies. *Emotion, Space and Society* 9: 1–3.

Boardman, B. (2007) *Home Truths*. London: Co-operative Bank/Friends of the Earth.

Borden, I. M. (2001) *Skateboarding, Space and the City: Architecture and the Body*. London: Berg.

Bosco, F. J. (2010) Play, work or activism? Broadening the connections between political and children's geographies. *Children's Geographies* 8(4): 381–390.

Brah, A. and Phoenix, A. (2013) Ain't I a woman? Revisiting intersectionality. *Journal of International Women's Studies* 5(3): 75–86.

Braidotti, R. (2011) *Nomadic Theory: The Portable Rosi Braidotti*. New York: Columbia University Press.

Briers R. A. (2013) Invertebrate communities and environmental conditions in a series of urban drainage ponds in eastern Scotland: implications for biodiversity and conservation value of SUDS. *CLEAN – Soil, Air, Water* 42(2): 193–200.

Bringolf-Isler, B., Grize, L., Mader, U., Ruch, N., Sennhauser, F. H., Braun-Fahrlander, C., the SCARPOL Team. (2010) Built environment, parents' perception, and children's vigorous outdoor play. *Preventive Medicine* 50(5–6): 251–256.

British Youth Council. (2014) About us: our work. Retrieved on 26 September 2014 from www.byc.org.uk/about-us/our-work.aspx.

Brown, G. (2011) Emotional geographies of young people's aspirations for adult life. *Children's Geographies* 9(1): 7–22.

Brown, M. (2012) Gender and sexuality I: intersectional anxieties. *Progress in Human Geography* 36(4): 541–550.

Bunge, W. W. (1973) The geography. *The Professional Geographer* 25(4): 331–337.

Burgess, R. and Jenks, M. (eds). (2002) *Compact Cities: Sustainable Urban Forms for Developing Countries*. London: Routledge.

CABE. (2007) *Sustainable Design, Climate Change and the Built Environment*. CABE: London.

CABE. (2008) *Civilised Streets*. London: CABE.

Cahill, C. (2000) Street literacy: urban teenagers' strategies for negotiating their neighbourhood. *Journal of Youth Studies* 3(3): 251–277.

Caillois, R. (2001) *Man, Play, and Games*. Chicago, IL: University of Illinois Press.

Catto, I. (2008) Carbon zero homes UK-style, *Renewable Energy Focus* 9(1): 28–29.

Cele, S. and van der Burgt, D. (2015) Participation, consultation, confusion: professionals' understandings of children's participation in physical planning. *Children's Geographies* 13(1): 14–29.

Chanan, G. and Miller, C. (2013) *Rethinking Community Practice: Developing Transformative Neighbourhoods*. Bristol: Policy Press.

Chawla, L. (2002) *Growing Up in an Urbanising World*. London: Earthscan.

Chawla, L. (2007) Childhood experiences associated with care for the natural world: A theoretical framework for empirical results. *Children Youth and Environments* 17(4): 144–170.

Chawla, L. and Cushing, D. (2007) Education for strategic environmental behaviour. *Environmental Education Research* 13 437–452.

Childs, C. R., Thomas, C., Sharp, S. and Tyler, N. (2010) Can shared surfaces be safely negotiated by blind and partially sighted people? Paper delivered at The 12th International Conference on Mobility and Transport for Elderly and Disabled Persons (TRANSED), Hong Kong, 2–4 June 2010.

Christensen, P. (1994) *Children as the Cultural Other*. Tema: Kinderwelten.

Christensen P. (1999) 'It hurts': children's cultural learning about health and illness. Etnofoor, Kids and Culture. *Journal of Anthropology* 12(1): 39–53.

Christensen, P. (2000) Childhood and the cultural constitution of vulnerable bodies. In A. Prout (ed.), *The Body, Childhood and Society*, 38–59. Basingstoke: Macmillan.

Christensen, P. (2003) Place, space and knowledge – children in the village and the city. In P. Christensen and M. O'Brien (eds), *Children in the City: Home, Neighbourhood and Community*, 13–28. London: Routledge.

Christensen, P. (2004a) Children's participation in ethnographic research: issues of power and representation. *Children and Society* 18(2): 165–176.

Christensen, P. (2004b) The health-promoting family: a conceptual framework for future research. *Social Science and Medicine* 59(2): 377–387.

Christensen, P. and James, A. (eds) (2000). *Research with Children: Perspectives and Practices*. London: Routledge.

Christensen, P. and Mikkelsen, M. R. (2008) Jumping off and being careful: children's strategies of risk management in everyday life. *Sociology of Health and Illness* 30(1): 112–130.

**196** References

Christensen, P. and James, A. (2017) Introduction: researching children and childhood. Cultures of communication. In P. Christensen and A. James (eds), *Research with Children: Perspectives ad Practices*, 1–10. London: Routledge.

Christensen, P. and Mikkelsen, M. (2009) Is children's independent mobility really independent? *Mobilities* 4: 37–58.

Christensen, P. and Mikkelsen, M. R. (2013) 'There is nothing here for us ..!' How girls create meaningful places of their own through movement. *Children and Society* 27(3): 197–207.

Christensen, P. and O'Brien, M. (eds) (2003) *Children in the City: Home, Neighbourhood and Community*. London: Routledge.

Christensen, P. and Prout, A. (2002) Working with ethical symmetry in social research with children. *Childhood: A Global Journal of Child Research* 9(4): 477–497.

Christensen, P., Mikkelsen, M. K., Sick Nielsen, T. and Harder, H. (2011) Children, Mobility and Space: using GPS and mobile phone technologies in ethnographic research. *Journal of Mixed Methods Research* 19(5): 227–246.

Cochrane, A. (2010) Exploring the regional politics of 'sustainability': making up sustainable communities in the south-east of England. *Environmental Policy and Governance* 20: 370–381.

Cochrane, A., Colenutt, B. and Field, M. (2014) *Spatial Policy, Urban Extensions and Volume House-Building: Lessons from a Growth Region*. Milton Keynes: Open University. Retrieved on 11 July 2017 from www.open.ac.uk/researchprojects/tensionsandprospects/commu nication-outputs/working-papers.

Cockburn, T. (1998) Children and citizenship in Britain: a case for a socially interdependent model of citizenship. *Childhood* 5(1): 99–117.

Cohen, S. (1972) *Folk Devils and Moral Panics: The Creation of the Mods and Rockers*. London, MacGibbon & Kee.

Collins, R. (2015) Keeping it in the family? Re-focusing household sustainability. *Geoforum* 60: 22–32.

Conroy, J. C. (2010) The state, parenting, and the populist energies of anxiety. *Educational Theory* 60(3): 325–340.

Cook, D. T. (2016) Disrupting play: a cautionary note. *Childhood* 23(1): 3–6.

Cook, V. A. and Hemming, P. J. (2011) Education spaces: embodied dimensions and dynamics. *Social and Cultural Geography* 12: 1–8.

Corsaro, W. A. (1997) *The Sociology of Childhood*. Thousand Oaks, CA: Pine Forge Press.

Cortés-Morales, S. and Christensen, P. (2015) Unfolding the pushchair: children's mobilities and everyday technologies. *Research in Education and Media* 6(2): 9–18.

Crenshaw, K. (1991) Mapping the margins: intersectionality, identity politics, and violence against women of colour. *Stanford Law Review* 43(6): 1241–1299.

Cresswell, T. (2005) *Place: An Introduction*. Chichester: John Wiley & Sons.

Cresswell, T. (2006) *On the Move: Mobility in the Modern Western World*. London: Taylor & Francis.

Cresswell, T. (2011) Towards a politics of mobility. In E. Pietrese and N. Edjabe (eds), *African Cities Reader II: Mobilities and Fixtures*, 159–171. Vlaeberg: Chimurenga.

Crossa, V. (2013) Play for protest, protest for play: artisan and vendors' resistance to displacement in Mexico City. *Antipode* 45(4): 826–843.

Dalby, S. (2014) After the Anthropocene: politics and geographic inquiry for a new epoch. *Progress in Human Geography* 38: 449–456.

Damerell, P., Howe, C. and Milner-Gulland, E. J. (2013) Child-oriented environmental education influences adult knowledge and household behaviour. *Environmental Research Letters* 8(1): 1–7.

Davies, H. and Christensen, P. (2015) Sharing spaces: children and young people negotiating intimate relationships and privacy in the family home. In S. Punch, R. Vanderbeck and T. Skelton (eds), *Families, Intergenerationality, and Peer Group Relations*, 1–23. Berlin: Springer.

DCLG. (2007) *Building a Greener Future, Department for Communities and Local Government.* London: The Stationery Office.

DCLG. (2017) First ever garden villages named with government support. Retrieved on 17 April 2017 from www.gov.uk/government/news/first-ever-garden-villages-named-with-government-support.

de Boer, N. (2005) *Polemische Beschouwingen over Staden Region*. Delft: Bouwkunde.

den Besten, O., Horton, J. and Kraftl, P. (2008) Pupil involvement in school (re)design: participation in policy and practice. *CoDesign* 4: 197–210.

Department for Transport. (2004a) *The Future of Transport: A Network for 2030*. London: DfT.

Department for Transport. (2004b) *Walking and Cycling: An Action Plan*. London: DfT.

Department for Transport. (2004c) *Policy, Planning and Design for Walking and Cycling*. London: Department for Transport.

Department for Transport. (2006) *National Travel Survey 2005*. London: DFT.

Department for Transport. (2007) *Manual for Streets*. London: Thomas Telford Publishing.

Department for Transport. (2011) *Shared Space*. London: TSO.

Department of the Environment. (1973) *Children at Play: Design Bulletin*. London: HMSO.

de Roo, G. and Miller, D. (eds). (2000) *Compact Cities and Sustainable Urban Development: A Critical Assessment of Policies and Plans from an International Perspective,*. Farnham: Ashgate.

Design Council UK. (2016) *The Value of Public Space*. London: CABE Space.

DETR. (1998) *A New Deal for Transport: Better for Everyone*. London: Department of the Environment, Transport and the Regions.

DETR. (2000a) *Our Towns and Cities: The Future. Delivering an Urban Renaissance*. London: DETR.

DETR. (2000b) *Quality and Choice: A Decent Home for All: The Housing Green Paper*. London: DETR.

Disney, T. (2015) Complex spaces of orphan care: a Russian therapeutic children's community. *Children's Geographies* 13(1): 30–43.

Dunn, K. and Farnsworth, M. S. (2012) 'We ARE the revolution': Riot Grrrl Press, girl empowerment, and DIY self-publishing. *Women's Studies* 41(2): 136–157.

Dwyer, C., Shah, B. and Sanghera, G. (2008) 'From cricket lover to terror suspect': challenging representations of young British Muslim men. *Gender, Place and Culture* 15(2): 117–136.

Dyson, J. (2014) *Working Childhoods: Youth, Agency and the Environment in India*. Cambridge: Cambridge University Press.

Ecclestone, K. and Hayes, D. (2009) Changing the subject: the educational implications of developing emotional well-being. *Oxford Review of Education* 35(3): 371–389.

Edwards, B. and Turrent, D. (eds). (2000) *Sustainable Housing: Principles and Practice*. London: Taylor and Francis.

Eriksen, S. H. and Mulugeta, E. (2016) Social networks for survival among working children in Addis Ababa. *Childhood* 23(2): 178–191.

Eßer, F., Baader, M. S., Betz, T. and Hungerland, B. (2016) *Reconceptualising Agency and Childhood: New Perspectives in Childhood Studies*. Abingdon: Routledge.

EU. (2007) *Leipzig Charter on Sustainable European Cities*. Retrieved on 3 May 2017 from http://ec.europa.eu/regional_policy/archive/themes/urban/leipzig_charter.pdf.

Evans, B. and Honeyford, E. (2011) Brighter futures, greener lives: children and young people in UK sustainable development policy. In P. Kraftl, J. Horton and F. Tucker (eds), *Critical Geographies of Childhood and Youth*, 61–78. Bristol: Policy Press.

**198** References

Evans, R. (2010) Children's caring roles and responsibilities within the family in Africa. *Geography Compass* 4(10): 1477–1496.

Evans, R. (2012) Sibling caringscapes: time–space practices of caring within youth-headed households in Tanzania and Uganda. *Geoforum* 43(4): 824–835.

Evans, J., Davies, B. and Rich, E. (2009) The body made flesh: embodied learning and the corporeal device. *British Journal of Sociology of Education* 30: 391–406.

Evans, J., Rich, E., Davies, B. and Allwood, R. (2005) The embodiment of learning: what the sociology of education doesn't say about 'risk' in going to school. *International Studies in Sociology of Education* 15: 129–148.

Farr, D. (2008) *Sustainable Urbanism: Urban Design with Nature*. Chichester: John Wiley & Sons.

Faulconbridge, J. (2013) Mobile 'green' design knowledge: institutions, bricolage and the relational production of embedded sustainable buildings. *Transactions of the Institute of British Geographers* 18: 339–353.

Ferré, M., Guitart, A. and Ferret, M. (2006) Children and playgrounds in Mediterranean cities. *Children's Geographies* 4: 173–183.

Fishman, R. (1999) *Urban Utopias in the Twentieth Century: Ebenezer Howard, Frank Lloyd Wright, Le Corbusier*. Cambridge, MA: MIT Press.

Flint, J. and Raco, M. (2012) (eds.) *The Future of Sustainable Cities: Critical Reflections*. Bristol: Policy Press.

Foucault, M. (1997) *The Essential Works of Foucault, 1954–1984, Vol. 1: Ethics, Subjectivity, and Truth* (ed. P. Rabinow, trans. R. Hurley et al.). New York: New Press.

Francis, M. (1987) The making of democratic streets. In M. A. Vernez (ed.), *Public Streets for Public Use*, 23–39. New York: Van Nostrand Reinhold.

Franklin, A. (2017) The more-than-human city. *The Sociological Review* 65(2): 202–217.

Gagen, E. A. (2004) Making America flesh: physicality and nationhood in early twentieth-century physical education reform. *Cultural Geographies* 11(4): 417–442.

Gagen, E. (2015) Governing emotions: citizenship, neuroscience, and the education of youth. *Transactions of the Institute of British Geographers* 40: 140–152.

Gehl, J. (2006) *Life Between Buildings: Using Public Space*. Copenhagen: Danish Architectural Press.

Geldens, P., Lincoln, S. and Hodkinson, P. (2011) Youth: Identities, Transitions, Cultures. *Journal of Sociology* 47(4): 347–353.

Geller, A. (2003) Smart growth: a prescription for livable cities. *American Journal of Public Health* 93(9): 1410–1415.

Geoghegan, H. and Woodyer, T. (2014) Cultural geography and enchantment: the affirmative constitution of geographical research. *Journal of Cultural Geography* 31(2): 218–229.

Gibson, J. J. (2014) *The Ecological Approach to Visual Perception: Classic Edition*. New York: Psychology Press.

Giddens, A. (1991) *Modernity and Self-Identity: Self and Society in the Late Modern Age*. California: Stanford University Press.

Gill, T. (1997) Policy review: Home Zones. *Children and Society* 11: 268–270.

Gill, T. (2006) Home Zones in the UK: history, policy and impact on children and young people. *Children, Youth and Environments* 16(1): 13.

Gill, T. (2007) *Can I Play Out . . . ? Lessons from London Play's Home Zones Project*. London: London Play.

Gold, J. R. (1997) *The Experience of Modernism: Modern Architects and the Future City*. London: E. & F. N. Spon.

Gold, J. R. and Ward, S. V. (eds). (1994) *Place Promotion: The Use of Publicity and Marketing to Sell Towns and Regions*. Chichester: John Wiley & Sons.

Goodchild, B., O'Flaherty, F. and Ambrose, A. (2014) Inside the eco-home: using video to understand the implications of innovative housing. *Housing, Theory and Society* 31(3): 334–352.

Government of India. (2016) Smart Cities Mission, Ministry of Urban Development. Retrieved on 24 November 2016 from http://smartcities.gov.in/content/innerpage/strategy.php.

Government of India. (2017) Smart Cities Mission, Ministry of Housing and Urban Affairs. Retrieved on 20 July 2017 from http://smartcities.gov.in/content.

Government of Singapore. (2012) *Tianjin Eco-City*. Singapore: Government of Singapore. Retrieved on 3 May 2017 from www.tianjinecocity.gov.sg/index.htm.

Gratton, P. (2014) *Speculative Realism: Problems and Prospects*. New York: Bloomsbury.

Grønhøj, A. (2006) Communication about consumption: a family process perspective on 'green' consumer practices. *Journal of Consumer Behaviour* 5(6): 491–503.

Grønhøj, A. and Thøgersen, J. (2012) Action speaks louder than words: the effect of personal attitudes and family norms on adolescents' pro-environmental behaviour. *Journal of Economic Psychology* 33(1): 292–302.

Grosz, E.A. (ed.). (1999) *Becomings: Explorations in Time, Memory, and Futures*. Ithaca, NY: Cornell University Press.

Grosz, E. (2011) *Becoming Undone: Darwinian Reflections on Life, Politics, and Art*. Durham, NC: Duke University Press.

Hackett, A., Procter, L. and Seymour, J. (2015) *Children's Spatialities*. Basingstoke: Palgrave Macmillan.

Hadfield-Hill, S. (2013) Living in a sustainable community: new spaces, new behaviours? *Local Environment: The International Journal of Justice and Sustainability* 13(3): 354–371.

Hadfield-Hill, S. (2016) Children and Young People in Changing Urban Environments in the Majority World, P. Kraftl., K. Nairn and T. Skelton (Eds.) *Geographies of Children and Young People: Space, place and environment, Springer Major Reference Work*, 3: 1–18.

Hadfield-Hill, S. and Zara, C. (2017) *Final Report: New Urbanisms in India: Urban Living, Sustainability and Everyday Life*. Birmingham: University of Birmingham.

Hall, P. and Ward, C. (1998) *Sociable Cities*. Chichester: John Wiley & Sons.

Hamilton-Baillie, B. (2008) Shared space: reconciling people, places and traffic. *Built Environment* 34(2): 161–181.

Hammersley, M. (2016) Childhood studies: a sustainable paradigm? *Childhood* 24(1): 113–127. doi: 10.1177/.

Handy, S.L., Boarnet, M.G., Ewing, R., Killingsworth, R.E. (2002) How the built environment affects physical activity: views from urban planning. *American Journal of Preventative Medicine* 23: 64–73.

Haraway, D. (2008) Companion species, mis-recognition, and queer worlding. In N. Giffney and M. Hird (eds), *Queering the Non/Human*, xxiii–xxvi. Aldershot: Ashgate.

Hardy, D. (1991) *From New Towns to Green Politics: Campaigning for Town and Country Planning, 1946–1990*. London: E. & F.N. Spon.

Harker, C. (2005) Playing and affective time-spaces. *Children's Geographies* 3(1): 47–62.

Hart, J. (2008) Children's participation and international development. *International Journal of Children's Rights* 16(3): 407–418.

Hart, R.A. (1979) *Children's Experience of Place*. Irvington.

Hart, R.A. (2013) *Children's Participation: The Theory and Practice of Involving Young Citizens in Community Development and Environmental Care*. Abingdon: Routledge.

Hart, R.A. and Moore, G.T. (1973) *The Development of Spatial Cognition: A Review*. New Brunswick, NJ: Aldine Transaction.

Hart, R.A., Moore, G.T., Downs, R.M. and Stea, D. (1973) Image and environment: cognitive mapping and spatial behaviour In R.A. Hart, G.T. Moore, R.M. Downs and

**200** References

D. Stea (eds), *The Development of Spatial Cognition: A Review*, 246–288. New Brunswick, NJ: Aldine Transaction.

Harvey, D. (2012) *Rebel Cities: From the Right to the City to the Urban Revolution*. London: Verso.

HCA. (2009) *Learning from Europe on Eco-Towns*. London: Homes and Communities Agency.

Hemming, P.J. and Madge, N. (2012) Researching children, youth and religion: identity, complexity and agency. *Childhood* 19(1): 38–51.

Hendrick, H. (1997) Constructions and reconstructions of British childhood: an interpretative survey 1800 to the present. In A. James and A. Prout (eds), *Constructing and Reconstructing Childhood: Contemporary Issues in the Sociological Study of Childhood*, 34–62. London: Routledge.

Henn, M.A.T.A., Pontes, A.I. and Griffiths, M.D. (2016) Young people, citizenship education, and political engagement. *Education Today* 66(1): 21–25.

Henricks, T.S. (2015) *Play and the Human Condition*. Chicago, IL: University of Illinois Press.

Heynen, N.C., Kaika, M. and Swyngedouw, E. (2006) *In the Nature of Cities: Urban Political Ecology and the Politics of Urban Metabolism* (Vol. 3). London: Taylor & Francis.

Hillman, M., Adams, J. and Whitelegg, J. (1990) *One False Move*. London: Policy Studies Institute.

Hinchliffe, S. (2008) Reconstituting nature conservation: towards a careful political ecology. *Geoforum* 39(1): 88–97.

Hinchliffe, S. and Whatmore, S. (2006) Living cities: towards a politics of conviviality. *Science as Culture* 15(2): 123–138.

Hobson, K. (2016) Bins, bulbs, and shower timers: on the 'techno-ethics' of sustainable living. *A Journal of Philosophy and Geography* 9(3): 317–336.

Holloway, S.L. and Valentine, G. (2000) Spatiality and the new social studies of childhood. *Sociology* 34(4): 763–783.

Home Office. (2014) Anti-social Behaviour, Crime and Policing Act 2014: Reform of anti-social behaviour powers – Statutory guidance for frontline professionals. Home Office. Retrieved on 23 February 2017 from www.gov.uk/government/uploads/system/uploads/attachment_data/file/352562/ASB_Guidance_v8_July2014_final__2_.pdf.

Hopkins, P.E. (2009) Responding to the 'crisis of masculinity': the perspectives of young Muslim men from Glasgow and Edinburgh, Scotland. *Gender, Place and Culture* 16(3): 299–312.

Hopkins, P. (2010) *Young People, Place and Identity*. London: Routledge.

Hopkins, P. and Pain, R. (2007) Geographies of age: thinking relationally. *Area* 39(3): 287–294.

Hörschelmann, K. and Colls, R. (eds). (2009) *Contested Bodies of Childhood and Youth*. Berlin: Springer.

Hörschelmann, K. and van Blerk, L. (2013) *Children, Youth and the City*. Abingdon: Routledge.

Hordyk, S.R., Dulude, M. and Shem, M. (2015) When nature nurtures children: nature as a containing and holding space. *Children's Geographies* 13(5): 571–588.

Horton, J. (2010) 'The best thing ever': how children's popular culture matters. *Social and Cultural Geography* 11(4): 377–398.

Horton, J. (2012) 'Got my shoes, got my Pokémon': everyday geographies of children's popular culture. *Geoforum* 43(1): 4–13.

Horton, J. and Kraftl, P. (2006a) What else? Some more ways of thinking and doing 'children's geographies'. *Children's Geographies* 4(1): 69–95.

Horton, J. and Kraftl, P. (2006b) Not just growing up, but going on: children's geographies as becomings: materials, spacings, bodies, situations. *Children's Geographies* 4: 259–276.

Horton, J. and Kraftl, P. (2008) Reflections on geographies of age: a response to Hopkins and Pain. *Area* 40(2): 284–288.

Horton, J. and Kraftl, P. (2009a) What (else) matters? Policy contexts, emotional geographies. *Environment and Planning A* 41(12): 2984–3002.

Horton, J. and Kraftl, P. (2009b) Small acts, kind words and 'not too much fuss': implicit activisms. *Emotion, Space and Society* 2(1): 14–23.

Horton, J., Christensen, P., Hadfield-Hill, S. and Kraftl, P. (2014) 'Walking . . . just walking': children's pedestrian practices in new urban developments. *Social and Cultural Geography* 15: 95–115.

Horton, J., Hadfield-Hill, S., Christensen, P. and Kraftl, P. (2013) Children, young people and sustainability: introduction to special issue. *Local Environment: The International Journal of Justice and Sustainability* 18(3): 249–254.

Horton, J., Hadfield-Hill, S. and Kraftl, P. (2015) Children living with 'sustainable' urban architectures. *Environment and Planning A* 47(4): 903–921.

Houston, D., Hillier, J., MacCallum, D., Steele, W. and Byrne, J. (2017) Make kin, not cities! Multispecies entanglements and 'becoming-world' in planning theory. *Planning Theory*, online. doi: 10.1177/2017092412000042.

Houston, D., MacAllum, D., Steele, W. and Byrne, J. (2016) Climate cosmopolitics and the possibilities for urban planning. *Nature and Culture* 11: 259–277.

Howard, E. (1898) *Tomorrow: A Peaceful Path to Real Reform.* London: Swan Sonnenschein and Son.

Howard, E. (1902) *Garden Cities of Tomorrow.* London: Swan Sonnenschein and Son.

Huckle, J. and Wals, A.E. (2015) The UN Decade of Education for Sustainable Development: business as usual in the end. *Environmental Education Research* 21(3): 491–505.

Huizinga, J. (1955) *Homo Ludens: A Study of the Play-Element in Cult.* Boston, MA: Beacon Press.

Hultman, K. and Lenz Taguchi, H. (2010) Challenging anthropocentric analysis of visual data: a relational materialist methodological approach to educational research. *International Journal of Qualitative Studies in Education* 23(5): 525–542.

IBM. (2015) Smarter cities: new cognitive approaches to long-standing challenges. Retrieved on 27 April 2017 from www.ibm.com/smarterplanet/us/en/smarter_cities/overview.

Imrie, R. (2012) Auto-disabilities: the case of shared space environments. *Environment and Planning A* 44(9): 2260–2270.

Imrie, R. and Kumar, M. (2011) Shared space and sight loss: policies and practices in English local authorities. Retrieved on 11 July 2017 from www.pocklington-trust.org.uk/project/shared-space-policies-fail-sight-loss.

Imrie, R. and Street, E. (2009) Regulating design: the practices of architecture, governance and control. *Urban Studies* 46(12): 2507–2518.

Ingold, T. (1995) Building, dwelling, living: how animals and people make themselves at home in the world. In Marilyn Strathern (ed.), *Shifting Contexts: Transformations in Anthropological Knowledge*, 57–80. London: Routledge.

Jackson, S. and Scott, S. (1999) Risk anxiety and the social construction of childhood. In D. Lupton (ed.), *Risk and Sociocultural Theory*, 86–107. Cambridge: Cambridge University Press.

Jacobs, J. (1961) *The Death and Life of Great American Cities.* New York: Vintage Books.

Jacobs, J.M. and Merriman, P. (2011) Practising architectures. *Social and Cultural Geography* 12(3): 211–222.

Jacobs, J., Cairns, S. and Strebel, I. (2007) A tall storey . . . but, a fact just the same: the Red Road high-rise as a black box. *Urban Studies* 44: 609–629.

James, A., Jenks, C. and Prout, A. (1998) *Theorizing Childhood.* Williston, VT: Teachers College Press.

James, A. and Prout, A. (eds). (2015) *Constructing and Reconstructing Childhood: Contemporary Issues in the Sociological Study of childhood.* Abingdon: Routledge.

**202** References

Jeffrey, C. (2012) Geographies of children and youth II: global youth agency. *Progress in Human Geography* 36(2): 245–253.

Jeffrey, C. (2013) Geographies of children and youth III: alchemists of the revolution? *Progress in Human Geography* 37(1): 145–152.

Jelsma, J. (2003) Innovating for sustainability: involving users, politics and technology. *Innovation* 16(2): 103–116.

Jenks, C. (2005) *Childhood.* London: Routledge.

Jenks, M., Burton E. and Williams, K. (eds). (1996) *The Compact City: A Sustainable Urban Form?* London: Taylor and Francis.

Jensen, J.O. (2002) Green buildings as a part of the infrastructure: supporter, symbol or stranger. *Built Environment* 28(1): 22–32.

Jones, H., Neal, S., Mohan, G., Connell, K., Cochrane, A. and Bennett, K. (2015) Urban multiculture and everyday encounters in semi-public, franchised cafe spaces. *The Sociological Review* 63(3): 644–661.

Jones, O. (2008) 'True geography quickly forgotten, giving away to an adult-imagined universe'. Approaching the otherness of childhood. *Children's Geographies* 6(2): 195–212.

Juris, J.S. and Pleyers, G.H. (2009) Alter-activism: emerging cultures of participation among young global justice activists. *Journal of Youth Studies* 12(1): 57–75.

Kallio, K.P. and Häkli, J. (2011a) Tracing children's politics. *Political Geography* 30(2): 99–109.

Kallio, K. and Häkli, J. (2011b) Are there politics in childhood? *Space and Polity* 15(1): 21–34.

Kallio, K.P. and Häkli, J. (2013) Children and young people's politics in everyday life. *Space and Polity* 17(1): 1–16.

Kallio, K.P., Häkli, J. and Backlund, P. (2015) Lived citizenship as the locus of political agency in participatory policy. *Citizenship Studies* 19(1): 101–119.

Karsten, L. (2005) It all used to be better? Different generations on continuity and change in urban children's daily use of space. *Children's Geographies* 3(3): 275–290.

Karsten, L. and van Vliet, W. (2006) Children in the city: reclaiming the street. *Children Youth and Environments* 16(1): 151–167.

Kashyap, R. and Lewis, V.A. (2013) British Muslim youth and religious fundamentalism: a quantitative investigation. *Ethnic and Racial Studies* 36(12): 2117–2140.

Katz, C. (2004) *Growing Up Global: Economic Restructuring and Children's Everyday Lives.* Minneapolis, MN: University of Minnesota Press.

Katz, P. (1993) *The New Urbanism: Toward an Architecture of Community.* New York: McGraw-Hill.

Kennedy, C., Pincetl, S. and Bunje, P. (2011) The study of urban metabolism and its applications to urban planning and design. *Environmental Pollution* 159(8): 1965–1973.

Kenway, J. and Youdell, D. (2011) The emotional geographies of education: beginning a conversation. *Emotion, Space and Society* 4(3): 131–136.

Kiili, J. (2016) Children's public participation, middle-class families and emotions. *Children and Society* 30(1): 25–35.

Kilbert, C.J. (2004) Green buildings: an overview of progress. *Journal of Land Use and Environmental Law* 19(2): 491–502.

King, M. (2007) The sociology of childhood as scientific communication observations from a social systems perspective. *Childhood* 14(2): 193–213.

Klocker, N. (2007) An example of 'thin' agency: child domestic workers in Tanzania. In R. Panelli, S. Punch and E. Robson (eds), *Global Perspectives on Rural Childhood and Youth: Young Rural Lives,* 83–94. New York: Routledge.

Koglin, T. (2009) *Sustainable Development in General in Urban Context: A Literature Review.* Lund: Lund University.

Kola-Olusanya, A. (2005) Free-choice environmental education: understanding where children learn outside of school. *Environmental Action Research* 11: 297–307.

Kraftl, P. (2006) Building an idea: the material construction of an ideal childhood. *Transactions of the Institute of British Geographers* 31(4): 488–504.

Kraftl, P. (2008) Young people, hope and childhood-hope. *Space and Culture* 11: 81–92.

Kraftl, P. (2010) Architectural movements, utopian moments: (in)coherent renderings of the Hundertwasser-Haus, Vienna. *Geografiska Annaler: Series B, Human Geography* 92(4): 327–345.

Kraftl, P. (2012) Utopian promise or burdensome responsibility? A critical analysis of the UK government's Building Schools for the Future policy. *Antipode* 44: 847–870.

Kraftl, P. (2013) Beyond 'voice', beyond 'agency', beyond 'politics'? Hybrid childhoods and some critical reflections on children's emotional geographies. *Emotion, Space and Society*: 13–23.

Kraftl, P. (2014) Liveability and urban architectures: mol(ecul)ar biopower and the becoming-lively of Sustainable Communities. *Environment and Planning D: Society and Space* 32(2): 274–292.

Kraftl, P. (2015) Alter-childhoods: biopolitics and childhoods in alternative education spaces. *Annals of the Association of American Geographers* 105: 219–237.

Kraftl, P. (2016) The force of habit: channelling young bodies at alternative education spaces. *Critical Studies in Education* 57: 116–130.

Kraftl, P., Christensen, P., Horton, J. and Hadfield-Hill. (2013) Living on a building site: young people's experiences of emerging 'sustainable communities' in England. *Geoforum* 50: 191–199.

Kubba, A. (2012) *Handbook of Green Building Design: LEED, BREEAM and Green Globes.* Waltham, MA: Butterworth-Heinemann.

Kullman, K. (2014) Children, urban care, and everyday pavements. *Environment and Planning A* 46(12): 2864–2880.

Kullman, K. (2015) Pedagogical assemblages: rearranging children's traffic education. *Social and Cultural Geography* 16(3): 255–275.

Kyttä, M. (2004) The extent of children's independent mobility and the number of actualized affordances as criteria for child-friendly environments. *Journal of Environmental Psychology* 24(2): 179–198.

Lacey, L. (2007) *Street Play: A Literature Review.* London: National Children's Bureau.

Lafferty, W. (2001) *Sustainable Communities in Europe.* London: Earthscan.

Lane, R. and Gorman-Murray, G. (2016) Introduction. In G. Gorman-Murray (ed.), *Material Geographies of Household Sustainability*, 1–15. New York: Routledge.

Langevang, T. (2008) Claiming place: the production of young men's street meeting places in Accra, Ghana. *Geografiska Annaler: Series B, Human Geography* 90(3): 227–242.

Lara, F. (2010) Beyond Curitiba: the rise of a participatory model for urban intervention in Brazil. *Urban Design International* 15: 119–128.

Latour, B. (2005) *Reassembling the Social: An Introduction to Actor–Network Theory.* Oxford: Oxford University Press.

Lawhon, L.L. (2009) The neighbourhood unit: physical design or physical determinism? *Journal of Planning History* 8(2): 111–132.

Lee, N. (1999) The challenge of childhood distributions of childhood's ambiguity in adult institutions. *Childhood* 6(4): 455–474.

Lee, N. (2001) *Childhood and Society: Growing Up in an Age of Uncertainty.* London: McGraw-Hill Education (UK).

Lee, N. (2008) Awake, asleep, adult, child: an a-humanist account of persons. *Body and Society* 14(4): 57–74.

Lee, N. and Motzkau, J. (2011) Navigating the biopolitics of childhood. *Childhood* 18: 7–19.

**204** References

Lerum, V. (2007) *High Performance Building*. Chichester: John Wiley & Sons.

Lester, S. (2015) Posthuman nature: life beyond the natural playground. In M. Maclean, W. Russell and E. Ryall (eds), *Philosophical Perspectives on Play*, 53–68. Abingdon: Routledge.

Lester, S. and Russell, W. (2014) *Children* 1(2): 241–260.

Little, C. (2015) The 'Mosquito' and the transformation of British public space. *Journal of Youth Studies* 18(2): 167–182.

Lobo, M. (2016) Co-inhabiting public spaces: diversity and playful encounters in Darwin, Australia. *Geographical Review* 106(2): 163–173.

Louv, R. (2005) *Last Child in the Woods: Saving Our Children from Nature-Deficit Disorder*. Chapel Hill, NC: Algonquin Books.

Lucas, K., Halden, D. and Wixey, S. (2010) Transport planning for sustainable communities. In T. Manzi, K. Lucas, T. Lloyd-Jones and J. Allen (eds), *Social Sustainability in Urban Areas: Communities, Connectivity and the Urban Fabric*, 121–140. London: Earthscan.

Lynch, K. (1981) *Good City Form*. Cambridge, MA: MIT Press.

Maclean, M., Russell, W. and Ryall, E. (eds). (2015) *Philosophical Perspectives on Play*. Abingdon: Routledge.

Malone, K. (2007) The bubble-wrap generation: children growing up in walled gardens. *Environmental Education Research* 13: 513–527.

Malone, K. (2012) 'The future lies in our hands': children as researchers and environmental change agents in designing a child-friendly neighbourhood. *Children's Geographies* 18(3): 372–395.

Malone, K. (2016) Theorizing a Child-Dog Encounter in the Slums of La Paz Using Post-humanistic Approaches in Current 'Child in Nature' Debates, *Children's Geographies* 14(4): 390–407.

Malone, K. and Hasluck. L. (2002) Australian youth. In L. Chawla (ed), *Growing Up in an Urbanising World*, 81–109. Paris/London: UNESCO/Earthscan Publications.

Malone, K. and Tranter, P. (2003) 'Hanging out in the school ground': a reflective look at researching children's environmental learning. *Canadian Journal for Environmental Education* 10: 196–212.

Manzi, T., Lucas, K., Lloyd-Jones T. and Allen J. (2010) Understanding social sustainability: key concepts and developments in theory and practice. In T. Manzi, K. Lucas, T. Lloyd-Jones and J. Allen (eds), *Social Sustainability in Urban Areas: Communities, Connectivity and the Urban Fabric*, 1–34. London: Earthscan.

Mapes, J. and Wolch, J. (2010) Living green: the promise and pitfalls of new sustainable communities. *Journal of Urban Design* 16(1): 105–126.

Marmot, A. (2002) Architectural determinism: does design change behaviour? *British Journal of General Practice* 52(476): 252–253.

Marres, N. (2015) *Material Participation: Technology, the Environment and Everyday Publics*. New York: Palgrave Macmillan.

Marsden, T. (ed.). (2008) *Sustainable Communities: New Spaces for Planning, Participation and Engagement*. London: Elsevier.

Massey, D. (2005) *For Space*. London: SAGE.

Matthews, H. (1987) Gender, home range and environmental cognition. *Transactions of the Institute of British Geographers* 12(1): 43–56.

Matthews, H. (1992) *Making Sense of Place: Children's Understanding of Large-Scale Environments*. New York: Barnes & Noble Books.

Matthews, H. (2001) *Children and Community Regeneration: Creating Better Neighbourhoods*. London: Save the Children.

Matthews, H. (2003) The street as liminal space: the barbed spaces of childhood. In P. Christensen and M. O'Brien (eds), *Children in the City: Home, Neighbourhood and Community*, 101–117. London: RouledgeFalmer.

Matthews, H., Limb, M. and Taylor, M. (1999) Reclaiming the street: the discourse of curfew. *Environment and Planning A* 31 10: 1713–1730.

Matthews, H., Limb, M., and Taylor, M. (2000) The street as third space. In S.L. Holloway and G. Valentine (eds), *Children's Geographies: Playing, Living, Learning*, 63–79. London: Routledge.

Matthews, H., Taylor, M., Percy-Smith, B. and Limb, M. (2000) The unacceptable flaneur: the shopping mall as a teenage hangout. *Childhood* 7(3): 279–294.

McKendrick, J. (2000) The geography of children: an annotated bibliography. *Childhood* 7(3): 359–87.

Middleton, J. (2011) Walking in the city: the geographies of everyday pedestrian practices. *Geography Compass* 5: 90–105.

Mikkelsen, M.R. and Christensen, P. (2009) Is children's independent mobility really independent? A study of children's mobility combining ethnography and GPS/mobile phone technologies. *Mobilities* 4(1): 37–58.

Millei, Z. and Joronen, M. (2016) The (bio) politicization of neuroscience in Australian early years policies: fostering brain-resources as human capital. *Journal of Education Policy* 31(4): 389–404.

Mitchell, K. and Elwood, S. (2012) Mapping children's politics: the promise of articulation and the limits of nonrepresentational theory. *Environment and Planning D: Society and Space* 30(5): 788–804.

Mizen, P. (2003) The best days of your life? Youth, policy and Blair's New Labour. *Critical Social Policy* 23(4): 453–476.

Mol, A. (2008) I eat an apple: on theorizing subjectivities. *Subjectivity* 22(1): 28–37.

Moody, S. and Melia, S. (2013) Shared space – research, policy and problems. *Proceedings of the Institution of Civil Engineers* 167(6): 384–392.

Morgan, D. (2011) *Rethinking Family Practices*. Berlin: Springer.

Mössner, S. (2015a) Sustainable urban development as consensal practice: post-politics in Freiburg, Germany. *Regional Studies* 50: 971–982.

Mössner, S. (2015b) Urban development in Freiburg, Germany: sustainable and neoliberal? *Die Erde* 146: 189–193.

Mössner S. and Miller V. (2015) Sustainability all in one place? Dilemmas of sustainability governance in the Freiburg Metropolitan Region. *Regions* 300: 18–12.

Mould, O. (2009) Parkour, the city, the event. *Environment and Planning D: Society and Space* 27(4): 738–750.

Nayak, A. (2003) 'Through children's eyes': childhood, place and the fear of crime. *Geoforum* 34(3): 303–315.

Nayak A. (2010) Race, affect, and emotion: young people, racism, and graffiti in the postcolonial English suburbs. *Environment and Planning A* 42(10): 2370–2392.

Nayak A. (2015) White lines: racist graffiti, skinhead youth and violence in the English suburbs. In R.E. Rinehart, E. Emerald and R. Matamua (eds), *Ethnographies in Pan Pacific Research: Tensions and Positionings*, 145–162. New York: Routledge.

Nayak, A. (2017) Purging the nation: race, conviviality and embodied encounters in the lives of British Bangladeshi Muslim young women. *Transactions of the Institute of British Geographers* 42(2): 289–302.

Neary, J., Egan, M., Keenan, P., Lawson, L. and Bond, L. (2013) Damned if they do, damned if they don't: negotiating the tricky context of anti-social behaviour and keeping safe in disadvantaged neighbourhoods. *Journal of Youth Studies* 16(1): 118–134.

**206** References

NHBC. (2008) *Zero Carbon?* Milton Keynes: National House Builders' Council.

O'Brien, M., Jones, D. and Smidt, S. (2000) Children's independent spatial mobility in the urban public realm. *Childhood* 7(3): 257–277.

ODPM (2000) *Our Towns and Cities: the Future – Delivering an Urban Renaissance*. London: Office of the Deputy Prime Minister.

ODPM. (2003a) *Sustainable Communities: Building for the Future*. London: Office of the Deputy Prime Minister.

ODPM. (2003b) *Proposed Change to Planning Policy for Influencing the Size, Type, and Affordability of Housing*, London: Office of the Deputy Prime Minister.

ODPM. (2004) *The Egan Review: Skills for Sustainable Communities*. London: Office of the Deputy Prime Minister.

Opie, I. A. and Opie, P. (1969) *Children's Games in Street and Playground: Chasing, Catching, Seeking, Hunting, Racing, Exerting, Daring, Guessing, Acting, Pretending*. Oxford: Clarendon Press.

O'Riordan, T. (2004) Environmental science, sustainability and politics. *Transactions of the Institute of British Geographers* 29(2): 234–247.

Osmani, M. and O'Reilly, A. (2009) Feasibility of zero carbon homes in England by 2016: a housebuilder's perspective. *Building and Environment* 44: 1917–1924.

Oswell, D. (2013) *The Agency of Children: From Family to Global Human Rights*. Cambridge: Cambridge University Press.

O'Toole, T. (2003) Engaging with young people's conceptions of the political. *Children's Geographies* 1: 71–90.

Pacini-Ketchabaw, V. (2013) Frictions in forest pedagogies: common worlds in settler colonial spaces. *Global Studies of Childhood* 3(4): 355–365.

Pacini-Ketchabaw, V. and Clark, V. (2016) Following watery relations in early childhood pedagogies. *Journal of Early Childhood Research* 14(1): 98–111.

Pain, R. (2006) Paranoid parenting? Rematerializing risk and fear for children. *Social and Cultural Geography* 7(2): 221–243.

Pellegrini, A.D. and Smith, P.K. (1998) Physical activity play: the nature and function of a neglected aspect of play. *Child Development* 69(3): 577–598.

Percy-Smith, B. (2010) Councils, consultations and community: rethinking the spaces for children and young people's participation, *Children's Geographies* 8(2): 107–122.

Percy-Smith B. and Burns, D. (2013) Exploring the role of children and young people as agents of change in sustainable community development. *Local Environment: The International Journal of Justice and Sustainability* 18: 323–339.

Percy-Smith, B. and Thomas, N. (eds). (2008) *A Handbook of Children and Young People's Participation*. Abingdon: Routledge.

Philo, C. (2011) Foucault, sexuality and when not to listen to children. *Children's Geographies* 9: 123–127.

Philo, C., and Parr, H. (2000) Institutional geographies: introductory remarks. *Geoforum* 31(4): 513–521.

Philo, C. and Smith, F. (2013) The child-body-politic: afterword on 'Children and young people's politics in everyday life'. *Space and Polity* 17(1): 137–144.

Pickerill, J. (2015) Cold comfort? Reconceiving the practices of bathing in British self-build eco-homes. *Annals of the Association of American Geographers* 105(5): 1061–1077.

Pickerill, J. (2016) *Eco-homes: People, Place and Politics*. London: Zed Books.

Pickerill, J. and Maxey, L. (eds). (2009) Low impact development: the future in our hands. Retrieved on 2 February 2012 from http://lowimpactdevelopment.files.wordpress.com.

Pike, J. and Kelly, P. (2014) *The Moral Geographies of Children, Young People and Food: Beyond Jamie's School Dinners*. Berlin: Springer.

Pinder, D. (2011) Errant paths: the poetics and politics of walking. *Environment and Planning D: Society and Space* 29(4): 672–692.

Platt, L. (2012) Parks are dangerous and the sidewalk is closer: children's use of neighbourhood space in Milwaukee, Wisconsin. *Children, Youth and Environments* 22(2): 194–213.

Pooley, C., Turnbull, J. and Adams, M. (2005) The journey to school in Britain since the 1940s: continuity and change. *Area* 37: 43–53.

Price, L. (2015) Knitting and the city. *Geography Compass* 9(2): 81–95.

Probyn, E. (2005) *Blush: Faces of Shame*. Minneapolis, MN: University of Minnesota Press.

Prout, A. (2005) *The Future of Childhood*. London: Routledge.

Punch, S. (2015) Possibilities for learning between childhoods and youth in the minority and majority worlds: youth transitions as an example of cross-world dialogue. In J. Wyn and H. Cahill (eds), *Handbook of Children and Youth Studies*, 689–701. Berlin: Springer.

Punch, S. and McIntosh, I. (2014) Food is a funny thing within residential child care: intergenerational relationships and food practices in residential care. *Childhood* 21(1): 72–86.

Pykett, J. (2012) Making youth publics and neuro-citizens: critical geographies of contemporary educational practice. In P. Kraftl, J. Horton and F. Tucker (eds), *Critical Geographies of Children and Youth: Policy and Practice*, 27–42. Bristol: Policy Press.

Qvortrup, J., Bardy, M., Sgritta, G. and Wintersberger, H. (1994) *Childhood Matters: Social Theory, Practice and Politics*. Aldershot: Avebury.

Raco, M. (2005) Sustainable development, rolled-out neoliberalism and sustainable communities. *Antipode* 37(2): 324–347.

Raco, M. (2007) *Building Sustainable Communities: Spatial Policy and Labour Mobility in Postwar Britain*. Bristol: Policy Press.

Raco, M. (2012) A growth agenda without growth: English spatial policy, sustainable communities, and the death of the neo-liberal project? *GeoJournal* 77: 153–165.

Raco, M. (2017) Critical urban cosmopolitanism and the governance of urban diversity in European cities. *European Urban and Regional Studies*, in press.

Rainio, A.P. and Hilppö, J. (2017) The dialectics of agency in educational ethnography. *Ethnography and Education* 12(1): 78–94.

Rapoport, E. (2015a) Globalising sustainable urbanism: the role of international masterplanners. *Area* 47: 110–115.

Rapoport, E. (2015b) Sustainable urbanism in the age of Photoshop: images, experiences and the role of learning through inhabiting the international travels of a planning model. *Global Networks* 15: 307–324.

Rautio, P. (2013) Children who carry stones in their pockets: on autotelic material practices in everyday life. *Children's Geographies* 11(4): 394–408.

Rautio, P. (2014) Mingling and imitating in producing spaces for knowing and being: Insights from a Finnish study of child–matter intra-action. *Childhood* 21(4): 461–474.

Rawlinson, C. and Guaralda, M. (2011) Play in the city: Parkour and architecture. Paper presented at the First International Postgraduate Conference on Engineering, Designing and Developing the Built Environment for Sustainable Wellbeing, Brisbane, Australia.

Reay, D. (2000) A useful extension of Bourdieu's conceptual framework? Emotional capital as a way of understanding mothers' involvement in their children's education. *The Sociological Review* 48(4): 568–585.

RIBA. (2003) *Sustainable Communities: RIBA Response to the Egan Review of Skills in the Built Environment Professions*. London: Royal Institute of British Architects.

Ridgers, N., Knowles, Z. and Sayers, J. (2012) Encouraging play in the natural environment, *Children's Geographies* 10: 49–65.

**208** References

Robinson, J. (2002) Global and world cities: a view from off the map. *International Journal of Urban and Regional Research* 26(3): 531–554.

Robinson, J. (2005) *Ordinary Cities*. London: Routledge.

Rogerson, R., Sadler, S., Green, A. and Wong, C. (2011) Learning about sustainable communities. In R. Rogerson, S. Sadler, A. Green and C. Wong (eds), *Sustainable Communities: Skills and Learning for Place-Making*, 1–22. Hatfield: University of Hertfordshire Press.

Rose, G. (1993) *Feminism and Geography: The Limits of Geographical Knowledge*. Minneapolis, MN: University of Minnesota Press.

Rose, N. (2009) *The Politics of Life Itself: Biomedicine, Power, and Subjectivity in the Twenty-First Century*. Princeton, NJ: Princeton University Press.

Rosen, R. (2015) 'The scream': meanings and excesses in early childhood settings. *Childhood* 22(1): 39–52.

Routledge, P. (2012) Sensuous solidarities: emotion, politics and performance in the Clandestine Insurgent Rebel Clown Army. *Antipode* 44(2): 428–452.

RUDI. (2013) *Case Study Revisited: Newhall, Harlow*. London: Resource for Urban Development International.

Rumford, C. (2008) *Cosmopolitan Spaces: Europe, Globalisation, Theory*. Abingdon: Routledge.

Ryall, E., Russell, W. and MacLean, M. (2013) *The Philosophy of Play*. Abingdon: Routledge.

Ryan, K. (2012) The new wave of childhood studies: breaking the grip of bio-social dualism? *Childhood* 19: 439–452.

Ryan, K. (2014) Childhood, biosocial power and the 'anthropological machine': life as a governable process? *Critical Horizons* 15: 266–283.

Satchwell, C. (2013) Carbon literacy practices: textual footprints between school and home in children's construction of knowledge about climate change. *Local Environment* 18: 289–304.

Satterthwaite, D. (ed.). (1999) *Sustainable Cities*. London: Earthscan.

Savills. (2008) Kids' dream home. Retrieved from www.kidsdreamhome.co.uk/Results.htm.

Schmidt, D. (2009) Low exergy systems for high-performance buildings and communities. *Energy and Buildings* 41(3): 331–336.

Schreiner, C. and Sjoberg, S. (2005) Empowered for action? How do young people relate to environmental challenges? In S. Alsop (ed.), *Beyond Cartesian Dualism: Encountering Affect in the Teaching and Learning of Science*, 53–68. Dordrecht: Springer.

Sharkey, A. and Shields, R. (2008) Abject citizenship – rethinking exclusion and inclusion: participation, criminality and community at a small town youth centre. *Children's Geographies* 6(3): 239–256.

Shaw, R., Colley, M. and Connell, R. (2007) *Climate Change Adaptation by Design*. London: Town and Country Planning Association.

Shove, E., Pantzar, M. and Watson, M. (2012) *The Dynamics of Social Practice: Everyday Life and How it Changes*. London: Sage.

Sibley, D. (1995) *Geographies of Exclusion: Society and Difference in the West*. London: Routledge.

Skelton, T. (2000) Nothing to do, nowhere to go? Teenage girls and 'public' space in the Rhondda Valleys, South Wales. In Sarah Holloway and Gill Valentine (eds), *Children's Geographies: Playing, Living, Learning*, 80–99. London: Routledge.

Skelton, T. (2007) Children, young people, UNICEF and participation. *Children's Geographies* 5(1–2): 165–181.

Skelton, T. (2013) Young people, children, politics and space: a decade of youthful political geography scholarship 2003–13. *Space and Polity* 17(1): 123–136.

Skelton, T. and Gough, K. (2013) Introduction: young people's im/mobile urban geographies. *Urban Studies* 50(3): 455–466.

SNE Architects. (2012) Rabalderparken. Retrieved on 11 July 2017 from www.snearchitects.com/project/rabalderparken.

SNE Architects. (Undated) About. Retrieved on 11 July 2017 from www.snearchitects.com/home/#a_About.

Snow, S., Vyas, D. and Brereton, M. (2015) When an eco-feedback system joins the family. *Personal and Ubiquitous Computing* 19(5–6): 929–940.

Social Exclusion Unit. (2000) *National Strategy for Neighbourhood Renewal: A Framework for Consultation*. London: Social Exclusion Unit.

Southworth, M. and Ben-Joseph, E. (2003) *Streets and the Shaping of Towns and Cities*. Washington, DC: Island Press.

Staeheli, L., Kafui, A. and Mitchell, D. (2013) Contested engagements: youth and the politics of citizenship. *Space and Polity* 17: 88–105.

Stallybrass, P. and White, A. (1986) *The Politics and Poetics of Transgression*. Ithaca, NY: Cornell University Press.

Staunæs, D. (2003) Where have all the subjects gone? Bringing together the concepts of intersectionality and subjectification. *NORA: Nordic Journal of Women's Studies* 11(2): 101–110.

Steinberg, L. (2015) Woonerf: inclusive and livable Dutch street. Retrieved from www.lvblcity.com/blog/2015/12/woonerf-inclusive-and-livable-dutch-street.

Stevens, Q. (2007) *The Ludic City: Exploring the Potential of Public Spaces*. London: Routledge.

Stratford, E. (2016) Mobilizing a spatial politics of street skating: thinking about the geographies of generosity. *Annals of the American Association of Geographers* 106(2): 350–357.

Susdrain. (2012) *Creating a Water Sensitive UK*. London: Susdrain.

Sutton-Smith, B. (2009) *The Ambiguity of Play*. Cambridge, MA: Harvard University Press.

Sutton-Smith, B., Mechling, J., Johnson, T. and McMahon, F. (1999) *Children's Folklore: A Source Book*. Boulder, CO: Utah State University Press.

Taylor, A. (2013) *Reconfiguring the Natures of Childhood*. London: Routledge.

Taylor, A. and Blaise, M. (2014) Queer worlding childhood. *Discourse: Studies in the Cultural Politics of Education* 35(3): 377–392.

Taylor, A., Blaise, M. and Giugni, M. (2013) Haraway's 'bag lady story-telling': relocating childhood and learning within a 'post-human landscape'. *Discourse: Studies in the Cultural Politics of Education* 34(1): 48–62.

TCPA. (2006) *Sustainable Energy by Design: A Guide for Sustainable Communities*. London: Town and Country Planning Association.

TCPA. (2007) *Climate Change Adaptation by Design: A Guide for Sustainable Communities*. London: Town and Country Planning Association.

TCPA. (2009) *Creating Low Carbon Homes for People in Eco-Towns*. London: Town and Country Planning Association.

TCPA. (2011) *Reimagining Garden Cities for the 21st Century: Benefits and Lessons in Bringing Forward Comprehensively Planned New Communities*. London: Town and Country Planning Association.

TCPA. (2014) *New Towns and Garden Cities: Lessons for Tomorrow*. London: Town and Country Planning Association.

Thomas, R. (1996) The economics of the New Towns revisited. *Town and Country Planning* 65: 305–308.

Thorne, B. (1987) Re-visioning women and social change: where are the children? *Gender and Society* 1(1): 85–109.

Thrift, N. (2000) Afterwords. *Environment and Planning D: Society and Space* 18(2): 213–255.

Thrift, N. (2004) Intensities of feeling: towards a spatial politics of affect. *Geografiska Annaler: Series B, Human Geography* 86(1): 57–78.

**210** References

Thrift, N. (2005). *Transactions of the Institute of British Geographers* 30: 133–150.

Tisdall, E. K. M., Davis, J. M., Hill, M. and Prout, A. (eds). (2006) *Children, Young People and Social Inclusion: Participation for What?* Bristol: Policy Press.

Turmel, A. (2008) *A Historical Sociology of Childhood: Developmental Thinking, Categorisation and Graphic Visualization.* Cambridge: Cambridge University Press.

Turner, V. (1967) *The Forest of Symbols: Aspects of the Ndembu Ritual.* New York: Cornell University Press.

UN-Habitat. (2009) *Planning Sustainable Cities.* Nairobi: United Nations Human Settlement Programme.

UN-Habitat. (2016) *Urbanisation and Development: Emerging Futures. World Cities Report 2016.* Nairobi: United Nations Human Settlement Programme. Retrieved on 16 March 2017 from http://nua.unhabitat.org/uploads/WCRFullReport2016_EN.pdf.

UNICEF. (2011) *Children and Climate Change.* Bangkok: UNICEF East Asia/Pacific.

UNICEF. (2012) *The State of the World's Children 2012: Children in an Urban World.* New York, UNICEF.

United Nations. (1987) *Report of the World Commission on Environment and Development.* New York: United Nations.

United Nations. (1989) Convention on the Rights of the Child. Retrieved on 28 April 2015 from www.ohchr.org/EN/ProfessionalInterest/Pages/CRC.aspx.

United Nations. (2013) *World Economic and Social Survey 2013.* New York: United Nations.

Uprichard, E. (2008) Children as 'being and becomings': children, childhood and temporality. *Children and Society* 22(4): 303–313.

Ursin, M. (2011) 'Wherever I lay my head is home': young people's experience of home in the Brazilian street environment. *Children's Geographies* 9(2): 221–234.

Uzzell, D. (1994) *Children as Catalysts of Environmental Change: Final Report.* Brussels: European Commission Directorate General for Science Research and Development Joint Research Centre.

Váhl, J. and Giskes, J. (1990) *Verkeerenstedenbouw: sameneenkunde apart.* Vanves: Amarcande.

Valentine, G. (1996a) Children should be seen and not heard: the production and transgression of adults' public space. *Urban Geography* 17(3): 205–220.

Valentine, G. (1996b) Angels and devils: moral landscapes of childhood. *Environment and Planning D: Society and Space* 14: 581–599.

Valentine, G. (1997) 'Oh yes I can' 'Oh no you can't': children and parents' understandings of kids' competence to negotiate public space safety. *Antipode* 29(1): 65–89.

Valentine, G. (2000) Exploring children and young people's narratives of identity. *Geoforum* 31(2): 257–267.

Valentine, G. (2008) Living with difference: reflections on geographies of encounter. *Progress in Human Geography* 32(3): 323–337.

Valentine, G. and McKendrick, J. (1997) Children's outdoor play: exploring parental concerns about children's safety and the changing nature of childhood. *Geoforum* 28(2): 219–235.

Valentine, G., Piekut, A., Winiarska, A., Harris, C. and Jackson, L. (2015) Mapping the meaning of 'difference' in Europe: a social topography of prejudice. *Ethnicities* 15(4): 568–585.

Vanderbeck, R. M. (2007) Intergenerational geographies: age relations, segregation and re-engagements. *Geography Compass* 1(2): 200–221.

van Gennep, A. (1960) *The Rites of Passage.* Chicago, IL: Chicago University Press.

van Loon, J. and Frank, L. (2011) Urban form relationships with youth physical activity: implications for research and practice. *Journal of Planning Literature* 26(3): 280–308.

## References

Walks, A. (2014) *The Urban Political Economy and Ecology of Automobility: Driving Cities, Driving Inequality, Driving Politics*. Abingdon: Routledge.

Walshe, N. (2013) Exploring and developing student understandings of sustainable development. *Curriculum Journal* 24(2): 224–249.

Ward, C. (1978) *The Child in the City*. New York: Pantheon.

Wasshede, C. (2017) The child of the common: governing children in the Freetown Christiania, Denmark. *Children and Society* 31(5): 403–413.

Watkins, M. (2011) Teachers' tears and the affective geography of the classroom. *Emotion, Space and Society* 4(3): 137–143.

Weller, S. (2003) 'Teach us something useful': contested spaces of teenage citizenship. *Space and Polity* 7(2): 153–171.

Weller, S. (2006) Situating (young) teenagers in geographies of children and youth. *Children's Geographies* 4(1): 97–108.

Weller, S. (2007) *Teenagers' Citizenship: Experiences and Education*. Abingdon: Routledge.

Wells, K. (2011) The politics of life: governing childhood. *Global Studies of Childhood* 1(1): 15–25.

Westerhoff, L.M. (2016) Emerging narratives of a sustainable urban neighbourhood: the case of Vancouver's Olympic Village. *Journal of Urban Research* 14.

Wheeler, S. (1996) *Sustainable Urban Development: A Literature Review and Analysis*. Berkeley, CA: Institute of Urban and Regional Development.

Wheeler, S. and Beatley, T. (eds). (2014) *The Sustainable Urban Development Reader*. Abingdon: Routledge.

Whyte, W.F. (1943) *Street Corner Society: The Social Structure of an Italian Slum*. Chicago, IL: University of Chicago Press.

Wilhelmsen, T. and Nilsen, R.D. (2015) Parents' experiences of diagnostic processes of young children in Norwegian day-care institutions. *Sociology of Health and Illness* 37(2): 241–254.

Williams, D.E. (2007) *Sustainable Design: Ecology, Architecture, and Planning*. New York: John Wiley.

Williams, K., Burton, E. and Jenks, M. (eds). (2001) *Achieving Sustainable Urban Form*. London, Taylor & Francis.

Williams, S. (2001) *Emotion and Social Theory: Corporeal Reflections on the (Ir)rational*. London: Sage.

Willis, P.E. (1977) *Learning to Labor: How Working Class Kids Get Working Class Jobs*. London: Saxon House.

Wirth, L. (1938) Urbanism as a way of life. *American Journal of Sociology* 44(1): 1–24.

Wood, B.E. (2012) Crafted within liminal spaces: young people's everyday politics. *Political Geography* 31: 337–346.

Wood, B.E. (2013) Young people's emotional geographies of citizenship participation: spatial and relational insights. *Emotion, Space and Society* 9: 50–58.

Wood, B. (2015) Border spaces: geographies of youth exclusion, inclusion, and liminality. In K. Nairn, P. Kraftl and T. Skelton (eds), *Space, Place and Environment, Geographies of Children and Young People*, 3. Singapore: Springer.

Woodyer, T. (2008) The body as research tool: embodied practice and children's geographies. *Children's Geographies* 6(4): 349–362.

Woodyer, T. (2012) Ludic geographies: not merely child's play. *Geography Compass* 6(6): 313–326.

World Commission on Environment and Development. (1987) *Our Common Future* ['the Brundtland Report']. Oxford: Oxford University Press.

## 212 References

Worpole, K. (2000) *Here Comes the Sun: Architecture and Public Space in Twentieth-Century European Culture*. London: Reaktion.

Worth, N. (2009) Understanding youth transition as 'becoming': identity, time and futurity. *Geoforum* 40(6): 1050–1060.

Wyness, M. (2000) *Contesting Childhood*. Falmer Press: London.

Young, I.M. (1990) *Justice and the Politics of Difference*. Princeton, NJ: Princeton University Press.

Youth Citizenship Commission. (2014) Youth Citizenship Commission: home. Retrieved on 28 April 2015 from www.youthcitizenshipcommission.co.uk.

Yusoff, K. (2013) Geologic life: prehistory, climate, futures in the Anthropocene. *Environment and Planning D* 31: 779–795.

Zeiher, H. (2001) Dependent, independent and interdependent relations: children as members of the family household in West Berlin. In L. Alanen and B. Mayall (eds), *Conceptualizing Child–Adult Relations*, 37–53. London: Routledge Falmer.

Zelezny, L. (1999) Educational interventions that improve environmental behaviours. *Journal of Environmental Education* 31: 5–14.

Zembylas, M. (2009) Global economies of fear: affect, politics and pedagogical implications. *Critical Studies in Education* 50(2): 187–199.

Zembylas, M. (2013) Mobilizing 'implicit activisms' in schools through practices of critical emotional reflexivity. *Teaching Education* 24(1): 84–96.

Zero Carbon Hub. (2013) *Zero Carbon Strategies*. Milton Keynes: National House Builders' Council.

Zheng, H., Shen, G. and Wang H. (2014) A review of recent studies on sustainable urban renewal. *Habitat International* 41: 272–279.

# INDEX

Page numbers in italics refer to figures.

abandoning 76–80
academic endeavour 29
accident prevention 97–8
activism 146
adult-child relations 27
affect 2, 15, 24, 29–37, 143, 149–50, 183, 186
affirmative community relations 108
affordability 143
affordable housing 104, 121
Alanen, Lena 27
American playground movement 30
actor–network theory (ANT) 22–3, 29–36;
  approaches 33
anthropology 6, 14, 17, 21–2, 40
anti-social behaviour 132
anxieties 72–6
architectural design of house 73
'auto-disabling' environments 90
automated private policing devices 132

belonging 112–20; intergenerational senses
  of 178–9
Bennett, Jane 35
biopolitics 32–5
biosocial dualisms 32
Blair, Tony 49
bodies shaping spaces 144–6
bodily vitalities 188–90
Braidotti, Rosi 35

Caillois, R. 150
canonical genealogy 46

car-owning households 82
child accident prevention 97–8
childhood/children: contemporary 34;
  embodiments of 33; mobilities 97; modes
  of ordering 34; playing and 153–74;
  social construction of 22–3, 29–30;
  social-scientific research on 14; and
  teachers 31
childhood studies 15–20; definition 14;
  embodiment 31–2; emotion/affect
  29–31; interdisciplinary 21–4, 182–4;
  materialities, biopolitics and nonhuman
  natures 32–5; mobilities 24–6; new wave
  of 15, 22–4; othering, intersectionality and
  intergenerationality 26–9; scholars 29–30;
  in (sustainable) urban contexts 18–21
children and sustainable urbanism 14–15;
  (re)constituting studies 22–35; critical
  appraisal of the vitalities of 35–8;
  interdisciplinary study of 21–2; social
  studies of 15–18; studies in (sustainable)
  urban contexts 18–21
China Sustainable Cities Programme 45
CHP *see* combined heat and power plants
  (CHP)
Christensen, P. 2, 18, 23, 26, 60, 111
citizenship 11; intergenerational senses of
  178–9
classroom 31
Code Level 6 buildings 61; Code Level
  6 homes 72, 74; eco-homes 64, 70; in
  Hettonbury 73

**214** Index

$CO_2$ emissions 81
combined heat and power plants (CHP) 59
commerce 41
communication 42; adult cultures of 141; young people's cultures of 146
communities 103–6; balanced 56; builders 58; children as creators of 108–20; with children in mind 106–8; community workshops as safe dialogical space 11; creation of 145; decision-making 181–2; designs of 71; development of 106; eco-materialities of 65; emergence of 120; exclusions and boundaries 120–8; funds 138; intense core of 105; living togetherness 108; 'mixed' or 'balanced' 56; narratives and discourses 71; neighbouring 123; in practice, qualities of 103; for public events and social gatherings 144; research 11; sense of 119; socio-material spaces of 121; spaces 132, 135; togetherness 103
connectivity 39
contemporary childhoods 34
conviviality 39, 81, 103, 148; convivial public spaces 55
cooperation 42–3
council houses 121–2
courtyards *93*, 95–6
culture 41
cyclists 86

decolonisation 34
design quality 42
domestic spaces 59
dormitory suburbia 103
dwelling perspective 14

eco-architectural features 69; 'weirdness' of 75
eco-architectural forms 62–3
eco-homes 59–60, 67
eco-housing 60, 75
eco-materialities 63–4
economy 41
eco-technologies 59, 61, 64, 70, 77; defined 60; design and tangibility of 67; in Hettonbury *61*; interactions and engagements with 64; lived experiences of 64; materialities of 74; 'unusual' appearances of 69
education 41; formal 63; scholars 31
education for sustainability (EfS) 62, 63; concerns of 71; pedagogic frames of 75; research 69
Egan wheel *44*, 45

electronic devices 68
embodiment 31–2
emotional/affective vitalities 29–31, 186–8
emotional knowledge 142–4
employment 41
environmental design 7
environmental issues 53
environmental knowledge, intergenerational transmissions of 63
ethnography 11, 16, 36, 101, 116, 153, 178, 187
European Union 40
'exemplar' developments 50

failures 76–80
fairness 42
Farr, D. 40, 43–4, 82; key principles from 43–4
faulty systems 77
feminisms 28
force drivers 86
formative visualisation 106
fostering community development 181
Freiburg Charter 40; principles of 41–3
frustrations 76–80

'Garden Cities' movement 47
'Garden City' 47, 103–4
Garden Village 103–4
geo-engineering 36–7
glass house 69
Goodchild, B. 67
Gorman-Murray, G. 60
GPS 11, 91, 94; data 96–7, 101; maps 88; research tools 12; technologies 11
green architecture 60
'GreenHome' 60
Grosz, Elizabeth 35

Hadfield-Hill, S. 11, 53
Harker, C. 30–1
heating system 78
Henricks, T. S. 149
Hettonbury 7, *8*, 66, 100; eco-technologies in *61–2*; haunted house 120; housing plan 144; interviews with participants in 89; road network 91; roads within 97–8; shared surface layout of 91; snow in *66*; spaces to play in *92–3*; street surfaces around park in *95*; urban extension of 124
Hobson, K. 67
home-based: consumption 71; technologies 77

Index **215**

'Homezone' 84–5; principles 83
Horton, J. 33
households, car-owning 82
house washing system 78
housing 10; affordable 104, 121;
   developments 5, 6, 52, 178;
   'shared-ownership' 10; social 121

'ideal' communities 47
identity 29; forms of 23
inbetweeness 141
'independent' mobility 25
Indian Smart Cities programme 45
India, vision for smart cities 45–6
indigeneity 34
Ingold, Tim 14
institutional spaces 31
interdependent relations 27
interdisciplinary: approach 35; childhood
   studies 14; conceptual framework 58
intergenerational and intersectional 4, 131
intergenerational community space 134–5
inter-generational conflicts 138
intergenerationality 26–9, 37; social
   languages of 29
intergenerational othering 121
intergenerational power relations 131
intergenerational relations 27, 29, 31, 36,
   112, 131
internationalisation 50
intersectionality 26–9, 28, 37; social
   languages of 29
intersectional power relations 131
intra-generational solidarity 114
investment in housing developments 6

Karsten study of generational change 25
Kraftl, P. 28, 30

lack of connectedness 63
Lane, R. 60
Lee, Nick 33
legibility 55
Letchworth 47–8
liveability 39, 56, 81, 148; political
   proclamation of 49
liveable spaces with children 182
living street 84
local knowledge 112–20

Marres, N. 60, 71
materialities 32–5, 63; of eco-technology
   74; of sustainable consumption 60
McIntosh, I. 28
Melia, S. 90

mews 96–7
Milton Keynes–South Midlands (MKSM)
   Growth Area 6
mixed community 56
mobile vitalities 184–5
mobilities 11, 24–6; distinct patterns of 91;
   forms of 26; planning 180–1
Moody, S. 90
multidisciplinary childhood studies 1
multistakeholder processes 133

Nannton: (case study development) 9, 10;
   and Tillinglow 126
nature 38
Nayak, A. 108
neighbourhood 133
neighbouring community 123
New Citizens: project 178; research 113
New Social Studies of Childhood (NSSC)
   14, 24, 32, 151; founding premises of 31;
   proponents 31; retaining and expanding
   36
new towns 49
New Towns Act 47
New Urbanisms, New Citizens (NUNC)
   project 5, 113, 149, 178; case studies 121;
   case study communities 132; objectives
   6; project 11, 12, 106, 108–9; research 12,
   22, 131; study 73
New Wave Childhood Studies 15, 22–4
nonhuman: agency 159–63; materialities 38;
   natures 32–5
'non-rough' spaces 127
NSSC see new social studies of childhood
   (NSSC)
NUNC project see New Urbanisms, New
   Citizens (NUNC) project

on-road parking 96
opening-up of community space 115
ordering process 100–1
orphanages 31
othering 26–9; children 27, 34; discourses
   of 138; intergenerational 121; processes
   of 37

Parish Council and Residents' Association
   meetings 139, 140, 142
park 92, 94–5
parking on-road 96
participation 42
partnership 42–3
pedestrians 86
photovoltaic (PV) panels 7, 10, 75
planning objectives 43

**216** Index

playing, and childhood 153–74; nonhuman agency 159–63; politics of vitality 167–74; public space 155–9; (re)essentialisation of 151; social relations 153–5
policy-makers, emergence of 43
policy-making processes 75
political engagement box 131
political engagement by children 136
political vitality 141
politics of vitality 167–74
practice, sustainable urbanism in 39
primary schools 107
private transportation 81
Prout, A. 22–3, 32–3
public events, community for 144
publicness of community spaces 134
public–private partnerships 133, 141
public space 59, 112, 155–9; experience of 132; politics of 132
Punch, S. 28
PV panels see photovoltaic (PV) panels

Rautio, P. 23
reality, social behaviours in 101
re-embody sustainable urbanisms 188
reliability 42
residential yard 84
road network, Hettonbury 91
Robinson, J. 57
Romsworth community (case study development) 7, 8; workshop 12
roughness 124, 126
rough spaces 127
rumours 72–6

scholars/scholarship 1, 46, 134
schools/schooling 31, 107
science 41
sense of community 109
settler colonialism 34
shared-ownership housing 10
shared sense of belonging 105
shared surface 55, 83–6; community spaces 85, 105; designs, application of 100; principles 86
shared surface street design 26, 82, 90–1; courtyards 95–6; mews 96–7; park 94–5; square 91–4
skateboarding 145
smart cities, India's vision for 45–6
smart solutions 59
social behaviours in reality 101
social cohesion 49
social difference 112, 163–8

social exclusion 132–6
social gatherings, community for 144
social housing 121
social inclusion 30
sociality 113
social networking 107
social practice theory 67
social relations 153–5
solar hot water tubing 64
solar hot water units 7, 10
solar panels 70
solidarity, intra-generational 114
spaces 141–6; bodies shaping 144–6; of eruption/disruption 148–9; of sustainable urbanism 10; of vitality 65
spatial exclusion 132–6, 136
'spatialise' childhood 21
square 91–4, *92*
subjectivity 29
suburbanisation 57
SUDS see Sustainable Urban Drainage System (SUDS)
sustainability 31, 63, 150; architectural geographies of 64; in community 70; notions of 148
sustainable architectures: lived experiences of 64
sustainable communities 141; components of 44; key constituents of 45; planning of 54; in UK 51–6
Sustainable Communities developments 55
Sustainable Communities plan 6, 10, 45, 49, 52, 53, 56–7, 83, 136; characteristic of 6–7; design parameters of 7
Sustainable Communities policy 131
Sustainable Communities projects 56
sustainable community transport networks 83
'sustainable' housing developments 5
sustainable mobilities 26, 81–3; contextualising 'shared surfaces' 83–6; shared surface design 97–101; shared surface street designs see shared surface street designs; with/in (sustainable) urban places 86–90
sustainable urban development 90; forms and principles of 6–7; principle of 40
Sustainable Urban Drainage System (SUDS) 7, 64, 65, 70, 72, 75; channels 10; form and function of 75
sustainable urbanism: importance of 52
*Sustainable Urbanism: Urban Design with Nature* (Farr) 43
sustainable urban technologies 59–62, 67; appearance and design of 64; children's

Index **217**

and families' engagements 69–71; education for sustainability 62–4; frustrations, failures and the danger of 'abandoning' 76–80; functional and technological complexity of 62; play, routine domestic practices and taken-for-granted interactions 64–9; routines and interactions with 67; weirdness, anxieties, rumours and wanting answers 72–6

sustainable urban/urbanism 31, 39–40, 43–4, 50, 57, 83, 143, 148–9, 152, 177, 190–2; agendas 49, 103; architectural forms of 59; architecture 39, 53; characterising play 149–53; childhoods 14; communities: liveliness of 65; studies of children in 12; concepts of 45; contexts of 13, 53, 57; Curitiba 50; description of 14; design, vitalities in 149; discourses of 45, 46; emergence of 43; environments 40, 63; existing 51–6; extension 7, 52; forms of 14, 133; impacts of 13; interdisciplinary framework for 182–4; internationalised emergence of 5–6; investment in 178; largescale delivery of 6; Malmö 50; 'mundane' forms of 51–2; need for research 56–8; neighbourhood 78–9; notions of 67; places 67, 143; playing and childhood 153–74; policy discourses and planning visions of 177; principles and visions of 40–51; principles for 7; spaces 10, 13, 134, 177–8, 179, 180–2; visions of 51, 54

sustainable urban vitality 178

thorny problematics 130
'throwntogetherness' 106
Tillinglow (case study development) 9, 10
tokenism 131
traffic 83
transportation 81
transport/transportation 180–1; forms of 82

UK's Code for Sustainable Homes 64
UK's Economic and Social Research Council 5

UK Sustainable Communities plan 52, 104
UNCRC *see* United Nations Convention of the Rights of the Child (UNCRC)
United Nations Convention of the Rights of the Child (UNCRC) 17, 131, 151
urban-based play 151
urban communities 56–7, 179
urban compactness 54
urban design of Hettonbury 65
urban development 41, 107
Urban Development Corporations 49
urban drainage systems 64
urban environments 25
Urbanisation and Development Programme 45
urbanism 51–6; sustainable *see* sustainable urban/urbanism
urban landscapes 86
urban life, 'sustainable' modes of 148
urban materialities 188
urban mobility 39
urban planning 47, 103; emergence of 43; 'sustainable' modes of 177; vision 46
urban policy and planning 180
urban spaces 27, 144; construction of 86

vehicular movement 86
viable community 106
visioning 42
visualisations 107
vital intersectionalities 185–6
vitality 103; non-romanticised politics of 141; space of 65
vital places 37
vital politics 130–2; formal political participation in sustainable communities 136–41; social and spatial exclusion 132–6; spaces, moments and stories 141–6
vital urbanisms 38, 131
vital urban places 153

walkability 55
weirdness 72–6; of eco-architectural features 75
Westerhoff, L. M. 78–9
woonerf ('living street') movement 84
'working' livelihoods 139